"Rochelle Scheuermann offers a much-needed resource to help the church move past its ignorance about image bearers with disabilities in our communities and churches. A missiologist and parent to a child with special needs, Scheuermann invites the reader into her lived theology toward meaningful and fruitful ministry."

Edward L. Smither, dean of the School of Missions and Intercultural Ministry at Columbia International University

"This book names with honesty the ways evangelism has too often excluded or overlooked people with disabilities and then offers a compelling alternative rooted in Scripture and informed by lived experience. Rochelle Scheuermann casts a vision of communities where God's mission is carried forward by the full body of Christ, in all its richness and diversity. *Disability and Evangelism* is a gift to the church and an invitation to deeper faithfulness and mutual flourishing."

Erik Carter, professor at the Baylor Center for Disability and Flourishing

"On this pressing topic of the church, there is no more tender pastor or wiser theologian than Rochelle Scheuermann. Her book invites us to share the good news with everybody, just as our incarnate God would have us do."

Beth Felker Jones, professor of theology at Northern Seminary and author of *Why I Am Protestant*

Rochelle Scheuermann

DISABILITY & Evangelism

THE GOOD NEWS OF THE FULLNESS OF GOD'S KINGDOM

An imprint of InterVarsity Press
Downers Grove, Illinois

InterVarsity Press
P.O. Box 1400 | Downers Grove, IL 60515-1426
ivpress.com | email@ivpress.com

InterVarsity Press® is the publishing division of InterVarsity Christian Fellowship/USA®. For more information, visit intervarsity.org.

Cover design: Faceout Studio
Interior design: Daniel van Loon
Images: Shutterstock: © Amovitania; © BOY ANTHONY; © Kozlik; © Miloje; © Kostin77; © nani888

ISBN 978-1-5140-0978-9 (print) | ISBN 978-1-5140-0979-6 (digital)

Printed in the United States of America ♾

Library of Congress Cataloging-in-Publication Data
Names: Scheuermann, Rochelle Cathcart author
Title: Disability and evangelism : the good news of the fullness of God's kingdom / Rochelle Scheuermann.
Description: Downers Grove, IL : IVP Academic, 2026. | Series: Center for Disability and Ministry books | Includes appendix. | Includes bibliographical references and indexes.
Identifiers: LCCN 2025041640 (print) | LCCN 2025041641 (ebook) | ISBN 9781514009789 paperback | ISBN 9781514009796 ebook
Subjects: LCSH: Church work with people with disabilities | Disabilities–Religious aspects–Christianity | Evangelistic work
Classification: LCC BV4460 .S34 2026 (print) | LCC BV4460 (ebook)
LC record available at https://lccn.loc.gov/2025041640
LC ebook record available at https://lccn.loc.gov/2025041641

32 31 30 29 28 27 26 | 13 12 11 10 9 8 7 6 5 4 3 2 1

For *I. M. S.*

Thank you for changing my life and teaching me about Jesus.

"I will give thanks to you, LORD, with all my heart;
I will tell of all your wonderful deeds.
I will be glad and rejoice in you;
I will sing the praises of your name, O Most High."

PSALM 9:1-2 NIV

Contents

Series Preface

BENJAMIN T. CONNER AND JOHN SWINTON

CENTER FOR DISABILITY AND MINISTRY books present fresh insights into ministry from the perspectives of disabled and nondisabled theologians and practitioners. The series editors, Benjamin Conner and John Swinton, are committed to creating resources to support congregations in identifying ableist theology and practices while offering frameworks for reimagining practices such as evangelism, the discernment of vocation, baptism, building community, leading communities, prayer, and children's ministry, to name a few.

Disability theology is an emerging theological discipline that has multiple interdisciplinary conversation partners, sources, and approaches. One aspect of theology that has received relatively little formal attention from disability theology is the discipline of practical theology. *Practical theology seeks to cultivate critical theological reflections on the practices of the church with a view to enabling more faithful participation in God's ongoing mission.* It is a discipline that takes formal, credal theology seriously, but seeks to examine and explore how such theology actually works itself out within, is refined by, and emerges from the experiences of the church in the world. A practical-theological approach to disability assumes that the specificities of human disability have theological and practical significance for our articulation and practice of the faith, and that reflection on such experience is necessary for the faithful ministry of the church.

In line with some of the thinking that has emerged from the field of disability studies, the series presumes that disability theology is committed to promoting the idea that the term *disability* is complex. At one level it is a way of naming difference. However, the nature of that difference is often socially constructed in ways that serve to stigmatize certain human differences. Such stigmatization inheres values and maps exclusion, thus filtering out disabled bodies and voices from important conversations. In a world where differences in mobility, processing, vision, and hearing, among others, are unexceptional and unsurprising, the series strives to overcome stigma and stereotypes and to point toward a way of living where difference is merely that: *difference.*

Using practical theology as a basic framework of understanding, this series seeks to initiate a range of conversations around key issues in disability theology with a view to increasing knowledge and creatively and faithfully shaping Christian practice. Books in the series will be supplemented by additional resources on the Center for Disability and Ministry website.

Acknowledgments

I HAD ALWAYS HEARD THAT HAVING KIDS will change your life. I could never have imagined how utterly life-altering the adoption of my son would be. He made me a mom. He filled a space in my heart that years of infertility had left empty. He captured me from the first glance of his big brown eyes. In every way my son is indeed a good and perfect gift from God (Jas 1:17). At first glance, many discount him because he has Down syndrome, but his extra chromosome is one of the things I love most about him. Yes, it brings challenges, but even in the tough moments I am still drawn to the heart of God. Doing life with my son has brought me face-to-face with my own shortcomings and vulnerability, it has pushed me to better understand the fullness and power of God's kingdom, and in capturing this expansive vision for what God's kingdom is, it has given me a greater zeal for helping the church be all she should be. My son has been a window to God because of his life. I believe he will be a window to God for others as well. I write this book because of him, for him, and with him. Thanks, sweet boy, for putting up with your mama and being patient through all of my faults. I love you to the moon and back!

Beyond my son, I am blessed by the love and tremendous support of my family. This book is not possible without their grace, cheers, and consolations. To my husband, Barrett, thanks for . . . *everything*. I am so grateful God brought you into my life at just the right moment and that we get to stumble and soar through this life together. I love you! To my daughter, who gives sweet and sass a whole new meaning, your sunshine fills my life with such joy. You are a gift from God. I love you, sweet girl!

I am also blessed by wonderful parents, Randy and Synthia, who have prayed and cheered and supported me every step of my life, and who have become colaborers with us in our work of love: raising children with and without disabilities. We couldn't do it without you. And Mom, thanks for reading everything I've ever written and providing sound editorial feedback. You deserve an honorary degree.

I am grateful for the community around me and want to thank in particular my colleagues who have journeyed with me as I've run headlong into the disability world. Thanks for helping me grow as a scholar, a missiologist, an evangelist, and a disciple. I am grateful too for your support of my sabbatical while I finished this book. Specifically, I want to thank Marc Cortez, John Dickson, Eunice Hong, Cassidy Larson, Wendy Larson, Michael Hakmin Lee, Heather Matthews, Rick Richardson, my teaching assistant Collin Glatz, and Wheaton College.

I am also extremely thankful for my new friends in the disability world who have pulled me into conversations, given me spaces to test my thoughts, and helpfully sharpened me. I am grateful for scholars who have been in this space far longer than I and whose work has particularly made an impact on me: Ben Conner, Erik Carter, Nathan John, John Swinton, Brian Brock, and the Lausanne Disability Group—Community of Practice. For those who have taken the time to be interviewed for this book (Abby, Andy, Chris, Hannah, Megan, and Rick), you have fundamentally reshaped my perspective and helped this book do what it needs to. Thank you for opening up your experiences to me and allowing me to share your remarkable lives, perspectives, and prophetic challenges with the world.

A big thank you to our church family, who has welcomed us unconditionally and given us a true home. Your impact on us, and especially my children, has taught me what church should be and time and again has demonstrated God's welcome embrace. Being with you is one of our favorite things and also one of our safest. It's hard to put into words how grateful we are. Pastor Mary, you *saw* our son and changed the trajectory of his life and ours. ¡Gracias!

Finally, to my editorial team (Jon Boyd, Rebecca Carhart-Mader, Ben Conner, and John Swinton) and my publisher, IVP Academic, thank you for your help, support, and encouragement and for believing in the message that people of all abilities are vital to God's work and witness.

To God be the glory.

Introduction

"I HAD THE MOST WONDERFUL THOUGHT I wanted to share with you. I was at prayer meeting this past week, and we were praying for God to heal a child of autism. I suddenly thought of you and wondered, *If God heals your son, do you think God would change your son's physical features?*"

The woman who said this had cornered me as I put hors d'oeuvres on my plate at a women's Christmas event for our church. I was there in hopes that I would connect better with the women at this church and start building relationships. Her comment pushed me away. She was earnest, eager, excited by the thought and did not seem to register the flood of emotions that rushed through me.

This was not the time and place for such a confrontation, and it was the first time someone had blatantly said my son's disability was an issue in the church. Did anyone else in the church share this belief? (I would find out soon that the answer was yes.) I was crushed, angry, flustered, and confused, and I didn't know how to respond. The entire comment was jarring. First, why would God need to heal a child of autism? Second, what did she think my son needed to be healed from? What was it about his physical features that she found so problematic?

CHRISTIANITY AND DISABILITY

My son was born with Down syndrome. An extra chromosome replicated in each of his cells affects him physically, mentally, and emotionally. Said this way, too many of us immediately assume problems: He has developmental delays, low muscle tone, a proneness to ear infections, and certain physical and behavioral traits that tend to run strongly in Trisomy 21. But my son's extra chromosome also affects him *positively*, and these effects are too numerous to count: empathy, tenderness, concern for others, an uncanny way of including everyone, freedom to just be himself, and so on. Too often these parts of his life get overlooked by a concern that his physical being and mental development are not *normal* or *typical.*

For Christians, there is an additional theological overtone to disability. Disability is seen as not just a physical problem but a spiritual one, requiring faith, repentance, and cure for my son and others like him to realize God's potential. For this woman, my son was not acceptable as he was. She thought it would be to God's glory for my son's genetic code to be rewritten so that he could be smart and quick and look like everyone else. She hadn't stopped to consider that she was praying away the very things that made him *him* and saying, in essence, that God messed up in making my son and needed to fix him. It seemed that in her world, disability was incompatible with God. Sadly, her view is very common in the church, so instead of welcoming disability, many Christians problematize it to the point that few people with disabilities find their way into the church. For those who do make their way in, many find themselves welcomed but not included, present but not full participants, recipients but not givers. This is a travesty.

Over one billion people in the world have a disability. Of these, 90 to 95 percent have not yet heard the gospel.[1] Erik Carter's recent research suggests that in the last month in the United States, 59 percent of people with disabilities did not attend a religious service.[2] If you consider that 28.7 percent of the adult US population has at least one disability, and that having a disability, particularly an intellectual or developmental disability, is a reliable predictor of whether people with disabilities *and their families* are in church, then we can take that 59 percent number and expand it considerably.[3] People with disabilities and their families are not

[1]Donna Jennings, "Those Who Seem to Be Weak: The Role of Disability Within a Missional Framework," *Mission Round Table* 12, no. 3 (2017): 30.

[2]Erik Carter, "From Barriers to Belonging: The Changing Landscape of Disability and Ministry" (virtual presentation to the Lausanne Disability Affinity Group—Community of Practice, March 22, 2023).

[3]Erik W. Carter, Elizabeth E. Biggs, and Thomas L. Boehm. "Being Present Versus Having a Presence: Dimensions of Belonging for Young People with Disabilities and Their Families," *Christian Education Journal* 13, no. 1 (2016): 128-29.

being reached with the gospel. And when they are, the church isn't doing a great job of incorporating them into the body as full-fledged, contributing, participating, and leading members.

Each of us, if we live long enough, will experience disability to varying degrees. In rejecting disabilities we find in others, we are at some point rejecting ourselves. However, we often approach disability as if it were a special ministry of the church and one churches can chose whether to take on. Not everyone is called to this space, we argue. We have a specific target for our church's outreach, and disability is just an add-on or extra we can choose to pursue or not. We rarely consider where disability fits in God's kingdom, if it fits at all. This reality doesn't jive with Scripture.

Hear this clearly: Disability matters. It matters to God; therefore, it should matter to us.

God wants people with disabilities in his kingdom as active participants in what he is doing in the world. The Bible is clear that God's kingdom is meant to be inhabited by people from every tribe, nation, language, and tongue (Rev 7:9), and from every walk of life, including those not highly regarded by worldly standards: children (Mt 19:13-15), slaves (Philem 15-16; Gal 3:28), and those with disabilities (Lk 14:15-24). If the church is truly meant to be a credible witness and foretaste of Revelation 7:9, then the church is also meant to reach and include people with disabilities within the church's works of evangelism and mission, not just as recipients but as active participants in and even leaders of this work as well. This is what *should* be. Why is it not?

Part of the problem is with our theology. When we don't fully understand God's story, we can struggle to tell the gospel message in a way that is good news for everyone. Most Christians don't know what to do with disability. Too often they tell the gospel story as if people with disabilities exist only because of sin and thus need heavenly perfection to be useful. It is easy to assume that people with disabilities (especially when it is an intellectual or developmental disability) cannot understand the gospel or even need to.

Part of the problem is with our practice. Our discomfort with disability and our misconception that we need advanced training to provide ministry to and with people with disabilities can easily move us to exclude disabled people from basic participation. Disabilities can make us uncomfortable because they often disrupt what we know of, believe about, and experience in the world. This can leave us unsure how to act or what to say, such that our best efforts toward inclusion can come off awkward, clumsy, and hurtful. Even when we do provide some welcome, it can be hard to overcome the assumption that disabilities disqualify people from certain tasks and responsibilities within the church. Both views—discomfort and disqualification—prevent us from having people with disabilities clearly in focus when establishing our mission and evangelism priorities and activities.

The bottom line is this: We aren't reaching people with disabilities (or their families), and when we do, we aren't benefiting from their gifts and ministries. The goal of this book is to reshape our evangelism theology and practice so that people with disabilities are central in all we think, say, and do. In being reshaped, we also discover the wonderful truth that including people with disabilities enriches our theology and practice, bringing it more in line with the gospel and the fullness of God's kingdom.

THE PATH OF THIS BOOK

We begin, in part one, with theology, refreshing our view of God's story so we know where people with disabilities fit in this story. Chapter one uses a missional hermeneutic to examine the Bible, uncovering how God's mission permeates the entirety of Scripture and how this understanding shapes our place and our work as part of his story. Because we often truncate God's story, it is important to spend time here, as this lays the theological and missional foundation for all that follows. Only as we understand God's story are we able to locate our lives, disabled and not, in God's story. With this foundation in place, we are able to start considering a guiding question of part one: *Where does disability show up in God's story?*

Chapter two makes sure we understand what we're talking about when we discuss disabilities. This chapter defines disability, explains popular ways we respond to disability, and dispels myths and misperceptions we have about disability. We put God's story and disability together in chapters three and four to discover that disability shows up in every aspect of God's story in surprising and wonderful ways. Closing out part one, we then consider how we can all live and speak a "disabled" gospel message. In chapter five, we uncover how God's story responds to the complexities of disability and provides the means and the message to share good news with people of all abilities.

Part two leans more into praxis, examining how to do evangelism among and with people with disabilities.

One of the unique aspects of this book is that multiple voices are heard in its pages. Chapter six introduces us to six people who were specifically interviewed for this book. Their voices and experiences cover a variety of visible and hidden disabilities and lead us to some important new ways for viewing evangelism. In fact, their voices have reshaped the ending of this book and the specific evangelism practices that are covered. Rather than throwing disability thoughts onto what we typically think of as evangelism practices, my conversations with these disabled friends called out new dispositional evangelistic practices that have the possibility to reshape our churches in beautiful and God-ward ways.

On our way to discovering these new dispositional practices, we make a few important stops. Chapter seven wrestles with important questions about what we mean by evangelism practices, making a distinction between activities we do and evangelism as a core practice, a core way, of the church that shapes us as disciples and witnesses. The next two chapters tackle questions we often have about evangelism and more severe intellectual and developmental disabilities. Chapter eight considers the use of words in evangelism and the witness of those who do not primarily have words. Chapter nine looks at conversion and how people make faith commitments. This is particularly important to understand so we do not inadvertently lower expectations or have incorrect assumptions about the need, means, and mode of conversion for people with disabilities, particularly if they have a developmental or intellectual disability. Our last stop before we get to practices is chapter ten, where we address what is often the elephant in the room: how we can overcome the "burden" of disability and evangelism.

Our final chapters get to the heart of practice as we consider three dispositional evangelism practices that surfaced within my interviews.

Chapter eleven looks at the practice of accommodation as a disposition of deference that disposes us to consider "the other" in all we do. Chapter twelve reminds us that we cannot evangelize if we do not properly see people. This chapter cautions us against the problematic foregrounding of disability over people and calls us to the practice of genuinely attending to people. Chapter thirteen examines a final evangelistic practice of interdependence. This chapter moves us to reconsider our own selves and the ways in which we relate to, need, and are integrated with one another. The conclusion draws everything together, calling us toward a new way of being church that embraces disability as a central part in all we believe, say, and do.

You will notice discussion questions at the end of each chapter. They are here to help you reflect on the concepts and consider your next steps. These can be used by individual people and groups. I hope that you will engage this book with others in your church and that your group will include people of all abilities. But even if it is just you, please do take the time to reflect and then act. Everyone with disabilities and their families should experience the hope, welcome, inclusion, and participation that is intrinsic to the gospel. If the information in this book can change the trajectory for one church or one family, it is worth it.

BEFORE JUMPING IN

Prior to our first section, I need to make a few additional comments.

First, I have tried to write this book with everyone in mind, hoping that it would challenge people who consider themselves abled and would resonate with those who have disabilities. This is an almost impossible task, and I admit that I have not accomplished this evenly.

Disability covers such a range of things that it is hard to hold all disabilities together. How we approach people with intellectual and developmental disabilities has similarities to and differences from how we work with people who have mobility, speech, visual, and hidden disabilities. I have tried to write for this expanse knowing that my experience is mostly with developmental disability due to my son. Even when I have not meant to, I am aware that I have this bias. I have tried to overcome this bias by including the voices of many different types of disability.

Second, in trying to effect change and call the church to see, welcome, embrace, and include people of all abilities in the church as central to the church's work and witness, I have spoken much more to the abled part of the church and on behalf of the disabled part of the church. This too sets up problems.

It inadvertently promotes an us-them divide that can easily be interpreted as establishing an abled norm against a disabled other. My goal is to overcome the othering that so often happens within disability. However, naming the problems of ableism requires honest conversation about what abled people assume, believe, do, and say, and how this affects disabled people. Bear with me as I stumble through the tough conversations. It is my hope that in naming what has kept us apart we will learn to see the beauty in all kinds of bodies and minds and embrace each person as a meaningful part of God's story and thus our story. The end goal is not to erase disability—we are not going to become disability-blind (just as we shouldn't be colorblind regarding race). The end goal is that we will think rightly about (dis)abilities and the ways in which people of all abilities contribute to all God is doing in the world.

Another problem with my voice is that it comes across as if I were the abled representative for disabled people and speaking on their behalf. I do not want to lump disability together as if there were a singular disabled experience, and I sincerely do not want to belittle or remove voice from people with disabilities. I am not a spokesperson for the disabled. I am a mom who has been deeply touched by disability (not just with my son but in my own ways and through experiences within my immediate family). I speak from my own experience. That said, I have spent much time studying disability and the church, interacting with a variety of disabled people and intentionally listening to their stories. I hope to be true to these voices. I also know I may be able to say some things abled people might hear from me that they may not hear from others.

Third, I have chosen to mostly use person-first language when naming disability (i.e., people with disabilities), but you will notice some mixing with disability-first language (i.e., disabled people, the disabled, autistic people, etc.). Scholars and people with disabilities are mixed on terminology. Some hold these terms loosely; others are adamant that their way is the most just and people-honoring way to speak. Person-first language helps me keep people in the foreground and honor their personhood. Especially when I'm talking in generalities or do not personally know someone, I use person-first language to honor the personhood of others. There are times, however, that disability-first language can force issues of justice, calling out the ableism that so often goes unnoticed. At times we need the sharpness that identifying some people as abled and others as disabled brings. Disability-first language can also help us see that our unique abilities are central to who God has made us to be and how he uses us. To always background disability can make it appear as if that part were expendable. It is not. Disabled people are an indispensable part of God's kingdom and not lesser than or in subordination to abled people.

Fourth, language itself can be problematic. In *Metaphors We Live By*, George Lakoff and Mark Johnson note that the metaphors within our language shape us into ways and modes of thinking and acting, often without our being fully aware of how these concepts affect our beliefs and actions.[4] If we're not careful, we can perpetuate judgments against and the othering of disability by indiscriminately using phrases that equate certain abilities with having desired qualities and a lack of certain abilities with lacking these desired qualities.

Consider, for example, the metaphor that equates sight with knowledge. When someone explains something to us and we understand them, we say, "I see." When we don't understand, we may say, "I fail to see your point." We want *insight*. We speak of *having vision*. We value people who can *see the big picture*. Conversely, we describe people who fail to understand something as *blind*. We also describe people who willfully ignore things as being *blind*. We describe people who are narrow-minded or lack intellectual knowledge as being *myopic*, *nearsighted*. This is so ingrained in us that when we meet someone who is physically blind, these kinds of judgment can easily shape our perceptions of the blind person to the point that we assume they lack intelligence and cannot

[4]George Lakoff and Mark Johnson, *Metaphors We Live By* (University of Chicago Press, 1980).

know things. And if they cannot know things and lack intelligence, it's an easy leap to assume they are disabled in all areas of life. The same is true for words related to hearing, movement, and speech.

It is almost impossible to avoid using these kinds of metaphors, but when we don't think about what we're saying, we will continue to problematize disabilities and the people who have them as broken, bad, inept, unintelligent, wrong, close-minded, and so on. I have tried to be sensitive to and cognizant of the problems in our language and avoid these kinds of metaphors as much as possible. However, there were times I could not find another word or phrase to express my meaning (e.g., the last paragraph of this introduction and naming our second evangelism practice "Seeing People"). I have not intended offense and ask for forgiveness where I do offend.

One last thing. I am not the final word on disability. I am disheartened that it took adoption for me to realize how much I need people with disabilities in my life and in the life of the church. I am growing in this space and have so much more to learn. For those of you just starting on this journey, I hope I can teach you some things that will help propel you forward. For those further along, forgive me if the limitations of my experience play out in these pages. I welcome your grace *and* correction. None of us ever arrives or will ever engage disability perfectly. We will make mistakes along the way. But perhaps that's the beauty of disability, too—it teaches us that we are all vulnerable and in need of grace from one another and most especially from God.

As we turn now to part one, I invite you to a moment of pause and prayer. This is going to be a deep discussion and at many turns challenging. This is especially true if you have strong feelings about disability, church ministry, evangelism, and healing. If this is your first foray into a disability conversation, I commend you for starting the journey. This book is for you. You will learn things that may contradict long-held beliefs and practices. You may find yourself feeling defensive or embarrassed, hopeful or sad. All these things are part of the journey into disability. Please don't become derailed by your feelings. Stick with it. The end goal is worth it! If this is your second, third, or one hundredth time in a disability-and-church conversation, I commend you for staying with the journey. I hope you will find things in this book that resonate and things that will challenge.

The best posture for entering this conversation is humility. You must have an open heart, mind, and spirit. Take a moment to quiet yourself and invite God's Spirit to guide you into truth, to bring conviction where it is needed, and to lead you into the just and righteous ways of *his* kingdom (Jn 16:8). Once you see, you can't unsee. Once you catch the vision for God's kingdom, there's no going back. It is life changing, beautiful, far more expansive than you ever thought possible, and it's completely upside down from this world.

PART 1

DISABILITY Within God's Story

1

God's Mission, Our Mandates

I STILL REMEMBER THE FEELING of intense obligation mixed with fear the Sunday night I walked into what was affectionately called Wilson's Chapel. A student from a local Bible college was offering an evangelism course at our church, and a sense of duty that I was supposed to "save people" led this introverted thirteen-year-old girl to spend the five o'clock hour before Sunday evening service in our church's old sanctuary learning how to be an evangelist. Only three or four people showed up (one of those being my older brother), and for the next four weeks, we worked through an evangelism curriculum that essentially taught us how to share the Romans Road with random strangers, with the goal of getting them to accept Jesus on the spot.[1]

I loved Jesus. I had believed in him my whole life. I wanted nothing more than to follow him and help others to follow him. But I became profoundly terrified by this approach to evangelism, and this made me feel guilty. *I know I'm supposed to do this, but I just can't!* When I sifted through my conflicted feelings, I latched onto a thought. *Maybe evangelism isn't my spiritual gift!* This thought quickly took root, and I was able to push my guilt to the background and focus on other gifts I might have. I soon concluded that I would embrace gifts of kindness, prayer, and helps and leave the work of evangelism to others. I never

---

[1]The Romans Road is an evangelism strategy that uses five key verses from the book of Romans to walk people through a basic salvation message. By presenting each verse, the evangelist can help listeners understand that they are sinners (Rom 3:23) who are separated from God and in need of rescue (Rom 6:23), that God has made the way of that rescue through Jesus (Rom 5:8), that we can respond to God's recuse by confession and belief (Rom 10:9-13), and that when we do, God will surely save us (Rom 10:13).

once stopped to consider that maybe I didn't fully understand evangelism or the many ways in which believers could participate willingly and joyfully in it.

I hear similar versions of this story from many people. With every new group of master's students in my school's Evangelism and Leadership and Ministry Leadership programs, I ask, "How many of you have the gift of evangelism?" Without fail, I never get more than one hand raised, and often it is none. When I make the case from Scripture that every Christian is called to participate in evangelism, the fear in the room gets palpable. Why is this?

The problem for many of us is that we have a reduced gospel. We emphasize that all people are sinful and headed to hell with no way to stop this trajectory on our own. We introduce Jesus as the one who steps into our place, taking our punishment and changing our destination to heaven. All we have to do is accept what Jesus has done and receive him as Lord and Savior of our lives. But this only tells a small portion of the story and, quite frankly, pulls Jesus' story out of context. For those hearing this message, they may wonder, *Who is Jesus, and why does he matter? What do I really gain by accepting this message? How does this really change the mess I'm in right now, the questions I have, the problems I see in the world? If Jesus is only good for helping me escape this world, then how and why do this world and my life really matter?* Ultimately people may ask, "How is this good news?"

And yet, when being introduced to Jesus, it *should* be good news. Mark opens his gospel by saying, "Here begins the Good News about Jesus the Messiah, the Son of God" (Mk 1:1). This opening line tells us several things. First, the good news is a story. It is not merely a set of propositions or truths. Second, it is a story about a particular person who lived in a particular time and is connected to a particular history. Third, this person is a man named Jesus who is connected to a people and history in which he is seen not just as the ultimate fulfillment of their expectations but also the ultimate answer for the world: This Jesus is Messiah and Son of God. This opening line sends us in two directions.

The first direction is backward into the past. Mark immediately situates this good-news story of Jesus within the Old Testament and the story of Israel. He notes that Isaiah prophesied about someone preparing the way for the Messiah, and Mark says this person Isaiah was talking about is none other than Jesus' cousin John the Baptist, who preaches repentance to prepare people for Jesus. When Jesus walks by one day, John the Baptist points to him as the one "who is greater than I am—so much greater that I'm not even worthy to stoop down like a slave and untie the straps of his sandals" (Mk 1:7). John the Baptist baptizes Jesus, and immediately the heavens split open, the Holy Spirit descends on Jesus like a dove, and God's voice booms from heaven "You are my dearly loved Son, and you bring me great joy" (Mk 1:9-11). In this dramatic, action-packed opening, Mark makes the important point that Jesus doesn't just appear out of thin air. He is a historical figure who is deeply connected to a story that has long been in the making.

The second direction Mark sends us is forward into the future. For the rest of his Gospel, Mark tells not only the story of how Jesus fulfills the story begun in the Old Testament but why this ultimately is good news for Israel, for the people in Jesus' immediate context, for us, and for all who come after us. Every story in Mark points to Jesus as the ultimate fulfillment of God's story and the promises God made about how God would fix a world that was created as good but had fallen into disarray because of disobedience. Jesus announces that the kingdom of God the Israelites had longed for is near (Mk 1:15). Jesus demonstrates his power as King and Priest by healing the sick, casting out demons, ruling over nature, and raising the dead. Jesus becomes the ultimate Prophet, denouncing the empty, legalistic rituals of the religious and announcing the fruits of hearts made new by his Spirit: fruits such as servanthood, love of God and neighbor, holiness, inclusion, sacrifice, and justice. Jesus becomes Savior of all, enacting God's justice against sin through his own death and inaugurating God's kingdom through his resurrection.

When you put these two trajectories together, you get a comprehensive *from-creation-to-new-creation story* that is good news from beginning to end or, more accurately, from eternity to eternity. The good news is the story of God and his work in the world, ultimately fulfilled through the person of Jesus Christ. It is a good-news story that makes sense of our world and brings help, wholeness, answers, and hope to the messes we are in, the questions we have, the problems we see in the world, and the need we have for our lives and the world to matter. When we go back and look at the whole story, from Genesis to Revelation, we see clearly that God is on mission, and we are invited into that mission in two grand and interrelated ways.

GOD'S MISSION

When we adopted our son, he received no fewer than five different children's Bibles as welcome gifts. These types of kid-edition Bibles didn't exist when I was born. My first Bible, a King James Version, was considered a kid's Bible simply because the front cover had a picture of Jesus with a group of children and the text included illustrations of popular stories. Most of the children's Bibles my son received summarize main stories of the Bible with easy prose and colorful pictures. What I observed about these Bibles is similar to what I've observed about how I was taught the Bible as a kid: They tell different happenings of the Bible as individual, self-contained stories but fail to connect the dots and discuss how these stories fit together in a bigger, more comprehensive narrative. Kids learn about Noah, Abraham, Moses, David, and Daniel but rarely know why these stories matter or how they fit together.

What is different about the Bible my son loves the most is that it doesn't hit all the Bible's highlights. Instead, it relays the big story of God's mission and work in the world. While I wish the people in the illustrations were brown and not white, and while I do want him and his sister to learn individual stories, what I love about my children's continual reading of this Bible is that they are learning to read the Bible missionally, as a big story of God, and not as isolated, "cool" stories of almost mythical heroes. With as many times as they have read *The Big Picture Story Bible*, I am convinced my children have a better grasp on missional theology than most adults in the church![2]

---

[2]David R. Helm, *The Big Picture Story Bible* (Crossway, 2004).

Reading Scripture missionally pushes us to see the Bible as a cohesive story and focuses our attention on the God around whom the story centers. Genesis opens, "In the beginning God created the heavens and the earth" (Gen 1:1), and Revelation 22 describes a new heavens and earth ruled by "the Alpha and the Omega, the First and the Last, the Beginning and the End" (Rev 22:13). In the middle, we follow God's "universal will and plan for his creation" as he seeks to make himself known to the people he has created and as he works to restore a creation that unravels in the aftermath of his people's rebellion.[3] This storied way of reading Scripture pulls us into a drama that, like any good story, has a good beginning that is corrupted by a problem and a good ending that showcases how the long struggle to overcome the conflict successfully resolves what is broken and leads to an even better future.[4]

There are many ways we can break up this drama. William Dyrness sees five acts, Craig Bartholomew and Michael Goheen six.[5] Scott Moreau, Gary Corwin, and Gary McGee count seven, as does Christopher Wright, but even they split the seven acts differently.[6] What holds all these visions of Scripture's drama together is a baseline of creation, fall, redemption, and new creation. This simplified way of splicing the text gives us the foundation and the latitude to draw out key anchor points within the grand narrative. Let us consider briefly what each part conveys.

In the first act, creation, we are introduced to the main characters of God's drama. We start with the God over all gods and unlike any other god, who is powerful and good and who creates everything that exists as a good extension of himself. He creates for his own pleasure, by his own power, and for his own purposes. Every creative act is seen as good until God gets to day six. On this day he forms man and woman and invests

---

[3]Craig Ott and Stephen J. Strauss with Timothy C. Tennent, *Encountering Theology of Mission: Biblical Foundations, Historical Developments, and Contemporary Issues* (Baker Academic, 2010), 58.

[4]Craig G. Bartholomew and Michael W. Goheen, *The Drama of Scripture: Finding Our Place in the Biblical Story*, 2nd ed. (Baker Academic, 2014); Christopher J. H. Wright, *The Great Story and the Great Commission: Participating in the Biblical Drama of Mission* (Baker Academic, 2023), 3.

[5]William A. Dyrness, *Let the Earth Rejoice! A Biblical Theology of Holistic Mission* (Crossway, 1983); Bartholomew and Goheen, *Drama of Scripture*.

[6]A. Scott Moreau, Gary R. Corwin, and Gary B. McGee, *Introducing World Missions: A Biblical, Historical, and Practical Survey*, 2nd ed. (Baker Academic, 2020); Wright, *Great Story and the Great Commission*.

his very image in them through his own life-giving breath. This creative climax results in the pronouncement of "very good" (Gen 1:31). The week ends on day seven with God resting from all his work (Gen 2:2).

If only the very good were enough. God birthed his creation out of unbridled love and with the desire that we would love him back wholeheartedly, but in act two, our tempter creeps into the garden hissing half-truths that birth doubts. "Did God really say?" (Gen 3:1). The whole garden is before them, and only one tree holds limits (Gen 2:16-17). But that one question followed by a declaration that essentially says, "God's just withholding power from you!" (Gen 3:5) leads Adam and Eve to view limitation as something bad. They didn't need to eat the fruit to "become like God." They had been made in God's image and were already God's imprint in the world (Gen 1:26-27). But somehow this truth doesn't prevail. It is limitation that becomes the concern, and with that, Eve reaches out, takes, eats, and gives. Adam reaches out, takes, and eats. And both immediately hide themselves in shame (Gen 3:6-7).

The consequences of this terrible act were swift and broad. God had created with the intent that all of creation would experience a shalom—a peace—that was all-consuming. It was not, as we think today, merely an absence of war, but rather a fullness of life, harmony, and things as they should be. People were to flourish as creatures. People were to flourish in relationship with one another. People were to help the world flourish. This was so because people were to live in the world as God's imprint.

The choice Adam and Eve make mars all this. In doubting God's word, they introduce distrust and disharmony into the world. Sin brings consequences: painful reproduction, difficult cultivation of the soil, and contentious relationships (Gen 3:16-19). The very things God imprinted his very good creation to do—be fruitful, multiply, fill the earth, and care for creation—those are still on the docket, but they are now complicated by difficulty, dismay, disruption, and death.

The amazing thing, however, is that the story isn't all bad news on this fateful day. In the midst of God revealing the consequences of sin, God inaugurates the third act—redemption—by announcing that a solution is coming. One day Eve's seed will crush the serpent (Gen 3:15). What God announces this day is an ultimate solution but not an immediate one. Through generation after generation, over the span of millennia, God continues to showcase his kingdom and his plan through particular moments and people of history. He covenants with Noah, Abraham, Moses, Israel, and David to be his set-apart people, not for their own sake but for his own sake. They are to mediate God's presence to the world and draw the world to God in worship (Ex 19:5-6), but, like their first ancestors, they cannot. They are captive to sin and cannot free themselves or those around them from the consequences of sin.

Then one day, as promised, God determines the time is right to enter his world as part of his creation—birthed from the womb of a virgin teenager—a fully God, fully human person (Gal 4:4). This baby is none other than the one announced by Mark as Jesus, the Messiah, the Son of God (Mk 1:1). As Word become flesh (Jn 1:14), Jesus grows in both wisdom and stature (Lk 2:52) to become a renowned teacher and healer, loved by many and hated by the religious. Through his teachings and miracles, Jesus always has his face pointed toward Jerusalem and his ultimate purpose. As the second Adam (1 Cor 15:45), the greater Moses (Heb 3:1-6), the eternal Davidic king (Acts 2:29-36) from the line of Abraham (Mt 1:1), Jesus comes to break sin, to restore lives, to bring justice, and to enable flourishing (Acts 4:14-20). He does this by taking on the weight of the world's sin and the consequences for the world's sin: He willingly dies at the hands of the religious leaders and is crucified (Mk 8:31; 9:31; 10:32-34; 14:12–15:47).

His death, however, is not an end. It is a beginning. As he predicted, he rises from the dead three days later, forever breaking the power of sin and our enslavement to its consequences, and writes the new future: a new creation in which God's judgments will deal the final blow to Satan sin, and death, and God's life will sustain his new people, called out from every tribe, nation, language, and tongue (Rev 7:9) as they dwell in a new city with a new garden, from which flows a river with the water of life (Rev 21–22). In this new future, God finds his home among his people, and his presence forever dissolves death, sorrow, crying, and pain as he makes all things new (Rev 21:3-5).

This final act, new creation, has an interesting position because it overlaps with the act of redemption. Israel's Scriptures had long foretold that one day God's kingdom would prevail. One day God would rule his people with justice and joy, infusing his creation with life and shalom (e.g., Mic 4). It was future. It was distant. When it came, a new age would dawn. But before his death, Jesus announces that God's kingdom is near and at hand. After his resurrection, the apostles wrestle with the implications of Jesus' life and conclude that their eschatology, their view about the end, needs adjustment. God's timeline wasn't strictly linear: creation to fall to redemption to new creation. Resurrection signaled the inbreaking of new creation into the present. The new age was already underway, even if the present time had not fully run its course. A day was coming when God would decisively bring about the fullness of his kingdom, but until that day, God's kingdom could be realized in small ways in the world, through the new people of God identified by their allegiance to Jesus Christ. As Gordon Fee notes, "The resurrection of Christ marked the beginning of the End, the turning of the ages." This *already-not-yet* reality means that people are both saved and being saved, with "God's final salvation of his people [having] already been accomplished by Christ" even though their "final salvation" has yet to be realized. This *already-not-yet* reality means that, as members of Christ's "end-time community" we also "live in the present as those stamped with eternity," being "empowered by the Spirit [to] now live the life of the future in the present age, the life that characterizes God himself."[7]

This is an interesting and grand story, but one that perhaps still feels a little disconnected to our lives. Why does Adam and Eve's act of disobedience matter for us? Why is God so concerned to send Jesus for us? What is God really trying to accomplish? If we leave our story here, with the outer shell, we can wonder where we fit, if at all. This is where the mandates given to human beings draw us in to the good beginning and the good ending in ways that make the *why* of God in the middle so compelling in its compassion and power. God has created us with vocational intent so we can participate in his good mission.

---

[7]Gordon D. Fee, *Paul, the Spirit, and the People of God* (Hendrickson, 1996), 51-52.

OUR MANDATES

We have just recounted the Bible through a missional hermeneutic. It is one of many ways we can approach Scripture and understand its themes and unity in diversity. It is a compelling way to engage the text because it tells us not just God's story but also our story. Through it, we come to know who we are, why we are here, how we should approach the world, how we should live, and how we should engage the world with the hope we have in God and his wonderful future.[8] Embedded within God's story are two visions for humanity.

Identity, existence, and purpose. The first vision comes right at the beginning. It is inseparable from our formation and the breath of God that warms this molded dust into living, breathing flesh. "Let us make human beings in our image, to be like us," God says. "They will reign over the fish in the sea, the birds in the sky, the livestock, all the wild animals on the earth, and the small animals that scurry along the ground" (Gen 1:26). Patterned after God himself, enfleshed as male and female (Gen 1:27), this new creation is blessed by God with the call to "multiply. Fill the earth and govern it" (Gen 1:28). Humanity shares in the creational wonder of all God has brought into existence. Like all creation, human beings are called to blessing, flourishing, and multiplication, but unlike the rest, human beings are given the command to rule created order, caring for it, culling life from it, and finding sustenance from it. In this way, human beings are called to enter God's mission as colaborers, as vice regents, imaging God in the world and bearing witness to God's lordship by how they live in the world and care for creation. Their rule and work are to be fully representative of God's rule and presence on and over the earth.

What is unique about this first mandate is that it does not differentiate between human beings. No person or group is excluded from this call. It is something given to all humankind. Through our ancestors Adam and Eve, God creates every human being in his image and with this charge to rule and serve. This *cultural mandate* (as it is often called) establishes God's design for diversity, culture, and relationship.

---

[8]Wright, *Great Story and the Great Commission*, 14.

We are distinctly created male and female and called to use this diversity to multiply and fill the earth. Our outward expansion across the many terrains and frontiers will naturally diversify our skills, knowledge, and perspectives. From one shared ancestral pair comes every ethnicity and culture. Diversity is built into God's plan for the world.

So is creative culture making. God's call for human beings to rule the world in his stead and as fully representative of his reign on earth entrusts the work of creation and culture making to his people. Following God, the first gardener, we are called to "imitate him by cultivating the initial gift of a well-arranged garden, a world where intelligence, skill and imagination have already begun to make something of the world."[9]

Ultimately, we are called toward community and relationship. Our Creator experiences perfect community in the triune Godhead, and he creates us to experience relational community both vertically and horizontally. This calling to community is meant to draw out unity in difference within marriages, families, friendships, neighborhoods, cities, and governments. Relational harmony and interpersonal communion should breed societal harmony and governing communion. We belong to one another and need one another.

This tripartite calling and mandate for humankind answers the questions of identity (who we are), existence (why we are here), and purpose (what we are meant to do/be). It is important to note that this mandate precedes the fall and prevails after the fall. Adam and Eve are not cut off from this calling when they sin. God announces that these callings go on, but now with difficulty, disruption, and division. Centuries later, when God wipes the slate clean and sends a flood in judgment of all humankind, he rebuilds through Noah and reiterates this same cultural mandate with him (Gen 9:1-7). The cultural mandate is part and parcel to what it means to be human. But while the fall does not dissolve our mandate, it does fundamentally change how successful we are in this endeavor.

Our lives after the fall are a testament to how we cannot live in relational harmony, in fully beneficent cultural making, or in diversity.

---

[9]Andy Crouch, *Culture Making: Recovering Our Creative Calling* (InterVarsity Press, 2008), 108.

After the fall, we fall apart and cause the world around us to fall apart. It is not that everything we do is bad, sinful, or faulty. We do many good things in the world, but our ability to live into God's calling with untainted compassion, humility, and deference is not possible. Sin crouches at the door (Gen 4:7), and our tempter continues to lure us beyond our limits and our calling. We are driven toward power and dominance and away from diversity. We are pulled toward endless toil that serves self more than others, humanity more than creation. We rebel against submission and seek to usurp our Lord. The vast majority of the Bible recounts this conflicted existence of creation bucking against Creator. Every human, from every walk of life, from every religion and ethnicity, from every (fill in the blank), is called to good work on earth, and every human has potential to do some good things. But no human, apart from God, can overcome the sin that infects our motivations, our thoughts, our desires, or our actions. We live in a world that can only proffer "a craving for physical pleasure, a craving for everything we see, and pride in our achievements and possessions" (1 Jn 2:16). The mandate goes on, even if we fail in carrying it out.

But all is not lost. All earthly existence points to a moment in time when God himself intervenes in his created world. It takes God, incarnate through the Virgin Mary as the fully God, fully human Jesus Christ, to set things right. Only through the entrance of Jesus into this earthly plane, and only by his own life, death, and resurrection, can our cultural mandate be redeemed. It is only through Christ that anyone can live into their human calling in a way that fulfills God's original design for flourishing, care, and shalom. Jesus alone makes God's calling possible. But Jesus does more than simply redeem our cultural calling. Jesus redeems our very lives as well, drawing us into a new vocational space.

God's faithfulness in history includes a people. The disobedience of Adam and Eve has devastating effects. Sin takes up residence in God's good world and manifests itself especially through the now-broken lives of Adam and Eve. But God has promised that he will redeem his people. Eve will produce an offspring who, though bruised in the process, will crush Satan's head. That offspring is a long way off. In the intervening space, as people multiply in the earth, God continually calls them toward obedience. A pivotal moment in this wooing comes when God chooses an old childless couple to be the antidote to the ruckus at Babel that begins with boastful, arrogant grasping for God's throne and ends in division and scattering (Gen 11:1-9).

The calling of Abraham is indeed surprising, but it is a calling that, as Christopher Wright argues, "is the beginning of God's answer to the evil of human hearts, the strife of nations, and the groaning brokenness of his whole creation. It is the beginning of the mission of God and the mission of God's people."[10] This calling has enormous scope because through it God promises blessing will come to all the nations of the earth (Gen 12:3). God specifically calls Abraham to *go* to a new land, to *expand* into a great nation, and ultimately to *bless all the peoples on earth* (Gen 12:2-3). In bringing about Eve's offspring, God chooses an unlikely man to birth a nation that is to grow and expand not for its own sake but for the sake of others. God keeps his promise, and within a few generations Abraham and Sarah grow from having no children to being the progenitors of the nation Israel, a nation over a million strong when they leave captivity in Egypt and move into Canaan, taking over the land God has promised as their inheritance.

God always draws back to this Abrahamic covenant as he calls each new generation of Israelites to follow him. God covenants with Israel that they should be a kingdom *of* priests. Not a kingdom *with* priests but a kingdom *of* priests.[11] This nation itself should be a sign and witness in the world of a holy and loving God, who blesses his people and through them blesses the world. But no matter how many judges, prophets, or priests the Lord sends, Israel can never maintain their witness or their focus. The pull of sin and idolatry, and the desire to be like their neighboring kingdoms, drags Israel down, leading to cycles of punishment and repentance until finally God can withstand them no more and sends his chosen people into exile. But even here God's mission does not end. Promises of Eve's offspring remain steady throughout Israel's history. In

[10] Christopher J. H. Wright, *The Mission of God's People: A Biblical Theology of the Church's Mission* (Zondervan, 2010), 66.

[11] Ott and Strauss, *Encountering Theology of Mission*, 8.

saving a remnant and bringing them back home from exile, God's mission is still possible, but it will be realized through a means Israel does not anticipate. The offspring of Eve enters the world as a baby, born in the small village of Bethlehem.

For thirty years Jesus' life seems unremarkable as he grows in physical stature and godly wisdom (Lk 2:52). There is nothing beautiful or majestic about Jesus' appearance, Isaiah prophesies, nothing to attract us to him (Is 53:2). And yet, Matthew (Mt 1:1) is sure to let us know that Jesus comes directly from the line of Abraham. Jesus is not there, however, to take over an earthly kingdom but rather to usher in the upside-down kingdom in which his own rejection, suffering, pain, and death will put an end to the power of sin and its ultimate propagator (Satan). Jesus is there to introduce a world in which he is King and Lord and in which people, through the empowerment of the Holy Spirit, can live in newness of life and participate in God's mission.

Something incredible takes place with Jesus' resurrection and ascension. Since Abraham, God has had a people, and this people was to manifest God's presence and blessing to the ends of the earth. This was not something every human on earth was called to. It was something God's people alone were called to. With their lives physically centered on the temple, in which God dwelled by his Spirit, they were to live in a way that beckoned the surrounding nations to come to the God of Israel. Sadly, they failed over and over and over again. So Jesus steps in to accomplish what they could not.

Replacing the death sentence that came with the first Adam's sin, Jesus succeeds where Adam failed, bringing righteousness to all who choose to die with Christ (Rom 5:18; 6:7-8). Jesus' death marks the end of sin and the victory over Satan. Jesus' death also ends the need for temple sacrifices and a nation physically centered on this temple. At the moment of his death, the temple curtain rips in two, from top to bottom (Mt 27:51), and Jesus himself becomes the "perfect sacrifice for our sins" (Heb 9:14), once and for all satisfying the penalty for our sins (Heb 10:12). With his death, Jesus takes care of the sin issue that has prevented his people from living into their God-given calling to be a blessing to the ends of the earth. With his resurrection, ascension, and sending of the Spirit, Jesus does something remarkable with his temple and his people. To understand this, we will start in Ephesians and end in Matthew.

In Ephesians 1, Paul argues that God's mission for the world was always in God's mind, even before God created the world. God had predetermined to seek the flourishing of creation: that men and women and all of creation would experience God's blessing, God's shalom. God had predetermined that he would have a people who would mediate this blessing to the world (Eph 1:4-5). Paul doesn't explicitly explain the intervening space in between God's plan and its fulfillment in Christ, but I have recounted it here at some length. Everyone from Adam and Eve through the most recent member of Israel had failed. It was only through his life, death, and resurrection that Jesus got God's mission back on track, winning the decisive victory over sin and death and beginning the work of establishing God's rule and reign once and for all.

Here Paul picks up the argument in Ephesians. God's plan has always been to bring everything in creation, everything in heaven and earth, under the rule and reign of Christ Jesus (Eph 1:6-10). Just because Israel cannot accomplish God's purposes on their own does not mean that God has abandoned his promise to Abraham. Rather, Christ resolves the sin issue by his death and resurrection and then reinfuses his promise of a chosen people with new life. Instead of his chosen people being an ethnic group made up of Jews, God has now determined it will be a new people made up of Jews and Gentiles. Paul is adamant about this point. Jesus is our peace. Though Jews and Gentiles have lived in hostility with one another, Jesus' death breaks down the wall of hostility that has separated them, and his resurrection inaugurates a new kingdom in which Jews and Gentiles are now made into one people (Eph 2:14-16). Now, as Paul says in Ephesians 2:18, "All of us can came to the Father through the same Holy Spirit because of what Christ has done for us."

Paul then breaks out some great imagery about what this means: For those who embrace Christ, we are now citizens of God's holy people, we are members of God's family, we are God's house, we are joined together like bricks in a building to become a holy temple for the Lord, we are now one body (Eph 2:19-22). Through Christ, Jew and Gentile are now being crafted into a new people, a holy temple for the Lord. No longer is God found in a physical temple in the center of one ethnic group. The Spirit of God now indwells anyone who is brought into Christ such that we, both individually and collectively, are now the temple of God. This means that everywhere God's people go, we carry with us the presence and home of God, called to attract others to know God through our work and witness (1 Pet 2:9-12). This brings fresh light to God's promises to Abraham.

As I have noted, Matthew's Gospel is concerned to place Jesus squarely as a "descendant . . . of Abraham" (Mt 1:1). Matthew fills his account with Old Testament Scripture, declaring over and over how Jesus fulfills the Scripture. It is not a surprise, then, that when Matthew ends his Gospel, he brackets it again with Abraham, this time showing the expanse of what Abraham's calling entails. We find the words in Matthew 28:18-20.

> Jesus came and told his disciples, "I have been given all authority in heaven and on earth. Therefore, go and make disciples of all the nations, baptizing them in the name of the Father and the Son and the Holy Spirit. Teach these new disciples to obey all the commands I have given you. And be sure of this: I am with you always, even to the end of the age."

There are precious and powerful parallels between this Great Commission—this gospel mandate—and God's original calling of Abraham. Go . . . expand . . . bless all the nations. Jesus announces that he has God's authority and in that power calls all his followers to make disciples in all their going. They are to teach everything they have learned from Christ—his words and his works—in order to form God's new people. They are to take this blessing, this message—that Christ Jesus is Lord and victor over all things and is making all things new, abolishing our punishment and giving us his Spirit so we can live into the fullness of God's intent for our lives—to the ends of the earth in order to make disciples of all the nations. "If humanity as a whole is subject to God's curse," Wright says, "then humanity as a whole must be reached by God's blessing."[12] Through Christ, we are made "true children of Abraham," inheriting his mission and promise (Gal 3:29) to be a blessing by taking Jesus to the ends of the earth until the end of the age (Mt 28:19-20).

---

[12]Wright, *Mission of God's People*, 71.

This isn't a work to be done in human strength and power. Rather, the Father and Son send the Spirit into the world to empower God's followers for this task. The Holy Spirit leads into truth (Jn 16:13), reveals God's kingdom with regard to sin, righteousness, and judgment (Jn 16:8), and gives each member of God's family gifts and means for growing God's church and witnessing to God's grace (1 Cor 12).

Renewed vocation in Jesus. Who is this new people, and what is their vocation? Everyone who places their faith in Christ Jesus and his death and resurrection is called to the family business of going, blessing, and working to make Jesus known to the ends of the earth, among every tribe, nation, language, and tongue (Rev 7:9). The apostles take this calling seriously, and Acts recounts the birth of the church, God's new covenant people, who, through the power of the Spirit, move out from Jerusalem, through Judea and Samaria, to the ends of the earth (Acts 1:8). This covenant people keep expanding and growing, through the centuries and millennia, right up to the present age.

You and I are now called into this vocational space not to fulfill just our creational calling but also our gospel calling. We are, as Peter reminds us, "a chosen people . . . royal priests, a holy nation, God's very own possession," called out for the express purpose that we can "show others the goodness of God" (1 Pet 2:9). The picture we get in Revelation is a beautiful bookend and fulfillment of all that has come prior. When every people group is represented in a great throng around God's throne, "as redeemed humanity, together with all angels and all creatures in creation, joins to celebrate [God's] great achievement," Wright imagines that God will turn to Abraham in that moment and say, "There you are. I kept my promise. 'All nations,' I said, and all nations it is. Mission accomplished."[13]

CONCLUDING THOUGHTS

God's story of creation to fall to redemption to new creation has many more layers than what I have expressed here. But what we can see so clearly is that God is a *God of love* who has created us to know him and live in his blessings. And God is a *God of love on mission* who relentlessly

[13]Wright, *Mission of God's People*, 77.

pursues the restoration of a created world that falls into utter catastrophe through sin that has tarnished every corner of creation. We know that Jesus has already won the victory, and yet we live in an age in which God's kingdom is breaking in but not fully realized. This in-between, already-not-yet space is not always easy to navigate. We know God is completing his victorious work, but we can't always see how things fit in the moment. Which leads us to ask a very important question, one that many people and families ask: Where do disabilities show up in God's story?

DISCUSSION QUESTIONS

1. In light of the opening anecdote, how have you tended to understand evangelism? What might it look like for every Christian to be an evangelist?
2. How does a missional reading of Scripture affect your understanding of the Bible?
3. What is the relationship between the cultural mandate and the gospel mandate? How do you find yourself participating in each?
4. Before reading on, how would you answer the closing question: Where do disabilities show up in God's story?

2

Understanding Disability

The first year we did taxes after adopting our son, we informed our tax agent that we had added to our family. His face widened into a huge grin, his voice moved up in pitch and volume, and he congratulated us heartily. Then we added, "We'll need to make sure we mark it as a special needs adoption because he has Down syndrome." Though our happy demeanor and celebratory tone did not change, his joy bubble seemed to pop upon this remark. Our agent's face immediately took on an expression of solemnity, and he dropped the volume and pitch of his voice to express, "I'm so sorry." We didn't quite know what to say because we weren't sorry and in fact had knowingly said yes to the extra chromosome when we said yes to our son. Our response of "We're not" morphed our agent's face once again into one of confusion. "Oh," he said, not sure of how to process this open embrace and even okayness with what so many perceive as a travesty. Herein lies one of the challenges that comes with a word and concept such as *disability*.

Just uttering the word can set a trajectory for how we consider the person on whom we apply this label. *Dis* as a prefix means *opposite of* or *absence* of, or simply *not. Disability*, in this light, then, is *opposite of ability*, or *absence of ability*, or simply *not ability*. This opposite and absence language easily biases us toward negative assumptions: (1) that something about the person is opposite of or at least devoid of aspects of "normal"; (2) that despite any other good thing, disability totalizes the person's experience, value, and purpose; (3) that disability is inherently bad or sad; and (4) that the person (and family) experiencing disability requires automatic pity and charity. Disability language as opposite language assumes we know what *normal* and *able* mean and then packs into the "dis" all the things we would be horrified not to have: mobility, speech, sight, intelligence, control, independence, socialization, and so on. To understand disability, we will start by interacting with the four assumptions listed above and then look at how various models of disability seek to address these.

DISABILITY IS ABNORMAL

Have you ever stopped to consider what a "normal" human being is? If you really think about it, any answer you give to this question is already fraught with challenges from the beginning because every answer requires qualification. Our age, our gender, our genetic makeup, our ethnic background, our culture, and our physical location all factor into what is normal at a particular point in time.

Consider my son's height, for example. Every doctor's visit we are told that he either doesn't show up on the "typical growth chart" or is somewhere in the 1 to 3 percent range. However, looking at a growth chart for boys with Down syndrome, he is somewhere around the 25 percent mark. What neither of these charts take into consideration, however, is that his birth parents are of an ethnicity whose height tracks smaller than that of white males. If there was a growth chart for this other ethnicity, he would be marked in another growth pattern altogether. So, what is he? Abnormal since he is in the lowest categories on a US growth chart that is largely based on white males? Is he normal when marked on a Down syndrome growth chart? Where might he fit in a different ethnicity's growth chart? Perhaps he would still be on the lower side but much more in a range that would be considered normal. What is more, regardless of which chart we put him on, isn't he still normal in that he is following an expected growth pattern that tracks with the growth curve? Do you see how elusive this is?

In many ways, normal is a social construct that we base on some "imagined entity" of what we think most people are like.[1] But "when disability is so 'obvious' or 'common sense,'" Benjamin Conner says,

[1]Brian Brock, *Disability: Living into the Diversity of Christ's Body* (Baker Academic, 2021), 20.

"people tend to forget how socially embedded notions of normalcy, ability, and disability can be."[2] Brian Brock, for example, argues that if we look at a range of numbers and determine the mean (the average) to be fifty, nothing suggests those numbers that are not fifty are "intrinsically inferior"—that is, until we assume that the mean is the norm. Once we take fifty to be normal, suddenly all those other numbers are now considered aberrations. In terms of disability, we think it's obvious what most people are like and assume this *mean* is actually the *norm*. When we do this, we inevitably make assumptions about people who are different: They are disabled because they are not normal. We rarely stop to consider whether the difference we perceive is good, even when the difference is "functional in its own particular and unexpected way."[3]

Asking questions about what is normal inevitably causes us to reconsider what is disability. It is easy to assume that disability is solely about a body that does not function in expected ways. However, disability advocates rightfully note that while we cannot ignore bodies, in many cases a body that is impaired in some way is not disabled until it comes up against a social or physical barrier that turns that impairment into a disability. It is the socially constructed expectations about how a person looks, what a person can do, and how they contribute to the whole that determine whether a person is disabled. This can be situational, leaving a person disabled in one circumstance and not another.

After my husband and I were married, we recounted our first date to someone, and I noted with humor that we both wore purple. My husband looked at me, shocked, and said, "Wait, my shirt was purple? I thought it was blue!" To my knowledge, I had never met a person with color vision deficiency until I met my husband. For most of our life together, his inability to see color is a nonissue. It doesn't affect our ability to converse, hike, cook, fold laundry, mow, or do so many of the other routine things that make up our everyday lives. However, when I talk in colors and try to point out the guy in the red sweater, when he's

---

[2]Benjamin T. Conner, *Disabling Mission, Enabling Witness: Exploring Missiology Through the Lens of Disability* (IVP Academic, 2018), 22.

[3]Brock, *Disability*, 20.

driving on particularly sunny days and can't determine whether the traffic light that is lit up is red, yellow, or green, or when he's asked by the cashier to "hit the green button," suddenly his impairment is turned into disability. Society expects that he can function with red/green distinction. It has built a world around red and green assuming it is normal for people to distinguish these colors. My husband can't do this, but until he's in a situation in which these colors become important, he doesn't experience disability.

We find great humor in my husband's color vision deficiency. He occasionally dresses the kids in some amazingly clashing ways and sometimes needs one of us to help him find the orange weed-eater string that falls into the grass, but overall my husband is not prevented from participating well in the world. For other disabilities, however, the stress on normalcy leads to false assumptions about the good of the person and their benefit to society.

DISABILITY IS ALL THAT MATTERS

Not long after we had adopted our son, a former employee of my husband's called while we were driving to the store. It had been a while since the two of them had caught up, and my husband happily shared our good fortune in adding to our family. As they chatted over the car speaker, it came up quite casually that our son had Down syndrome. For the rest of my life, I will be able to tell you the exact spot we had reached on Fabyan Parkway when the man responded, "Ohhhhh, so he's retarded!" I honestly don't believe this gentleman was ill-intentioned, just more informed of a much earlier era in which labels like *retarded* were standard fare. But still, my mouth fell open and I made the "I'm smacking his head between my hands" motion to my husband as my eyes bugged out.

Most people don't use "retarded" language with us, but it is a perception that my son will have to fight the rest of his life. It is true that my son experiences cognitive and physical delays and challenges that our daughter has not. At four years his junior, she is already mastering things that remain a struggle for him. We don't deny that the extra chromosome affects every area of his life in some interesting, wonderful, and difficult ways. But his disability is not all there is to him. I will admit that this is sometimes hard to remember, even for us as his parents. We recently hit a rough behavior patch and had to be reminded that this was an age-appropriate challenge that his peers were also navigating. It takes thought, reflection, and time to parse out. As parents, we are committed to this completely.

However, even when people are well-intentioned in the world, many do not take the time to know our son or engage in this hard and discerning work. For many who see our son, he is disabled. Totally and completely. There is no consideration of whether a presenting issue is related to his extra chromosome or not. There is no consideration of whether he is functioning in a more healthy, well-adjusted, and honest way than others. There is no consideration of whether he is in fact smart even when he presents with cognitive delays. What seems "obvious" is that he (sometimes) looks like he has a disability and therefore must be treated as if this were the most pressing, important, and totalizing part of him. Sadly, this experience is not unique to him.

Many people who deal with disabilities find themselves totalized by their disability in at least two ways. First, it is not uncommon for someone who is deaf, is blind, has speaking difficulties, presents with physical challenges, is autistic, or is dealing with mental illness to be thought of as disabled in every area of life. A friend with cerebral palsy is thought to have low IQ because his speech isn't always clear and his hand movements at times are unsteady. A friend who is blind faces continual surprise at the common, everyday things he can do without assistance. A friend in a wheelchair regularly has people make assumptions about her needs and desires as if she lacks the ability to advocate for herself.

Second, the disability, whatever it is, often is considered the most important and salient feature of a person and their most pressing concern. When a person with a disability comes forward for prayer, if people aren't listening carefully, they will assume the request is for healing of the disability when in most cases it isn't. When churches establish groups for meaningful interactions, people with disabilities of all types are often placed together and given their own space without asking whether age, gender, or other factors should be weightier considerations for group assignment.

This totalizing problem comes in part because *disability* is not a discerning label. We use it indiscriminately as if it means something clear, but we pack so much into that one concept that we fail to see the immense diversity that exists within its borders. Disability could refer to something temporary or permanent. It could identify something inherited or acquired. It could affect a person physically, mentally, and/or socially.

I recently participated on a disability panel representing my son, a person with an extra chromosome that affects various aspects of his physical and cognitive function. This panel included a person who was in a wheelchair as a result of an accident as an adult, a person with severe mental illness as a result of trauma, and a person who developed a neurological issue that manifested in involuntary neck spasms that, though having no cure, can be minimized through treatment. We all represented *disability*, but not all the disabilities were visible or obvious. We all represented *disability*, but we came at it from different directions. For some their experience was one of loss. For some it was one of affliction. For others it was so constitutive of their identity that it was hard to fathom existing without the disability, and indeed, in my son's case, it is something he doesn't know he has. But regardless of how visible our disability is or whether we came into the disability world obliviously or reluctantly, we are now marked with a label that leads the conversation for others, even when we don't lead with it ourselves.

This reveals another way we totalize a disability: People who do not see themselves as having a disability cannot help but *other* the other. When some people set themselves apart from others on account of a disability, they are functioning under the belief that *difference* is the most important way to identify how they relate to others. This fails to recognize how much more similar people with and without disabilities are. Perhaps there are ways in which people with a disability need extra support, additional tools, or more time in one area or another, but this does not negate the inherent sameness and likeness that people with and without disabilities share. Erik Carter poignantly notes,

> Although labels usually highlight differences, people with and without developmental disabilities share almost everything in common. *Like everyone else*, people with developmental disabilities need support to live a good life. However, this support sometimes must be a bit more intensive, deliberate, or lasting. *Like everyone else*, people with developmental disabilities have wonderful strengths and gifts that exist alongside their limitations. Yet, these incredible capacities too frequently are overlooked. *Like everyone else*, people with developmental disabilities will struggle in some contexts and shine in others. Unfortunately, they usually are viewed only in terms of what they cannot do. And *like everyone else*, people with developmental disabilities want to express their spirituality and belong to a community. But these needs and connections are regularly overlooked.[4]

Carter reminds us that no person thrives without the help of others, and no person lives without a mixture of abilities and inabilities. But once the disability label attaches itself to a person, their strengths, abilities, and sameness get overly lauded or overlooked. When overly lauded, people with disabilities face the constant surprise and shock that they can do "normal" things. When overlooked, the differences, delays, difficulties, and deficiencies become disproportionately emphasized.

In his book *Vulnerable Communion*, Thomas Reynolds argues that social systems require people to participate in meaningful and valuable ways that support the corporate vision of good and contribute to expected ways of dwelling together in order to achieve membership and belonging.[5] Each system develops its own *cult of normalcy*, which governs the expected practices, attitudes, languages, and contributions of its members. Within such systems, individual people earn *body capital* by being able to "sell" themselves as useful in providing good for others and purchasing good (e.g., autonomy, freedom, and equality) for self. John Swinton notes that societies that "thrive on meritocracy and processes of valuing . . . are contingent on the exchange of particular social, psychological or material goods." When people with disabilities

---

[4]Erik W. Carter, *Including People with Disability in Faith Communities: A Guide for Service Providers, Families, and Congregations* (Paul H. Brooks, 2007), 3.

[5]Thomas E. Reynolds, *Vulnerable Communion: A Theology of Disability and Hospitality* (Brazos, 2008), 56-62.

do not have body capital or are unable to participate in meritocracy in ways others expect, they are excluded as aberrant and unuseful. And "within a society that uses the criteria of independence, productivity, intellectual prowess and social position to judge the value of human beings," the value of people with all types of disabilities, but especially those with developmental disabilities, will be questioned.[6] Without considering the myriad of ways that people with disabilities contribute meaningfully to society and also defy norms such that their ways of being in the world are actually *better*, a cult of normalcy totalizes people with a disability as *disabled other*. When this happens, Reynolds concludes, people with disabilities lose the ability to be "subjects of their own experiences" because the "cult of normalcy tells people with disabilities who they are, forcing them by various societal rituals to bear a name that is depersonalizing."[7]

DISABILITY IS INHERENTLY BAD AND SAD

Without a doubt, disability presents us with paradox. I must readily confess that some parts of the disability experience are different for my husband and me because we came into it initially through choice. We did not experience the disequilibrium of becoming pregnant and having a vision of our lives going one direction, only to find shockingly one day that it was going to be different. We went into disability with our eyes wide open, making a conscious decision to embrace it, even when we didn't foresee the magnitude of what we were embracing (both good and challenging). The blessing of this is that we have never once had to contend with the thought, *I didn't sign up for this.* We don't hit rough patches and think, *It's not fair that our son was born with a disability.* His birth and his life are not threatened with thoughts like, *Why him? Why us? Why this?* For some people and families, this is a real part of the struggle. Disability can be an overwhelming gut punch. On the tougher days, it can be hard to not give into these thoughts.

---

[6]John Swinton, "The Body of Christ Has Down Syndrome: Theological Reflections on Vulnerability, Disability, and Graceful Communities," *The Journal of Pastoral Theology* 13, no. 2 (2003): 69, 67.

[7]Reynolds, *Vulnerable Communion*, 62.

However, even willingly taking on a disability does not erase the frustration, the fatigue, or the heightened feelings that come when facing challenges you just can't love away. For people with disabilities and their caregivers, disability is a mixture of joy and sorrow, easy and tough, sunshine and darkness. There is no denying or glossing over this. There is no scenario in which we can or should minimize the burdens of this. However, too often people without disabilities impute judgment and suffering on people with disabilities, forgetting that living between the highs and lows is not an experience unique to people with disabilities. Living in a paradox of joy and sorrow, easy and tough, sunshine and darkness is to be human.

Disability takes on the sad and bad trope when we cannot jettison the grip of our cult of normalcy. Every time we embrace the temptation to compare our lives against disabled others, we make false assumptions about ourselves and those we cannot help but pity. Our vision about ourselves is skewed because we can imagine only one way of being in the world. Any reduction in our abilities feels like a travesty because it would require a loss of capability in areas we can't imagine living without. When we consider disability only as loss for us, we can't imagine it as anything but loss for others as well.[8] We should never diminish the real difficulties, pains, and suffering that can come with disability; however, we err when we project difficulty, pain, and suffering on another.

The first few years my son went through holidays, I didn't think much about his disinterest in gifts or things such as trick-or-treating. When he got into kindergarten, however, it was important for me to get him the right birthday gifts, Christmas gifts, and Halloween costume. I just *knew* that this year these things would matter because when I was in kindergarten, these things mattered. However, I struggled when he didn't want to put on his costume or walk the neighborhood for candy. I felt let down that he didn't tear through his gifts, raving in excitement about them and looking for more. It was all we could do to get him to tear the wrapping paper and open gift bags. As I tried to parse through my feelings, I told my husband, "I'm just sad that he is missing out on

[8]Brock, *Disability*, 23.

these key childhood experiences." Then it hit me. I was the only one who was sad.

I assumed my son was experiencing loss by lacking interest and that he would live with a lifetime of regret. I assumed this because this is how I think about a few key moments in my life when I compare my experiences with others and regret my shyness or reluctance to be daring. My son is not caught by all of this. His great contentment with whatever is right in front of him, his comfort in his own skin, his being okay with knowing who he is and what he likes, means he doesn't live in the materiality that so besets our world. It means that he doesn't feel the need to compare his life and experience with others to assess how successful he is. It means that he doesn't get tripped up trying to be someone else. It means that he finds joy in the moment and is not haunted by regrets. This is a beautiful way of living in the world. It becomes sad or bad only when the disability is magnified such that the person is diminished. By using disabilities as the sole lens with which to evaluate a person's life, many of the good things about the person get reimagined or erased.

DISABILITY NEEDS PITY AND CHARITY

When we impute all manner of badness and sadness to disability, we end up imputing badness and sadness to the people with disabilities as well, leading us to see people as "tragic and pitiable" and in need of charity.[9] A natural outcome of elevating the disability over the person, then, is a loss of personhood. Disability that is seen "as an *abnormal* part of life in a *normal* world" requires remedy: fixing, healing, supplementing.[10] But when people are reduced "to a function of their disabilities rather than vice versa," they lose autonomy over their needs and desires as well as their bodies.[11] Too often, people without disabilities feel empowered to make decisions about what people with disabilities need and want without consulting the people living with the disabilities.

---

[9]Bethany McKinney Fox, *Disability and the Way of Jesus: Holistic Healing in the Gospels and the Church* (IVP Academic, 2019), 99.

[10]Stephanie O. Hubach, *Same Lake Different Boat: Coming Alongside People Touched by Disability*, rev. and expanded ed. (P&R, 2020), 26.

[11]Reynolds, *Vulnerable Communion*, 25.

Normate assumptions about what all people should have, do, or desire leads to actions that invalidate the perspectives, opinions, and experiences of people with disabilities.[12] This kind of charity mindset annuls any hope of reciprocity or mutuality by assuming the trajectory is always one of abled *to* disabled. This gives the abled the power to decide what people with disabilities need and the power to decide how they will address those needs. Too often, this leads to making decisions based on criteria such as the burden, cost, time, and discomfort such accommodations will have on the abled.

For example, when the American with Disabilities Act was being drafted and passed into law, religious organizations successfully lobbied for exemption from its stipulations, arguing that compliance would be too costly and "create an 'undue hardship' on their constituents."[13] As Deborah Creamer notes,

> Accommodations that have become standard in other places (stores, banks, schools, etc.) are still lacking in many churches. Religious organizations are "simply out of step" with other organizations, leading some to observe that access for people with disabilities has become for churches "a matter of benevolence and goodwill, rather than a prerequisite for equality and the foundation on which the church as a model of justice must rest."[14]

When churches assume that people with disabilities need ministry and service, full stop, they forget to look for the gifts and contributions people with disabilities have to offer. This strips people with disabilities of agency and relegates them to the role of passive recipient.[15] Without intentionality, people with disabilities become trapped inside the circular logic of normalcy because once a group establishes the norms by which it functions, it not only becomes resistant to the inclusion of the nonnormal, but it also assumes the nonnormal are incapable of participating.[16]

---

[12]Amos Yong, *The Bible, Disability, and the Church: A New Vision of the People of God* (Eerdmans, 2011), 11-12.

[13]Deborah Beth Creamer, *Disability and Christian Theology: Embodied Limits and Constructive Possibilities* (Oxford University Press, 2009), 130-31n4.

[14]Creamer, *Disability and Christian Theology*, 76.

[15]Fox, *Disability and the Way of Jesus*, 99.

[16]Reynolds, *Vulnerable Communion*, 27.

MODELS OF DISABILITY

Our response to disabilities is often dictated by whether we locate disability in individual bodies or in society. The *medical model* emphasizes the limitations of bodies and minds in comparison to socially and medically created norms about how a body or mind should work. People *are* disabled. The goal is to fix bodies so they can function as normally as possible. The *social model* emphasizes the ways that environments, attitudes, and social expectations bar people from full participation. People *become* disabled when they encounter prejudice and exclusion. The goal is to adjust physical spaces, social attitudes, systems, and points of access. While some might try to pit these models against each other as an either-or, the reality is that disability is both/and. People with disabilities experience a range of difficulties in tandem with, apart from, or solely due to social limitation.

There are moments when we do need to focus on bodies, but we need to be cautious in our assumptions about what actually needs fixing or what will constitute wholeness. What is more, we should never problematize bodies to the point of using impairments as the basis for automatically disqualifying someone from participating meaningfully in communal life. Erin Raffety reminds us that even when able-bodied people are confronted with clear examples of ableism, they most often respond with, "Yes, but . . ." because they cannot help but believe that disabled people are invariably different and their bodies problematic.[17]

There are also moments when we do need to focus on social, physical, and attitudinal barriers that prevent people from entering spaces, but we need to be cautious in assuming that access is enough. The goal should never be to let people in so they can simply get along like the rest of us. If not tempered, this can elevate sameness over diversity.[18] Additionally, if we're not careful, we can easily substitute present for presence, and consider our benchmark the number of disabled bodies in attendance rather than how we are receiving and benefiting from disabled people's

[17]Erin Raffety, *From Inclusion to Justice: Disability, Ministry, and Congregational Leadership* (Baylor University Press, 2022), 1-2.

[18]Jana M. Bennett and Medi Ann Volpe, "Models of Disability from Religious Tradition: Introductory Editorial," *Journal of Disability & Religion* 22, no. 2 (2018): 123, https://doi.org/10.1080/23312521.2018.1482134.

meaningful contributions. Again, Raffety challenges our assumptions that access and inclusion are the end goals. After inclusion, she asks, "Then what?"[19]

Navigating the diversity models on their own is challenging. Within the church, however, medical and social ways of understanding disability become even more complicated because of the theological layers that get added to each. Christians have theological beliefs about the world, bodies, relationships, gifts/talents, and work that come out of their understanding of creation, fall, redemption, and new creation. This gives spiritual overtones to any decision the church and the people in it make concerning the lives and inclusion (or not) of people with disabilities. While there are shining lights within the church, past and present, too often people with disabilities find their lives spiritualized as either sinner or saint and used as point of warning or inspiration for others. Not only does this relegate people with disabilities to objects for others to avoid, admire, ponder, or pity, but it also robs them of personhood.[20] When this happens, the church rarely sees people with disabilities as a priority for evangelism, discipleship, and church leadership roles or as needed members of the body through whom evangelism, discipleship, and leadership take place.

When we don't know where people with disabilities fit into God's story, it can be easy to speak and sermonize about disabilities in ways that make the good news something that excludes, discounts, demonizes, and objectifies bodies and the owners of those bodies. Might there be another way to understand God's story that shifts what is so often not-so-good news for people with disabilities into something glorious?

DISCUSSION QUESTIONS

1. What experiences do you have with disability (either yourself or through someone else)?
2. What are your initial responses to disability? How do they resonate with the typical responses listed in this chapter?

---

[19]Raffety, *From Inclusion to Justice*, 2.
[20]Creamer, *Disability and Christian Theology*, 50.

3. How has your church approached disability? What kinds of disability are in your church? Does your church talk about disability? What does it teach? What practices and ministries does it have?
4. How do the medical and social models of disability help you better understand responses to disability? Do you resonate more with one? If so, why?
5. How is your understanding of disability expanding or shifting?

3

Disability and God's Mission

A FALL-CENTERED STORY?

HAVING NOW LOOKED AT DISABILITY, it is time to pick up the question with which we ended chapter one: Where do disabilities show up in God's story line of creation, fall, redemption, and new creation? Think about it for a moment. When you think *disability*, what instinctively comes to mind? Not what you think the right answer *should* be, but what really stands out as your first impression?

Whenever I teach about disability and the church, I ask this question. When I do, the room suddenly gets very still and quiet, and people immediately avert their eyes. The pregnant pause is often broken by a squeaking chair when someone shifts, an uncomfortable cough, or one person who tentatively says, "Creation?" No one ever confidently says, "Creation," and no one ever dares to voice "The fall," even though Christian arguments and actions suggest that this is what comes to most people's mind by default.

WHY WE FOCUS ON THE FALL

Why is it that we locate disability in the fall? One reason stems from the way we understand God's story line, which also affects where we place our emphasis. Let's review the evidence we have for locating disability in the fall and consider the underlying principles we use to support this kind of reading and the consequences this has for people with disabilities. From there, we are positioned to think more critically about disability in God's good-news story.

I teach a course on apologetics, and every semester we inevitably get to the question of suffering and evil in the world. Without fail, when I ask students to consider how they would respond to someone asking about their child's disability or a friend's illness, the students I teach all recount the same type of story with slightly varying words:

> The world as we see it is not what God intended. The world God created was perfect and didn't have any sickness or disability or brokenness in it. Sadly, our sin messed it all up, and all the suffering and evil we see now is a result of sin. But there is good news. Because Jesus died and rose again, God will someday make it all right, and we will get back to a perfect Eden in heaven, where we will all have perfect bodies and there won't be any suffering or evil.

Scripture has much to say to support this. In the initial aftermath of Adam and Eve's sin, we find the first pronouncement that the time after the fall includes "intense pain and suffering," which Eve will now experience as she bears children (Gen 3:16). I used to think this referred only to physical pain, but there is much emotional pain and suffering that comes in rearing children as well. So, we can read this introduction of pain and suffering as including bodies, minds, hearts, and emotions.

In the postfall narrative we find barrenness, leprosy, blindness, muteness, lameness, stuttering, stillbirth and death through birth, fevers, depression, boils, infections, blood disorders, psychosis, seizures, intestinal issues, bodies broken and destroyed through sinful acts toward self or through sinful acts inflicted by others, and so much more. For Paul, all of this is explained in the fact that "against its will, all creation was subjected to God's curse" and has experienced "death and decay" (Rom 8:20-21). Creation and people alike groan to be "released from sin and suffering" and to experience the newness that awaits us in the glorious future God promised us (Rom 8:22-24). For people, this newness includes the end of bodies that die, decay, and disappoint and the receiving of bodies that are eternal, full of glory, and full of power (1 Cor 15:42-44). Though we don't fully know what these glorious, heavenly bodies will be like, we do know that they will be like Christ's (1 Cor 15:48) and free from death, sorrow, crying, and pain (Rev 21:4). What is more, we will live in a new heavens and earth, where threat of violence, sexual assault, murder, and other forms of inflicted sin and exclusion are not allowed (Rev 22:15). There is solid evidence to think disability originates in the fall and is a clear indicator of a world gone wrong.

But let's go back and consider this rendition of God's story piece by piece. When talking with our friend or neighbor, we start the story in the fall: What we see is not what God intended. Then we back up in the story to emphasize the perfection of creation, that Eden offers us a sublimely peaceful, perfectly ordered, perfectly functioning world, where perfect bodies are put to work and where the people housed in those bodies live at peace with one another. Then we start forward again, showing how sin destroyed perfection, prevented us from fixing it, and required a perfect sacrifice (Jesus) to reclaim it. We end by exulting in the restored perfection where sin will no longer have reach. What do you notice?

First, this story starts in the fall. We look at the world in front of us and start with what we see: It's all broken. And it's broken because of sin. Second, to remedy our brokenness, we tell the beginning and end of the story in a way that emphasizes perfection. It is perfection that is God's supreme act in creation, and it is perfection that becomes the ultimate reward in the end. Third, this story seems to emphasize humans. Yes, God creates, redeems, and rewards, but the real focus of this story is our perfection, our brokenness, and our hope for perfection once again. Somewhere in there we lose the fact that this is God's story and everything about it should relate to his purposes, his actions, and his wholly *and holy* other existence, power, and glory.

While in premise it is true that we lose Eden when we sin, that sin does break things in the world, and that God, through Jesus Christ, will soon usher in a new heaven and earth, what this narrative does, when unexamined and told in this way, is push us toward ideals and language that problematize rather than privilege people with disabilities.

For example, in *The Reason for God*, Tim Keller says, "Disease, genetic disorders, famine, natural disasters, aging, and death itself are as much the result of sin as are oppression, war, crime, and violence."[1] As a mom

---

[1]Timothy Keller, *The Reason for God: Belief in an Age of Skepticism* (Penguin Books, 2008), 177.

of a son with a genetic disability, I struggle to see how an extra twenty-first chromosome is of the same substance as war, violence, and oppression. Why does the presence of an extra chromosome inherently locate my son's life in the fall? Though Keller is trying to explain that sin broke the perfectly working systems in the world, from people to nature to relationships, his wording assumes a medical model of disability by believing that somehow an extra chromosome is a body problem that can be separated from the person in whom that extra chromosome exists. Greg Boyd in *Is God to Blame?* makes this even more explicit by arguing that because Satan tampers with God's good plan, God has no part in disabilities. For Boyd, Scripture unequivocally affirms that "infirmities such as muteness or blindness originate from Satan," and God's role is "to empower human mediators to free people from these afflictions."[2] For both writers, disability, as a byproduct of sin, is located in individual bodies and as such inherently results in physical suffering and affliction.

If what Keller and Boyd say is true, then of course we would want to free individual people from sin and the consequences of sin that distort God's intended plan for the human body and from the inherent suffering disability brings. But when we hold to the belief that disability is always connected to sin, that disability is always paired with physical suffering and affliction, and that it is always God's will to heal broken bodies and minds, it leads to real-life practices of praying for everyone to be healed of their disability, of laying blame for continued disability on the hidden sin of individual people, and of proclaiming without reservation that heaven will most assuredly eradicate all forms of disability. This kind of thinking is prevalent in the church and assumes that disability can be neatly carved away from a person without any unintended consequences.

However, disability doesn't have such easily delineated boundaries. Some disabilities are so constitutive of a person's identity that when we assign disability squarely to the camp of sin and use this as our starting point, we cannot help but convey the message that the person housing that disability belongs in the sin camp as well. *A fall-centered story leads us to fall-centered assumptions about disabled people and fall-centered*

---

[2]Greg A. Boyd, *Is God to Blame? Beyond Pat Answers to the Problem of Suffering* (IVP Academic, 2003), 188.

solutions that diminish much of the goodness of the good news. Before we can get to a different reading of the text, we need to first sift through some of these assumptions in order to pull away the strands of conjecture that will continue to lead us down the wrong path.

FALSE CONJECTURES ABOUT DISABILITY AND THE FALL

Conjecture 1: People with disabilities are more affected by sin than those who consider themselves able-bodied. Not true. Scripture is clear on this point:

> When Adam sinned, sin entered the world. Adam's sin brought death, so death spread to everyone, for everyone sinned. (Rom 5:12)

> God looks down from heaven
> on the entire human race;
> he looks to see if anyone is truly wise,
> if anyone seeks God.
> But no, all have turned away;
> all have become corrupt.
> No one does good,
> not a single one! (Ps 53:2-3)

> All of us, like sheep, have strayed away. (Is 53:6)

> For everyone has sinned; we all fall short of God's glorious standard. (Rom 3:23)

> Our bodies now disappoint us. . . . They are weak . . . [and] these perishable bodies of ours are not able to live forever. (1 Cor 15:42-43, 50)

Sin corrupts and destroys, period. One person is not more sinful or more affected by sin than another. When we're guilty, we're guilty. Jesus' brother James reminds us that "the person who keeps all of the laws except one is as guilty as the person who has broken all of God's laws" (Jas 2:10). To commit one sin is to "have still broken the law" (Jas 2:11). And to experience the consequence of one sin is to have experienced the consequences of all sin: death in progressive and sometimes immediate ways (Rom 6:23).

While we should acknowledge that the consequences of sin in this world are not even, with some sins causing much more physical, social, emotional, and spiritual harm than others, my point here is that we should be cautious in assuming that disability is an instant marker of sin or a considerably worse consequence of sin. All of us are affected by sinful attitudes, actions, and aspirations. All of us have bodies that will break down at some point. However, it is a non sequitur to elevate a "broken" body or mind as being more evident of sin than a seemingly normal body or mind that is also in a state of decay. Social attitudes and physical barriers by the "normal" are often the real reason impairments become disabilities. Which, then, is the greatest evidence of sin?

Conjecture 2: Disability always has a direct linkage to sin. No, it doesn't. Though we could draw on other passages and themes (e.g., Gen 32:22-31; Ex 4:10-17; Lk 13:1-5), perhaps no scriptural text is more illustrative of this than John 9. The scene opens with Jesus' disciples voicing a popular belief that disability always finds its origin in disobedience. "Why was this man born blind?" they ask of the blind chap they encounter. "Was it because of his own sins or his parents' sins?" (Jn 9:2). Jesus counters, to their surprise, that no one sinned; rather, this blindness is so that "the power of God could be seen in him" (Jn 9:3). The narrative goes on to demonstrate that physical blindness does not disable someone from having spiritual sight. It is the sighted Pharisees who cannot "see" the Jesus right in front of them and recognize that he is their long-awaited Messiah. The blind man, however, doesn't need his sight to recognize that Jesus is the Son of Man.

Even the Old Testament includes testimony from God that the Creator "decides whether people speak or do not speak, hear or do not hear, see or do not see" (Ex 4:11). What matters, God says, is the power of God at work in and through people. This premise gives comfort to a likely disabled Paul, who finds solace and peace in the notion that God's power "works best in weakness" (2 Cor 12:8). "For when I am weak," Paul says, "then I am strong" (2 Cor 12:10).

Conjecture 3: Disability equates unequivocally to suffering and affliction. Not so. Disability is the height of paradox, bringing with it tremendous challenge as well as blessing. As we have already said, we cannot and should not ever diminish the pain, loss, or frustration that disability brings. Brokenness often includes physical, emotional, and social pain, and at times it is beyond our ability to comprehend just how much. Raffety is adamant that church and church member ministry with disabled people requires a willingness to "come close to the suffering and the pain," by listening well and acknowledging the significance of the pain that is experienced in bodies, minds, and social realms.[3] However, we should never make the assumption that people with disabilities must necessarily suffer, that they suffer all the time, or that they wish their disability to go away so they can experience relief.

When we stand outside a particular disability, we can only imagine the loss, fear, or anger we would experience if we went from having a particular thing to not having it. If we acquire a disability later in life, we experience the pains of moving from one normal to finding a new normal (which in itself may feel elusive). Even our language that disability is caused by brokenness, malfunction, deformation, abuse, or accident pushes us toward these themes of despair, pain, and suffering. Such beliefs almost always center on a medical model of disability because they locate disability within a disabled body.

But this is not the experience of everyone with a disability. For people in the Deaf community, their language (sign language), culture, and heightened use of other bodily senses (sight, touch, smell, and taste) are causes for celebration and pride, not sorrow and regret. For people like my son who might not even be aware that they have one extra chromosome, they don't suffer on a day-to-day basis. My son embodies a different way of being in the world that may include slower development, a need for simplified and visualized commands, and a heightened attention to bodily functions to catch other impairments that are often associated with Down syndrome. But these things are not afflictions or sufferings in and of themselves. For him, the greatest source of affliction comes from *outside*, from attitudes and systems that bar him from participation or from the well-meaning but faulty attempts of my husband and me to always decipher his communication patterns or respond well to his frustrations.

---

[3]Erin Raffety, *From Inclusion to Justice: Disability, Ministry, and Congregational Leadership* (Baylor University Press, 2022), 78.

It should be pointed out here that when we assume disability equals suffering, it doesn't just lead us to pity people with disabilities for all they go through and assume the worst about their lives. It also can lead us to wrongly elevate people with disabilities as examples of supreme love, joy, and contentment from whom we should draw inspiration. I cannot tell you the number of times well-meaning people have suggested that people with disabilities have so much to teach others because "look at how joyful and loving they are." What this sentiment implies is that people with disabilities who show any measure of joy or contentment must have these qualities in abundance because only a truly extraordinary person could still be happy when they suffer so much. People with disabilities do not exist to be an object lesson for those who consider themselves able-bodied. They do not often suffer as much as the able-bodied assume or have copious amounts of joy from which the able-bodied are to draw inspiration.

Conjecture 4: People with disability want and thus seek out healing above all else. False. In fact, this is a very narrow view of disability that assumes disability is something that simply happens *to* someone. When disability is seen as an acting force that distorts created order, it is easily separated from the person on whom it acts. But disability has a much more complex relationship with people, often becoming a core part of how a person knows and experiences the world and of how they know and experience themselves. It can be hard to separate out disability from identity, even when a person wants to be known for more than their disability. This is why many people with disabilities do not seek healing for their disability, and when they do, it is often for a very nuanced aspect of relief rather than their disability in toto.

How a person comes into disability often (though not always) affects their views here. Brock, in *Disability*, recounts the juxtaposition between the eschatological hopes of Joni Erickson Tada (a woman who became an influential Christian after a diving accident left her quadriplegic) and his friend Chantel Huininck (who has cerebral palsy and has used a wheelchair since a childhood). Joni's hope centers on a restoration of her legs so she can run, walk, and climb the expanse of heaven; Chantel's centers on a specially designed jetpack that will make her heavenly wheelchair fly.[4]

We should also note that in the Gospels, Jesus is careful to not assume physical healing is topping a person's wish list and even asks once, "What do you want me to do for you?" when a person asks for Jesus to "have mercy on me" (e.g., Mk 10:47, 51; see Mk 7:33; Jn 5:6). Some of Jesus' healing encounters centered and started on spiritual needs, with physical healing being a secondary matter (e.g., Mk 2:5).

Conjecture 5: Impairment, by default, will be eliminated in heaven. Probably also false. There are many things about the new heaven and new earth that we can say with assurance. There will be "no more death or sorrow or crying or pain" (Rev 21:4), and "nothing evil will be allowed to enter" (Rev 21:27). Resurrected bodies will be imperishable, immortal, raised in glory and power, and changed (1 Cor 15:42-58). Like Jesus' glorified body, there will be points of resemblance and divergence with our mortal bodies (Jn 20:11-16, 19-20; Lk 24:13-16, 30-32). Society will also be transformed, with the last (Mt 20:1-16), the least (Lk 14:15-24), and the little (Mt 19:13-15) being honored, with divisions and points of exclusion eradicated, with the one new humanity and peace that is forged through Christ's death, resurrection, and glorification (Eph 2:14-22).

What is surprising to some, however, is that these assurances do not necessitate impairments are gone in their entirety. If true pain and suffering along with physical and social barriers that bar participation are all eliminated in heaven, does impairment necessarily need to be? What is more, when that disability is so constitutive of one's identity, how does eliminating the disability not eliminate the person as well?

New creation will have wonders that far exceed our ability to imagine, yet it is an eschaton in which our glorified Jesus still carries marks of disablement. Jesus' eternal and glorified scars, Nancy Eiesland, argues, are the means by which the resurrected Christ "is making good on the incarnational proclamation that God would be with us, embodied as we are, incorporating the fullness of human contingency and ordinary life into God," thus proving that "the disabled God is not only the One from

---

[4]Brian Brock, *Disability: Living into the Diversity of Christ's Body* (Baker Academic, 2021), 34-37.

heaven but the revelation of true personhood, underscoring the reality that full personhood is fully compatible with the experience of disability."[5]

Retentionists, such as Amos Yong, agree with Eiesland that Jesus' glorified and scarred body frees us from the requirement that bodies "be free of the marks of our present impairments" (especially those that are so closely associated with a person's identity).[6] What is more, Yong suggests disabilities will themselves be redeemed in new creation, becoming the means through which "divine power, wisdom, and glory are . . . most clearly and finally magnified," showcasing, as Louise Gobell puts it, a "'transvaluation' of disability in the resurrection body [that] is not unique to Jesus' resurrection."[7]

We should note, however, that not everyone believes impairments can exist in any form in heaven. Eliminationists such as James Gould, for example, are adamant that Jesus' scars are irrevocable proof that Jesus is healed from his wounds, and thus only by heaven's elimination of every flaw (that came from sin) does Jesus finally eliminate evil.[8] Perhaps the middle way, suggested by Maja Whitaker, is helpful here. Because only a person with a disability can truly determine how defining impairments are to their identity, she wonders whether some disabilities will be retained and others not. She is confident, however, that "in the case of our own resurrection, we will not be in doubt as to our identity or existence when the time comes."[9]

When we pull out these conjectures, we are left with some key principles that are ready to find location within God's story. First, people

---

[5]Nancy L. Eiesland, *The Disabled God: Toward a Liberatory Theology of Disability* (Abingdon, 1994), 100.

[6]Amos Yong, *The Bible, Disability, and the Church: A New Vision of the People of God* (Eerdmans, 2011), 122.

[7]Yong, *Bible, Disability, and the Church*, 135; Louise A. Gosbell, "Space Place, and the Ordering of Materiality in Disability Theology: Locating Disability in the Resurrection and the Body of Christ," *Journal of Disability & Religion* 26, no. 1 (2022): 151, https://doi.org/10.1080/23312521.2021.1976697.

[8]James Barton Gould, "The Hope of Heavenly Healing of Disability Part 1: Theological Issues," *Journal of Disability and Religion* 20, no. 4 (2016): 324, www.doi.org/10.1080/23312521.2016.1239153; James Barton Gould, "The Hope of Heavenly Healing of Disability Part 2: Philosophical Issues," *Journal of Disability and Religion* 20, no. 4 (2017): 98-116, https://doi.org/10.1080/23312521.2016.1270177.

[9]Maja Whitaker, "Perfected Yet Still Disabled? Continuity of Embodied Identity in Resurrection Life," *Stimulus*, 26, no. 2 (2019), https://hail.to/laidlaw-college/article/sRNklJP#_edn20.

with disabilities are people. Perhaps this is too obvious of a statement, but the fact that too often people with disabilities are seen as everything but people makes this necessary. Personhood matters. Even when the disability is a marker of pride, identity, and embodiment, we are still talking about people. Second, disability relates to people in a host of ways that make simplified answers impossible. We cannot make broad, sweeping generalizations about disabilities and assume a single answer solves the complexities of disablement. Third, disability involves bodies and environment, physical realms and social realms. Encountering God's story necessarily requires we address both. With these points in mind, let's return to our biblical narrative and consider what happens when we start where the text starts.

DISCUSSION QUESTIONS

1. How does centering disability in the fall resonate (or not) with your experiences or understanding of disability?
2. What conjectures have you held? Are you surprised by the answers given here?
3. Do you think it's possible to locate disability in a different part of God's story? Why or why not? What might this look like?

4

Disability and God's Mission

A CREATION-CENTERED STORY

"In the beginning God . . ." (Gen 1:1).

The first act of the Bible starts with the one actor who is outside all time and creation: God. By showing God before all time and as the one who creates everything that exists—the heavens and the earth—we are pulled beyond the limitations of our earthly sight and physical boundaries to enter God's story. Though people end up factoring largely in the narrative that proceeds from the creation story, the opening of the story reminds us that people (and their bodies) are not the beginning, center, or end. God is. With this, we are forced to step out of the center and rethink the purpose and impetus of the story. It is all about God and God's desire to create a world from which to draw glory and through which to display his glory. This corrects our usual story line that a perfect world and creation dominate the conversation. It is God who is the central character, actor, power, and purpose of creation, and this understanding serves as the anchor point for how we consider all the subsequent acts within creation through to new creation.

CREATED WITH LIMITATIONS AND DIVERSITY

One of the first things we notice as we move from God to God's first act—creation—is that the beginning surprisingly centers on limits. The moment the boundless God creates, what God creates must necessarily have limits. Form comes out of nothing. Light is separated from darkness. Sky is separated from water. Land establishes boundaries for the waters. Moon and sun are set to govern different times of day. Life on land and in sea is constrained by where it lives and constrained to reproduce within its own kind. Perhaps more surprisingly, God calls these limits good. Brock contrasts the formlessness of Genesis 1:2 with the bounded distinctions of created things and suggests that "to have embodied limits is a marvelous gift."[1] For Creamer, having limits is a characteristic shared by all humanity. Our lack of omnipotence, for example, is not a cause for woe. Having limits with regard to our power is simply to recognize that we are each a bounded creature with limits that are both inherent and necessary.[2]

When we recognize limits as being an unsurprising and intrinsic aspect of human existence, they move from being a negative evil to something "*good* or, at the very least, not evil."[3] This corrects our story line that emphasizes perfection as the goal of creation and the pinnacle of redemption as realized in the eschaton. Rather than idealizing bodily perfection and visible beauty, "the presentation of the goodness of limited creatures" allows us instead to "dwell on the beauty of [our] place within the ecology of God's good working." Like Creamer, Brock suggests that our shift toward the valuation of embodied limits introduces the idea of *vulnerability* into the creation narrative as another good, allowing us to then "speak about creatures who have unfamiliar forms without reference to the fall." Having different bodily forms and limited bodily forms is not a threat or problem but rather a good. Where the real work lies is in coming to terms with our "given form and limitations" so we can "learn to hear God's pronouncement over what God has created: 'It was very good' (Gen. 1:31)."[4]

Second, within God's desire to create a world for his glory, we find the valuation of extreme diversity. There is not merely one light in the sky, one type of terrain, or one type of water, and there is not merely one type of inhabitant within these spaces. Diversity oozes forth in creative forms and functions that God speaks into existence and then empowers to continue developing (e.g., "Let the earth produce every sort of animal, each producing offspring of the same kind," Gen 1:24).

---

[1]Brian Brock, *Disability: Living into the Diversity of Christ's Body* (Baker Academic, 2021), 66.

[2]Deborah Beth Creamer, *Disability and Christian Theology: Embodied Limits and Constructive Possibilities* (Oxford University Press, 2009), 93-94.

[3]Creamer, *Disability and Christian Theology*, 94-95.

[4]Brock, *Disability*, 67.

Though we will address the issue of *imago Dei* (image of God) in a moment, it is important to recognize here that God explicitly notes the necessity of diversity for understanding God. For God's image to be clearly on display, humankind must be formed as male and female. The call for all of creation to "be fruitful and multiply and fill the earth" also speaks to the diversity God desired through the natural expansion of genetic codes that cause each animal, plant, and person to be "of its own kind" and yet unique among its own kind.

When we start in creation, we find that many (though not all) things we say only the fall could have caused (limits, different ways of thinking, speaking, seeing, and experiencing the world) are actually part of God's design. We all experience limits and diversity because we are all created by God with this purposeful composition. With bodily limits and diversity as a given of creation, then, we are moved to consider the physical and functional goodness of all types of bodies. But this in and of itself is not enough. We also need a *theological* accounting "of the *goodness* of people's lives *as they are*."[5]

CREATED IN THE IMAGE OF GOD

This leads us to the third and perhaps most surprising thing we find in the creation account: God chooses to "make human beings in our image, to be like us" and subsequently "created human beings in his own image. . . . Male and female he created them" (Gen 1:26-27). Our familiarity with this idea of *imago Dei* has probably anesthetized us to "the fabulous nature of this assertion," but Marc Cortez reminds us of the power (and perhaps even absurdity?) of this declaration by noting, "At the beginning of a work founded on the belief in an invisible God who cannot be depicted by images and who transcends human understanding, God declares his intent to image himself in finite, physical, and imperfect human beings."[6] This is revolutionary and, for most theologians, central to how we can understand human beings, both in essence and in function.

---

[5]Brock, *Disability*, 96.

[6]Marc Cortez, *Theological Anthropology: A Guide for the Perplexed* (T&T Clark International, 2010), 14.

The four models. For centuries, theologians have debated what *imago Dei* entails and ascribes. For those looking for a way to theologically situate people regardless of ability, this concept becomes a way to "affirm the value and intrinsic worth of every human being." However, without considering the full implications of each view of *imago Dei*, well-meaning supporters of disability have, in Brock's words, "gotten into trouble."[7] What does being made in the image of God say about humankind?

There is general consensus among scholars that, among other things, imaging God includes every human person, involves reflecting God in creation, and is "a work in progress" for imperfect humanity due to the fall.[8] Beyond this, however, Cortez identifies four main ways that theologians have diverged in how they view *imago Dei*.

The structural approach centers on certain human capacities that are thought to set humans apart from other animals and to reflect God's own being and capabilities in some way (e.g., rationality, self-determination, moral agency). Because structuralists view the image as "an essential aspect of the human person, a part of human nature," they believe the fall does not destroy God's image in people (since their capacities remain postfall) even while the fall may mar the ways in which people carry out the actions and thoughts that come from this essential part of their humanness.

Though having the most historical popularity, most contemporary scholars reject the structural approach on several grounds. It lacks exegetical support, fails to adequately set humans apart from animals, struggles to identify universal capacities that are true of all people of all time, overly emphasizes individuals, and can easily jettison capacity from embodiment. When capacity (particularly rational thought or self-determination or self-fill-in-the-blank) is foregrounded, people who are young, old, or otherwise disabled don't just get backgrounded; they often get left out altogether. Imperfections and/or inabilities can easily lead to assumptions that the people with these are incapable of imaging God.[9]

[7] Brock, *Disability*, 106.
[8] Cortez, *Theological Anthropology*, 16-17.
[9] Cortez, *Theological Anthropology*, 18-21.

And as Brock notes, regardless of which capacity we highlight, it will always leave out someone regardless of their abilities.[10]

The functional image approach shifts imaging from something people *are* to something people *do*. Focusing on the *and* that connects the "let us make people in our image" clause with the "they will reign" clause (Gen 1:26 NLT 2015), this view suggests that people are to rule in the world in ways that reflect and represent God's divine rule. Said another way, because people are made in God's image, they are to rule in the world in ways that reflect God's own godly rule. As with the structuralist view, *imago* remains after the fall, but due to sin it is carried out in ways that are often fraught with sinful pulls toward power, oppression, domination, and hierarchy.

While having much more exegetical backing, the functional view can sometimes separate Genesis 1 from the rest of the canon and lose sight of the other important qualities of imaging that show up in Genesis 2 and beyond, as well as the ways in which the New Testament reorients our understanding. Any reading of Genesis 1:26-28, Cortez says, must always situate our understanding of *imago* "in such a way that it finds its ultimate fulfillment in Jesus Christ and its final manifestation in the eschatological union of Christ and his church."[11] Additionally, by making imaging a task, we are in danger of excluding people who struggle with or lack some ability to engage in "ruling" acts or culture creation.[12]

The relational image approach moves past inherent capacities or tasks to the relationality that is embedded in humanity. Namely, humans were created as male and female, called into relationship with one another in a way that (1) mirrors the relationship found within the Trinity and (2) extends to creation through roles viewed less as ones of dominion and power and more ones of stewardship and interdependence. It is in the God-human-creation dimensions of relationship that humans best image God, "who is himself a relational being."[13] The fall mars this imaging of God because the fall destroys our ability to "live in Christlike

---

[10]Brock, *Disability*, 107-8.

[11]Cortez, *Theological Anthropology*, 21-23.

[12]Brock, *Disability*, 108.

[13]Cortez, *Theological Anthropology*, 24.

ways toward one another." This undermines the assumption that we "securely possess the image of God" and calls us toward transformation and sanctification as we seek to "conform to *Christ's* image."[14] Brock argues that the relational view finds its greatest home in the New Testament and helps to expand the understanding of *imago Dei* to something more than "'human rights' or 'universal human worth.'" "Humans are valuable," Brock says, "not because they have God's image but because God made them in order that they should display Christ's love in the world."[15] Despite some exegetical concerns, which Coretz notes, the relational view remains a viable means for understanding *imago Dei*.[16]

For those scholars not satisfied with a structural, functional, or relational approach, one solution has been to attempt a blending of these into a multifaceted approach by drawing on the best parts of each to articulate a more robust vision overall. Arguing that the creation narratives do not limit themselves to one understanding of the human person (i.e., to capacity, function, or relationship), the better way to see *imago Dei* is by relating it to the whole human person and the "variety of different things about God" humans can image. While we retain the broader aspects of this approach after the fall (e.g., all our human capacities "that have an analogical parallel to the divine being"), our ability to reflect God's glory (the narrower aspect) is completely lost in the fall. While this seems to capture the best of all worlds, Cortez notes that this approach takes on the weaknesses of the structural approach and struggles to smooth out the inherent differences that offset the functional from the relational approach.[17]

Representational, personal, and covenantal. Where do we go from here? Because an understanding of *imago Dei* has such important implications for how we understand people and the ways that disabilities relate to God's story, wrestling with *imago Dei* is an important exercise we cannot bypass or gloss over quickly with overly used tropes or sayings. Here's what we can say.

---

[14]Brock, *Disability*, 108.
[15]Brock, *Disability*, 109.
[16]Cortez, *Theological Anthropology*, 24-27.
[17]Cortez, *Theological Anthropology*, 28-29.

The creation account, and the subsequent evidence in the canon, promotes the idea that *imago Dei* extends to all human persons. There is not an attendant quality, capacity, ability, or other characteristic that must be met for someone to be touched by the image of God. As such, any view that disqualifies or calls into question some persons and not others is not a valid reading of the text.

Because *imago Dei* extends to all humanity, every human being is included in the verses that suggest imaging includes relational and role aspects. Genesis 1 and Genesis 2 both stress that imaging God is not a solo thing. Imaging is necessarily communal. Only as male *and* female does humanity reflect/pattern God (Gen 1:27). Genesis 1 and Genesis 2 also both stress that in this community, humankind should rule and tend the earth. It should not be a lordly rule but rather a representational rule. As those patterned after God, humanity should care for the earth in a manner patterned after God as well.

For Cortez, these truths are best expressed in terms of *presence* and how God makes himself known in the world through representational, personal, and covenantal ways. First, God invites human beings into his work as representatives who manifest God's presence in creation. Because humanity serves as "a unique locus of the manifestation of God's glorious divine presence in creation," this should affect how humans rule and exercise dominion within creation.[18] Second, God's desire for his personal presence to be known in creation requires "personal beings through whom he can manifest himself personally in creation." This leads God to surprisingly conclude that it is not good for man to be alone (Gen 2:18). Only with a suitable helper who shares the same flesh and calling can humanity (as male and female) carry out representation fully and "constitute the interpersonal relationality in which God has chosen to manifest himself." Third, God makes his image most known "in and through his covenantal relationships with his people, Israel and the Church." Human beings do not exist outside God's story line, a story line ending with a new humanity and eschatological community. Only within this covenantal relationship can representation and personal imaging be understood.[19]

[18]Cortez, *Theological Anthropology*, 31-33.
[19]Cortez, *Theological Anthropology*, 33-35, 37.

This representational, personal, and covenantal understanding of *imago Dei* has important implications for not just how we understand human beings but how we understand disability as well. Among the seven implications Cortez highlights, we are reminded, first, that any understanding of *imago Dei* must necessarily start with the fact that "*Jesus Christ is the revelation of true humanity.*" Even in understanding ourselves as mysterious beings who are both part of and unique within creation, we can never make *us* the starting place for understanding God's image.[20] Jesus alone holds this position. And Jesus, as God's image, showcases a radically upside-down kingdom in which suffering and service identify God's Son (Mt 20:25-28), in which obedience is learned through suffering (Heb 2:17-18; 5:8), and in which, as I have noted elsewhere, Jesus also retains the scars and marks of disability within his glorified, resurrected, and transformed body (Jn 20:20, 24-29).

Second, human beings are both "*ecclesial being[s] constituted in and for relationship*" and "*responsible beings*," with the attendant freedom and moral responsibility to relate and respond to others and most especially to God.[21] Though these are two separate points for Cortez, it is important that we closely relate them here. We are created as personal beings and called to express this through our relationships with others (God, humans, and creatures). Ability does not arbitrate who has this constitution. We are all meant for relationship, which means we all have capacity to give as well as receive regardless of what abilities we have. At the same time, we must also remember that no matter how much dependence a person with disability requires, disability does not rob a person of the human freedom to relate and respond to God. Too often Christians have discounted this aspect of humanity from applying to people with disabilities on the assumption that the disabled are *holy innocents* who lack moral culpability. This is not true. People with disabilities are responsible to God and able to move toward or away from him as an expression of their freedom.

I recognize that, as I have argued both points here (humans are relational *and* responsible), I have implicitly suggested that people with

[20]Cortez, *Theological Anthropology*, 38-39.
[21]Cortez, *Theological Anthropology*, 39.

disabilities have agency. They contribute to the personhood of others; are vital for how relationship is carried out in, through, with, and to them; and have moral responsibility (even if we might argue that the level of this responsibility may relate in some way to capacity). But by implying agency, it might be assumed that we should therefore reject any sense of dependence or interdependence as being antithetical to agency. This is not so.

In a very important work called *Becoming Friends of Time*, John Swinton wrestles with the ways in which people with profound intellectual disabilities might confess belief in God and experience growth in discipleship. Drawing on Medi Volpe's suggestion that many of our problems in how we understand discipleship spring from the ways in which we have individualized Christian practice, Swinton suggests we have individualized and intellectualized discipleship to the point of not really needing the corporate. We make out salvation, vocation, gifts, and choices to be *mine*, independent of community, even to the place of assuming we are the ones who choose Jesus from a position of "self-made freedom" and after a "process of intellectual reflection wherein we discern the rational basis for making such a personal choice."[22] This is not what we read in the Gospel narratives.

The action in the Gospel narratives always centers on *Jesus* calling the disciples (who follow even without understanding who Jesus is or what he is fully calling them to). Understanding comes only later, through their being together. As Swinton puts it, "It appears that the essence of discipleship has first and foremost to do with being with Jesus and learning to trust him." Similarly to the creation story, we find here that Jesus is the one who is, who calls, who gifts, and who knows far more than we ever will, which calls us, then, in a way to what Swinton terms "a process of *unknowing*" as we relinquish what we think we know to the one who actually does know it all.[23] This does not mean we give up on intellect or the pursuit of doctrinal understanding. But in noting that doctrine does not save us, Volpe says, "Not being able to imagine God

[22]John Swinton, *Becoming Friends of Time: Disability, Timefullness, and Gentle Discipleship* (Baylor University Press, 2016), 99.

[23]Swinton, *Becoming Friends of Time*, 101, 103.

does not hinder anyone from approaching God, because God is the one doing the approaching! God gives the gift of doctrine to those who require it; God does not demand understanding of doctrine from those who do not need its discipline."[24] If this is so, then it is within community that those who don't have doctrinal understanding and those who do are held together and sustained by each other. It is through the mutuality of diverse bodies and modes of knowing formed together in God's body that God's love can be fully known. This eliminates the assumption that the discipleship of people with profound disabilities is "a poor approximation of the discipleship of others within the Body." Only by being in mutually sustaining community is God's inexhaustible love revealed.[25]

This has been a long argument from Swinton. What does it have to do with the fact that humans are relational and responsible? Just this: Our relationships with others can have profound impact on how others respond to God. Even though we recognize *imago Dei* extends to all humanity, we can struggle to understand how the agency we are given to relate and respond works out for people with profound intellectual disabilities. Swinton's perspective is to say, first, God is the actor who creates, calls, and equips. Second, how we understand God's calling and equipping might need adjustment. Third, God who is himself in community and who creates us in this image uses the community of people to help others hear God's voice and respond.

Swinton concludes that for the most profoundly disabled among us, faith very much depends on the community of Christ faithfully and fully embodying a love that in turn helps all others to experience and trust in God's goodness. When the body of Christ fails to reflect and embody God's love, the opportunity for faith is taken away. "It may be that people with profound intellectual disabilities are deeply implicated in and influenced by sin," Swinton says, but rather than it being because of their own acts of disobedience, "sin may well be located within their communities' inability to share embodied love."[26]

---

[24]Medi Volpe, "Saving Knowledge: Doctrine and Intellectual Disability" (revised paper presented at DThM summer school, University of Durham, UK, September 2013).

[25]Swinton, *Becoming Friends of Time*, 108.

[26]Swinton, *Becoming Friends of Time*, 112.

This leads to our final two implications of a representational, personal, and covenantal understanding of *imago Dei*: Human beings are embodied beings who are also broken. *Imago Dei* doesn't just touch all humanity; it also touches all our humanity. This is vitally important to understand because we tend to embrace gnostic thinking when we consider what it means to image God.

One of the prominent features of gnostic thinking is a duality between the spiritual and the material, in which secret spiritual knowledge and rationality are elevated as good, and materiality, including created bodies, is considered sinful and flawed. If imaging God is gnostic, the spiritual nature of imaging (invisible, spiritual knowledge and rationality) is counted as good, whereas the bodily nature of imaging is discounted altogether. But imaging God is not and can never be a gnostic endeavor.

Our bodies matter immensely for how we image God in a physical world and through our relationships within that world. However, we must also remember that these bodies (which include mind, soul, and flesh) also experience brokenness because of sin. We can never fully or perfectly image God in the world because all humanity and all our humanity is also touched by sin.

SUMMING UP: IT MATTERS WHERE WE START

So, what does starting our understanding of disability in creation do for how disability shows up in God's story? First, in terms of creation, our understanding of God's design for this world allows us to place some differences and limitations (in mind, body, emotion, sociality, and/or functions) within creation. This does not mean that all disability is located prefall. As we have already noted, disability is complex, and we can't discount how sin integrates with bodies, minds, and relationships. But by starting with creation, we can pull ourselves away from the usual anthropocentric view of disability that centers disability and people with these disabilities in the fall. The story is not about individual bodies, the sin that broke bodies and minds and distorted nature, and what needs to happen to fix this and get these bodies back to some idealized sense of perfection. Yes, sin has broken aspects of the world, but when we start the conversations in the fall, we overlook the beginning of the story, which is that God centers our lives and vocations in creation and in community and relationship.

When we start in creation, we keep the fall in perspective and limit its ability to undermine the "it is very good" of creation, and we limit its ability to dictate the rest of the story in a person-ward way.[27] Diversity, limitation, calling, vocation, and imaging all flow out of God and God's purposes and pleasures for creation. Only with God as beginning, center, and end will we ever understand our place, for "To confess the Christian God as Creator means concretely, to be liberated not to *transcend* creation"—which was the sin of Adam and Eve—"but to *receive one's true being in Christ* . . . by learning what it means to be a creature, that is, to recognize and freely embrace loving relations with other persons as and where they are, with all their brokenness and angularity."[28] This puts everyone on the same plane. There are not some humans who are better, more perfect, or more ideally created. Rather, all humans are created by God with a variety of differences and limitations, and all humans are touched by God's image and given ways in which to image God in the world through relationship and representation.

Second, in terms of the fall, we can speak more circumspectly about it: Sin affects every human life equally. Period. The wages of sin is death (Rom 6:23), and the consequences of living in a sinful world lead to all sorts of calamities and challenges, from broken bodies to broken social spaces that problematize some bodies and minds over others. The fall gives us a space to make sense of the tragedies and complexities of life, to call sin *sin*, and to name the ways that disability might relate to living in a fallen world. Sin can damage bodies in irreparable ways, and everyone's body will eventually present problems.[29]

But for all the fall can do, it can never overtake the start of the story, that creation and existence are good. The fall can never overtake God or God's pronouncement of goodness over what was created. In this way, no one is ever born as a tragedy of sin. All of us, no matter how we are

---

[27]Brock, *Disability*, 106.

[28]Brian Brock, *Wondrously Wounded: Theology, Disability, and the Body of Christ* (Baylor University Press, 2020), 154.

[29]Brock, *Disability*, 104, 106.

embodied in the world, are "fearfully and wonderfully made" (Ps 139:14 NIV) because God creates, and what God creates is good.

Third, in terms of redemption, we are drawn away from the human-centric notion that redemption is all about getting us to heaven with perfected souls housed in perfected bodies. If God is the start, then God is also in the center of how he goes about addressing our rebellion and what this does for us. Paul tells us in Ephesians 1:3-10 that God's plan was something he had already established before the world began, so the moment sin entered, there was already a solution in motion. The *protoevangelium*, as it is called, is the first announcement of the gospel message: Through one of Eve's offspring, God is going to crush Satan (Gen 3:15). But note that this pronouncement announces that the offspring will not triumph unscathed. Satan will bruise this offspring's heel; thus, the one who will redeem the world will himself be marred by the world. This offspring is Jesus Christ, the true human who is fully God and fully man.

As the true human, Jesus experienced all the same temptations we faced though without sin (Heb 4:15). Jesus was marked by humanness and sin, with his body experiencing the wear and tear of life and the crushing, bruising, and violence of sin as enacted in his brutal murder on the cross. This is an important point. As Carmen Imes argues, "If the ideal human is an able-bodied, virile male, then the aging process automatically erodes a man's humanness." But when we look at Jesus, we discover "that this cannot be the case. Being human on this side of the garden entails frailty, weakness, and dependence. Jesus experienced these things in his aging body without losing an inch of his status or dignity."[30] With his resurrection, Jesus dealt the final blow to sin and opened the way for us to receive full life in him. And yet Jesus' resurrected body carries the marks and scars of his life and death forward in a transformed and glorified way.

What this tells us is that bodies matter, both now and in the resurrection. Jesus is the firstborn of the dead (Col 1:18), and because of how his body is retained and transformed in his resurrection, we can be confident of

[30]Carmen Imes, *Being God's Image: Why Creation Still Matters* (IVP Academic, 2023), 110.

the fact that our *bodies are not bad*; "we simply need to remove the sin that's spurred on by evil desires so we can reflect God's glory to the world (Colossians 2:11; 3:5; cf. Ephesians 4:22)."[31] God creates bodies and redeems bodies but never problematizes some bodies as being aberrant, worthless, or insignificant. Even the most egregious marks that come from another's sinful hand are no match for God's redemptive power. For Jesus and for us, our scars may not be erased, but they will be transformed, and we can be assured that our resurrection body will never die, will never disappoint us, and will be full of glory and power (1 Cor 15:42-43).

This leads us, then, to new creation. When we understand disability from a creational aspect, we are no longer focused on the need for the elimination of problematic bodies in heaven and the creation of something utterly new. Rather, we can rejoice in the ways that God's redemptive power brings renewal, restoration, and healing to all creation so we can fully live out God's creational intents for relationship, shalom, and vocation. New creation is not about finally realizing some Hollywood-idealized idea of a human body. New creation will instead be about a new heaven and earth in which everyone participates in a redeemed creation in which diversity continues to reign (Rev 7:9).

The ramifications of new creation are cosmic and will include the eradication of prejudice, exclusion, and social alienation. It will be God's kingdom come and God's will done (Mt 6:10), which again pulls humans out of the center and realigns them as members of God's family who reclaim their roles as God's agents and image bearers over a restored and renewed creation.[32] The first creation does not exclude the goodness of all created humanity, nor demand perfection of body or mind in order to take on the gifts of imaging God through right relationships and right representation. How much more is this true of new creation, in which disability is not eradicated as a matter of course. Rather, along with all parts of humanity, disability will find itself transformed, glorified, and fitted into God's kingdom as a valuable and important part of the grand diversity of God's family and contributor to all the diversity of good works God expects in his eternal shalom. Only within this new creation

[31]Imes, *Being God's Image*, 134.
[32]Imes, *Being God's Image*, 179.

will humanity in all its ethnic, cultural, social, gendered, *and* bodily difference "do what it has been designed to do from the beginning: serve [God] by reigning as his ambassador."[33]

What I have argued for here is grand and deserving of whole volumes in order to mine the depths of this wonder. God uses all of us with our limitations and through our limitations to image his perfect, infinite, and transcendent self. And God, knowing our limitations, works out his beautiful plan through the marring of his perfect Son to deal with our limitations and transform us into a people who can experience his goodness in its fullness and manifest his goodness through a diversity of bodies, minds, and experiences in unfettered glory. This is good news! And it is good news for everyone. However, it has not always been clear how this has been good news for people with disabilities.

John Steinbeck once said, "If the story is not about the hearer, he [*sic*] will not listen. And here I make a rule—a great and interesting story is about everyone, or it will not last."[34] God's story is truly about everyone, but we have not always shared it in ways that people with disabilities recognize is about them. We have more often shared the story in ways that discount and problematize disabled bodies and the people who own them. When we grasp the true nature, beauty, and grandeur of God's story, and learn to find people with disabilities in the goodness of creation rather than the cursedness of the fall, we can tell God's story as it truly is and as one that people with disabilities recognize is a great and interesting story about them. Taking everything we have discussed in these first four chapters, let us now attempt to tell this God story as the good-news-for-all story it is.

DISCUSSION QUESTIONS

1. How does the idea that limitation is an innate part of a finite, created existence affect the way you understand the experiences of disability?

2. How have you understood the idea of being made in the image of God? How does disability challenge or expand your understanding?

---

[33]Imes, *Being God's Image*, 175.

[34]John Steinbeck, *East of Eden* (Penguin, 1980), 268.

3. Do you think impairment will persist in the new creation? Why or why not? How does your view shape the ways in which you respond to disability in the present?
4. Before reading on, in light of all you've learned so far, what do you think are some of the unique challenges and opportunities in doing evangelism among and with people with disabilities?

5

Living and Speaking the "Disabled" Gospel Message

Our journey these last four chapters has taken us on some winding paths and perhaps even a few seeming rabbit trails, but if there is anything that strikes me in all that's been said, it's this. First, disability is complex, without easy definition or description. Disability introduces great gifts into the world and deep suffering. People enter disability in different ways and subsequently experience disability in different ways. To know one person with a disability is to know one person with a disability. There are some ways to make broader statements about disability, but overall there are no grand, sweeping generalizations that are true of all people within the disability label. To honor people with disability and their families, we must honor the complexities and paradoxes they inhabit.

Second, God's story is big enough and grand enough to handle all the complexities of disability. It does not force everyone into one mold. It does not isolate the experience of disability into just one point in the narrative. It does not overembellish the joys or gloss over the pains. It allows for ambiguity, questions, and different perspectives. It really is good news for everyone. So how can we live and speak a "disabled" gospel message in practical ways?

To begin with, let's make sure we know what we mean by *the gospel.* Many of my incoming students feel quite confident they know the gospel when they start their first class. Let me summarize what they usually say in one sentence: Jesus died for our sins so we can go to heaven. Yes, they give a few more details than this (we're all sinners, we need to accept

Jesus into our hearts and ask him to forgive us), but it really does boil down to this. While this hits on one of the major truths and blessings of the gospel—Jesus really did do something dramatic in order to deal with sin and offer us forgiveness—it approaches the gospel story in a rather Marcionic fashion (i.e., it leaves out the Old Testament and makes it practically unnecessary), and it also suggests that reaching some ethereal, otherworldly place is the express reason Jesus died.[1]

What you and I have learned together so far is that God's story starts way back in the beginning and has a much bigger purpose and more amazing outcome than just "Jesus died for our sins so we can go to heaven." The gospel is not "good advice" or "a business deal."[2] It is a good-news story that centers on Jesus Christ, who, out of all of humanity, was the one who alone fulfilled God's purposes and plans for humanity and who, through his life, death, resurrection, postresurrection appearances, and ascension, took on the sins, brokenness, and failures of the world and defeated them.

It is a historical story: Jesus was a real human who lived in a real time and place, and his life connects with Israel's story and all that God purposed for the world and also purposed specifically through that nation.[3] It is also a theological story: Jesus was God incarnate, the Word made flesh, fully God and fully human. Jesus did something cosmic when he came into the world and dealt personally with the world's powers and principalities. Jesus inaugurated something new that is real in the present even while we don't see it fully realized. Jesus is King, Lord, and the one with all authority (Mt 28:18). Through the work of the Spirit, he is at work in our present reality, bringing about his kingdom. He is

---

[1]Marcion, who lived in the second century, suggested that the official texts of the church should, among other things, exclude the entire Old Testament on the point that God's character in the Old testament is irreconcilable with the New Testament God who was revealed through Jesus Christ.

[2]N. T. Wright, *Simply Good News: Why the Gospel Is News and What Makes It Good* (HarperOne, 2015), 39; Darrell L. Bock, *Recovering the Real Lost Gospel: Reclaiming the Gospel as Good News* (Broadman & Holmes, 2010), 125.

[3]See, for example, Scot McKnight, *The King Jesus Gospel: The Original Good News Revisited* (Zondervan, 2016); David M. Gustafson, *Gospel Witness: Evangelism in Word and Deed* (Eerdmans, 2019); Sam Chan, *Evangelism in a Skeptical World: How to Make the Unbelievable News About Jesus More Believable* (Zondervan Academic, 2018); Wright, *Simply Good News*; Bock, *Recovering the Real Lost Gospel.*

also at work behind the scenes, preparing the fullness of his kingdom to come on earth as it is in heaven (Mt 6:10), to renew all things and establish his home with us (Rev 21:3).

Said another way, in Jesus Christ, "something has happened as a result of which the world is a different place."[4] The *something that has happened* is that God entered this world in the person of Jesus to get his purposes for people, creation, and the cosmos back on track. The *something that has happened* is that through Jesus Christ, God defeated Satan, sin, and death. The world as a result is now *a different place* because God is restoring, healing, and renewing all the brokenness that came because of our sin. God is setting things right, and he is doing so through Jesus Christ. Yes, Jesus died for our sins, but it was not simply for personal benefit or a passport out of this world. Jesus died for all of the sin and brokenness of creation, and he did it for our personal, corporate, and cosmic benefit so that we can get back toward our original vocational calling. That is to live in the shalom of God in the eventual new heavens and earth that gets established right here, as God makes his dwelling with us in a world in which death, decay, and suffering have no place (Rev 21:1-5).

For those who believe this message, perhaps you are having a brief "Hallelujah!" moment as you bask in the good news of this story and consider the power and wisdom of God on display in Jesus Christ (1 Cor 1:18, 24). For those who don't believe this message, however, the response to this good-news story will be mixed. Paul reminds us that the gospel is "a stumbling block to Jews and foolishness to Gentiles" (1 Cor 1:23 NIV). For people with disabilities, too often we have added to the stumbling blocks through the ways we have told the gospel story and considered the disabled experience. Even if we get the gospel "right," we can still package it in ways that create unnecessary hurdles. When we don't understand the disabled experience and learn to listen, our gospel storying can attempt to answer questions the people in front of us are not asking and leave their deep concerns untouched.

I am more cognizant of this today than I was yesterday. Most days with my son have the typical ups and downs experienced by families with

---

[4]Wright, *Simply Good News*, 16.

early elementary-age kids. You know, the sibling squabbles as they learn to share, the displays of independence that challenge the household rules, the energy that just doesn't get burned before bed, leading to whining and resistance when you try to turn out the lights. But on some days, my son gets emotionally dysregulated in ways we just can't figure out. The overwhelm he feels and his inability to communicate these feelings or deal with them is both heartbreaking and exhausting. Everyday tasks that are normally fleeting thoughts become monumental obstacles, and the coping strategies that worked last time often don't work this time.

Yesterday my son was undone. I don't know how else to say it. When I picked him up early from school to take him to a weekly occupational therapy appointment, I knew instantly that something was wrong. He was wearing different pants. As I spoke to his assistant, she confirmed it was a tough day, filled with whining, refusal, resistance, and two bathroom accidents. He was slow to take my hand as I led him toward the car and began to resist as soon as he realized we were not going home. He tried to push me away when I buckled him into his car seat, and he kept saying, "Stop it." I tried everything I could to calm him down, but talking made him more upset. So I drove quietly, but that didn't work either because every turn I made got him more agitated. He began whining and yelling about which direction I should go. Nothing I did was right. We got to occupational therapy, and I literally had to drag him through the door. (Thankfully occupational therapy is one safe space where no parent judges you because we're all there to deal with disabilities.)

Occupational therapy went well, but in leaving I could sense his calm was tenuous. The moment he realized we weren't going to my parents' house, he was totally undone again. Sadly, today was a day we had two more medical appointments. The first was lab work. I mentally cried because my husband was out of town for a business trip and couldn't be there to help. My son is strong, and on a day like this day, I needed my husband's physical and emotional strength. But he was gone, and I was on my own. My son, who normally barely acknowledges blood draws, was flailing and yelling. It was all I could do to keep him in the chair as two techs worked to complete the simple procedure. By the time it was done, I was sweaty, and my son was missing his shoes. But this wasn't the end. The next stop was to the hospital, to have an ultrasound on his thyroid. On the way, I called my parents and asked them to pray.

When we got to the hospital, my son sat down in the middle of the parking lot, refusing to budge, and anxiously gnawed on his fingers (these are two of his coping mechanisms when he's overwhelmed). I had to deadweight pick him up and carry him the length of the hospital to the outpatient department. He calmed in the waiting room, but the moment we were called back, the resistance, crying, and yelling resumed. He dropped to the floor outside the room, and I held tightly to his leg to keep him from bolting. Eventually I had to drag him in the room by his foot. I had had this grand notion that I could just put a video on my phone and he'd calm down, but today that was a total fail. Instead, the phone, loudly playing *Toy Story* clips, lay abandoned on the foot of the exam table as I lay on the bed with him, my legs wrapped around his, my arms trying to contain his, my head trying to trap his head. I tried to speak in a quiet, soothing voice as he raged and squirmed. Eventually I slow counted to one hundred. We got the ultrasound done with much effort and walked out covered in the ultrasound goo, sweaty and tired.

We walked out . . . or I should say I walked out, carrying him the full way back to the car. Again, he resisted my attempts to put him in his car seat, whined all the way to my parents' house, and then refused to get out. The evening got a little better as he played with his sister and was entertained by Papi and fed his favorite meal by Nana, but the emotions leaked out in impulses and outbursts. Putting him in bed that night, I could only pull the hair back from his face and pray that God would calm his spirit and give him rest. A new day was coming, and hopefully it would be better, but there was no guarantee.

So why spend all this time behind the curtain of our lives? First, because people need to know about what everyday life is like in homes where there is disability. We had good yesterday, we truly did. But it was a tough day. My dean called me today, and his first question was, "How did the tests go yesterday?" All I could say was, "It was a rough day." I sometimes fear he'll think we live in chaos, but I'm learning the importance of naming real-life experience so I can help normalize disabled experience for others and also help people not yet touched by disability to become aware of just how much people and families with disability carry in ways not often on display to the public. Second, days like yesterday make me think afresh today about how I am trying to answer the question I've set out here: How can we live and speak a "disabled" gospel message in practical ways? I don't want people to ignore the nitty-gritty of our lives and only focus on soul saving and passports to a heaven where nothing about our present life will remain. If the good news is good news, it will say something meaningful about times when my son is totally dysregulated and flailing on the parking lot asphalt and about times when his tenderness and love radiate in ways that are practically otherworldly.

Sam Chan, in his book *Evangelism in a Skeptical World*, argues that any time we make a gospel presentation, it should say something about (1) who Jesus is, (2) the individual and corporate blessings that come from this, and (3) what our response must be.[5] It can be easy to lock in on one way of telling this story or think that the way in which the gospel message first connected with us is how it will connect for everyone. This simply isn't so. We should be clear here that the story of Jesus *doesn't* change; however, there are many ways to tell this story, and what we choose to emphasize within that story should very much depend on who is listening and what will connect with them.

Consider, for example, the New Testament Gospels. Each Gospel writer emphasizes different aspects of Jesus, our sinful state, and what we are called to do. Within John's Gospel, we find Jesus presenting himself through different metaphors as a way to meet the present need of the person in front of him. To the woman at the well, he is living water (Jn 4:14). To the crowd who has eaten their fill of the loaves yet find themselves still hungry, he is the bread of life (Jn 6:35). To people living in darkness and bound by sin, he is the light of the world (Jn 8:12). To the Pharisees who are blinded by their slavery to the law, he is the gate for the sheep (Jn 10:7) and the good shepherd (Jn 10:11). To Martha, whose brother just died, Jesus is the resurrection and the life (Jn 11:25). To the disciples who are grappling with Jesus' warning that he is about to go away, he is the way, the truth, and the life (Jn 14:6). To Jesus' followers,

[5]Chan, *Evangelism in a Skeptical World*, 68.

who must persevere in godliness after he leaves, Jesus is the vine (Jn 15:5). Each picture calls us to understand something about who Jesus is, and each says something about our sinful state and what our response should be. If we need water, we live in a state of thirst in this world. The call is for us to drink. If we need light, we live in a spiritual state of blindness and need God's illumination. If we are wandering, we need to find the way. When he appears, our response is to follow.[6]

Over and over again, Scripture provides different metaphors and ways of seeing Jesus, seeing ourselves, and finding the right response. This should give us comfort and freedom to "explore a variety of gospel presentations . . . looking for the one that will best connect with our audience existentially, emotionally, and culturally."[7] So what does the good-news gospel story give to families like mine and families who face even more challenges and exhaustion than we do? Following Chan's model, let's consider a few starting points, remembering that these are just examples and the ways in which you enter a Jesus conversation can be vast and varied and should be based on what the person in front of you is needing.

FULLNESS OF LIFE FROM OUR CREATOR

I think back to the day we adopted our son. The first hold. The first realization he was *ours*. The joy of filling a long-empty crib with a tiny bundle. And I think back to the many initial responses people had when they heard he had a disability. *Oh! I'm so sorry. Poor kid. I guess that's why his birth parents didn't want him. You are extra-special people for adopting him.* People celebrated with us, but in some circumstances, there was this underlying message of pity, tragedy, and a dismissal of this little life as something not valuable, desired, or needed in the world. What I wanted in those moments was a way to celebrate life in all its embodied forms even while recognizing the reality that we were heading into unknown challenges both big and small. What the gospel story has given us in these moments is a real reason to celebrate.

---

[6]Chan, *Evangelism in a Skeptical World*, 63-99. Chan offers numerous examples of how to craft a gospel presentation in both chart and narrative form. Readers are encouraged to spend time in his chapter, savoring the richness of the gospel and the many ways in which it can be told.

[7]Chan, *Evangelism in a Skeptical World*, 85.

Through Jesus, God created all things, and God has plans and purposes for all he created. This tells us that there is an inherent goodness in being created and a valuation of life in all its embodied forms. God created us, and God loved our creation so much so that "he gave his one and only Son" so we could find eternal life through him (Jn 3:16). This disbands the assumption that disability evokes automatic pity. People are to be celebrated because God was at work in their creation and has given each one his image. This also adamantly counters the belief that some genetic potentialities that are discovered in utero are legitimate grounds for destroying that budding life, or that when those lives come to fruition they can be viewed as dispensable. Even when our bodies present problems, we are fearfully and wonderfully made and should be honored as such.

Everyone finds themself in the creation story (and subsequently in the rest of God's story too). This means that we don't have to assume a posture of grief and solemnity the moment we hear a baby is born with a disability. This also means that when people develop a disability later, we do not suddenly see their life as tragic and pitiable even when the circumstances and outcomes may indeed be tragic. Their lives are still to be celebrated because, even in this, God is present, at work, and manifesting himself through this life.

Celebrating life does not negate the real truth that some disabilities cause pain, concern, disappointment, anger, and sadness, but it does mean that we can never discount that life simply because of a disability. Life is good because life is from God. Because life is from God, God loves that life enough to do all that is necessary for that life to experience the fullness of existence that can only come by following him. God is Creator. He has made a way for us to experience eternal, full, complete, and fruitful life in him through the life, death, and resurrection of Jesus. Our response is to embrace his life and surrender to his Spirit's transforming work.

FREEDOM FROM SIN THROUGH OUR REDEEMER

The gospel story doesn't just relish the highs. The gospel story takes sin very seriously, and much of the Bible is spent recounting the innumerable ways in which sin steals, kills, and destroys (Jn 10:10). Every person is found guilty and wanting because of their collusion with sin and their disobedience of God. This disbands the assumption that people with disabilities are holy innocents and lack culpability. All have sinned (Rom 3:23). People with disabilities need to hear this message. We cannot overemphasize this point. We will discuss the question of culpability for the more severely intellectually and developmentally disabled in chapter six. The point here is that we can easily overlook the need for people with intellectual and developmental disabilities to know Jesus by falling back on assumptions that they lack guilt (much like a child before the age of accountability). The gospel takes everyone and their sin, however it manifests, seriously.

There are times when it is challenging for us to know whether my son's disobedience is a matter of his not understanding what he is to do or whether it is willful rebellion. This week, however, I observed the most deliberate exercise of his own disobedient will that I had no doubt. "I *will* do this," he said in complete contradiction to my definitive no. And sure enough, he did. Yep, my son is under the curse of sin too. And he, like all of us in the human race, has chosen freedom from God, trying to take over God's position by exercising his will outside God's. The result of our rebellion has been destruction in every way imaginable. We fail to carry out our relationships and responsibilities in fully God-honoring ways, leading to strife, jealously, greed, and selfishness. The playing out of these and so many other sinful impulses has corrupted relationships, our care of the earth, and subsequently our care of our own bodies. Things are falling apart. For people with disabilities, there will also be points at which understanding the consequences that sin in general has wrought in the world will help make sense of the experiences of disability, particularly the points at which people experience pain, suffering, and heartache, and the points at which exclusion, prejudice, and injustice make impairment something problematic.

The good news is that God already had a plan in motion to deal with the vast consequences of sin before Adam and Eve ate the fruit. Through the work of Jesus Christ, God has dealt a cosmic blow to sin, rendering justice for all our mistreatments of self, others, society, and creation, erasing sin's punishment by giving forgiveness and life to all who call on his name, and restoring true shalom. Jesus is Redeemer. He has provided a cosmic solution to a cosmic problem. Our response is to repent.

A PLACE TO LAMENT WITH IMMANUEL—GOD WITH US

In taking sin seriously, the gospel story also gives us the means to face the pains, sorrows, difficulties, and injustices of life head-on. Most of God's story, as we read it in the Bible, is the long road of redemption in which God is wooing and calling us toward him. It is a story that showcases God's incredible love and desire for his people, and it is a story that bleeds with brokenness and failure as God's people cannot free themselves from sin's grip. We see victory on the cross. As Paul testifies, "Christ died for our sins, just as the Scriptures said. He was buried. . . . He was raised on the third day, just as the Scriptures said" (1 Cor 15:3-4), and he is now exalted as Lord (Phil 2:9-11). This victory reorients our perspective to see that God's redemption is bringing a new heavens and earth, a renewal of mind and bodies, and the establishment of a new and diverse people inhabited by God's Spirit. It is a work that has started but is not yet at its fullness. In this space, we deal with pain, suffering, and grief even as we hope for the future to come, and beautifully, God has given us the gift of lament for such a time as this.

We don't often tell the gospel story and center it on lament, but the story gives us a space to call out the brokenness and injustice we see, to rage at it, to throw our hurts and frustrations and anger at God, to name and condemn specific ways in which bodies and people and societies break down. The gospel doesn't offer pithy statements or easy solutions to this lament. Indeed, our God actually sits with us in all that mixed-up space, "attentive, actively listening, crying, grieving, and being with us in our pain."[8]

The gospel story presents God as one who is concerned for our afflictions and moved by our troubles, so much so that he becomes Immanuel—God with us (Mt 1:23; Is 7:14), stepping into our world in a finite human body to take sin and destruction head-on. If we think God

---

[8]Erin Raffety, *From Inclusion to Justice: Disability, Ministry, and Congregational Leadership* (Baylor University Press, 2022), 101.

came into the world at the top of the social ladder, loaded with money, influence, and power, with the right pedigree and the world handed to him on a silver platter, we need to think again. The prophet Isaiah (Is 53:3-4) notes that Jesus was "despised and rejected—a man of sorrows, acquainted with deepest grief. We turned our backs on him and looked the other way. He was despised, and we did not care. . . . We thought his troubles were a punishment from God, a punishment for his own sins!"

For many people with disabilities, this has been their own experience: being despised and rejected, experiencing pain and suffering, held in low esteem, being the ones other people stare at or quickly avert their eyes from, accused of sin and even getting what they deserve. The lament of disability includes physical and mental pain but also the wounding of a world that considers different embodiment as something to be despised, condemned, rejected, and shunned. To this experience of disability comes Jesus, a man who embodies the very suffering, pain, rejection, and exclusion experienced daily by the disabled, to take up everyone's pain and bear our suffering, to be physically marred and crushed for our transgressions and iniquities, and to bear wounds by which we all can find healing (Is 53:5-6). The gospel story centers squarely on Jesus, who fulfills God's promises made to Adam and Eve, Noah, Abraham, Moses, Israel, David—promises that have something to say to the world about how God is in the business of righting the wrongs by redeeming our lives and our world. This Jesus is the one who, in taking on our bodily form, steps squarely into the fray of everyday life, experiencing life as we experience it, taking on the scars from it.

When we sit with people with disabilities and their families, understanding this place of lament and the gospel's ability to name the wrongs should keep us from turning the Bible into motivational sound bites that ignore context and promote false positivity. Please, do not tell people with disabilities that God gives his greatest challenges to his strongest soldiers or that God will never give them more than they can handle. Please, do not rush to Romans 8:28 without first stopping and sitting in the brokenness, frustration, and groaning of Romans 8:18-27. Yes, God is at work, but not in a way that discounts how difficult everyday life can be. God's love remains and we are never separated from it, even when we walk through "trouble or hardship or persecution or famine or nakedness or danger or sword" (Rom 8:35 NIV).

In your gospeling, sit with lament for as long as it takes. Name the hurts and pains and injustices. Consider the medical, financial, emotional, and relational toll of disability. And show people how Jesus really does get it—he was called crazy, he was an embarrassment to his brothers, he was despised, rejected, accused, excluded, and marred. Jesus knows, and because he knows, he can also be near to the disabled in ways that only those who have also experienced disability can. Jesus is Immanuel—God with us. By identifying with our greatest griefs, pains, and sorrows, he not only understands the disabled experience, but he takes that experience to the cross in order to set things right. Our response is to let Jesus take up residence with us so we can "walk the road" with him (Mk 1:17 First Nations Version).

FINDING HOPE IN OUR DISABLED GOD

My grandmother was a wonderful, strong, Christian lady who was about as physically twisted up as one can get. Early-onset rheumatoid arthritis made a mess of her joints, and by the time she passed, she had had numerous hand, foot, neck, knee, and hip surgeries to replace joints, fuse bones, and implant so much metal that she would light up security when she walked through metal detectors. My Pentecostal grandfather always joked that he'd like to be next to her when the rapture took place so he could see what stayed and what went. My grandma always longed for heaven, where she would get back working hands and feet and a body that did not scream with pain day in and day out. She held firmly to the hope that "by his wounds we are healed" (Is 53:5 NIV).

Having grown up in this same Pentecostal tradition, a lot of people I know have this hope: Heaven will reverse it all. But in having my son and having people approach us about his need for healing, I began to wonder whether there was good news in a story that said everything *we deem* imperfect in our bodies must necessarily be erased. It wasn't good news to me to think that my son will cease to be so much of who he is when God's kingdom comes into its fullness.

The extra chromosome does present challenges (we are constantly having to monitor a number of his body systems and behaviors), but it has also given him a way of being in the world that truly seems much healthier than all those who think they are normal. His empathy and tenderness are unmatched. He always has a song in his heart and isn't afraid to belt it out. He loves to dance and doesn't care where he is when the need to dance overtakes him. At a minor league baseball game two weeks ago, he heard the music as people were leaving and started dancing wildly to it in the middle of the lane where people were exiting. "Mama, dance with me!" he shouted. My self-consciousness kicked in, and I worried, *What will everyone else think?* Then I looked at him and thought, "No, I need to worry less about others," and so awkwardly I began to dance with him. The ways he engages with the world teach me a whole new way of seeing, being, thinking, and living. Why would I ever want that to go away?

With two entirely different ways of seeing God's victory for our bodies, is there a way to capture a good-news story that embraces both? It is here we can turn to the Disabled God, an idea first coined by Nancy Eiesland.[9]

We have already said that as Immanuel, God took on the contingencies of human bodies, experiencing the social exclusion that is so often part of the disabled life. Eiesland pushes this further by suggesting that Jesus experienced disablement in his crucifixion and that when he resurrected, he did not remove these impairments or marks from his body. Rather, "Paradoxically, in the very act commonly understood as the transcendence of physical life, God is revealed as tangible, bearing this representation of the body reshaped by injustice and sin into the fullness of the Godhead." It was in the scars that remained postresurrection that God was truly with us, being "embodied as we are, incorporating the fullness of human contingency and ordinary life into God."[10] It was through these scars that the disciples' doubt turned to belief.

For people with disabilities, this marks the good-news story with a very real sense that disability does not contradict God or find itself at odds with God's kingdom. Eiesland reminds us that the resurrection revealed the true meaning and significance of Jesus' earthly life, and it

[9]Nancy L. Eiesland, *The Disabled God: Toward a Liberatory Theology of Disability* (Abingdon, 1994).
[10]Eiesland, *Disabled God*, 99-100.

was "in the resurrected Jesus Christ [that the disciples] saw not the suffering servant for whom the last and most important word was tragedy and sin, but the disabled God who embodied both impaired hands and feet and pierced side and the imago Dei."[11] Disability does not exclude one from being God's image, and disability does not exclude one from experiencing resurrection life.

For my grandmother, who lived at such odds with her body, the Disabled God is one who identifies with her pains and did something about it. Jesus was crushed, bruised, and disfigured so that her pains—both spiritual and physical—would be eliminated. Jesus' postresurrection scars became her hope that she would one day carry scars and *imago Dei* in a body that, like Jesus' body, was a "new model of wholeness."[12] For my son, whose very essence is so tightly bound to his disability, Jesus' postresurrection scars are my son's (and our) hope that he will one day retain his extra chromosome in a redeemed body that retains the Down syndrome "scars" and the *imago Dei* in a way that, like Jesus' body, is a "new model of wholeness."

The good-news story tells us that God created us with purpose, that God redeemed us through the marring of his son so that we might have life, and that we have eternal purposes that are now restored because of Jesus' work. This includes disability from beginning to end. Jesus is the Disabled God. He provides us hope "that our nonconventional, and sometimes difficult, bodies participate fully in the imago Dei, and that God whose nature is love and who is on the side of justice and solidarity is touched by our experience."[13] Our response is to place our hope in Jesus Christ, our Disabled God, receiving the fullness of his life and resurrection that comes solely by means of his cross.

LIVING OUT THE DISABLED GOSPEL

As we wrap up this chapter, I want to make one final point. In each of our four examples of how to speak a disabled gospel message, it is impossible to separate this from how to live a disabled gospel message. Whether

---

[11]Eiesland, *Disabled God*, 99.
[12]Eiesland, *Disabled God*, 101.
[13]Eiesland, *Disabled God*, 107.

we're considering celebration, sin, lament, or hope, we cannot enter these conversations without first experiencing the nearness of disability. Let me say this next bit especially to those who consider themselves abled. We need to be present and involved with one another in deep ways, learning from the many beautiful gifts and postures that people with disabilities have so that our gospeling comes from one of *interdependent relationship* rather than a charity mindset that makes evangelism a one-way trajectory *from* us *to* them, *from* the abled *to* the disabled.

Hans Reinders says pointedly that we do not choose to share in life with the disabled, particularly those who are intellectually disabled, because "they are generally not seen as people we want to be present in our lives" and even more because we believe "we don't need them."[14] Sadly, as Ben Conner notes, "Even the church, instead of imagining life together with people with intellectual disabilities and considering that our mutual encounter might result in changes in discipleship, ministry, and witness, Christians tend to follow the marginalizing approaches that Schreiter describes as homogenizing, colonizing, demonizing, romanticizing, or pluralizing."[15] We cannot speak a disabled gospel message if the only time we're engaging in the life of disabilities is when we are trying to "save" someone. Disability demands nearness, honesty, transparency, discomfort, rawness, dependence, interdependence, humility, and being okay with paradox. Until and unless we are willing to participate in relational life in these ways, we will have no platform or trust from which to speak the gospel.

The beauty of seeing disability and embracing people with and without disabilities is that all of us become better people, able to see and experience God's kingdom in its fullness and as it was meant to be lived. In Jesus' kingdom, the weak, the lowly, and the humble are exalted. In Jesus' kingdom, value is found not in position, possessions, or power but rather in postures, dispositions, and habits that exude love, joy, peace, patience, kindness, goodness, faithfulness, gentleness, and self-control (Gal 5:22-23). In Jesus' kingdom, we are each given gifts and callings,

---

[14]Hans Reinders, *Receiving the Gift of Friendship: Profound Disability, Theological Anthropology, and Ethics* (Eerdmans, 2008), 142.

[15]Benjamin T. Conner, *Disabling Mission, Enabling Witness: Exploring Missiology Through the Lens of Disability* (IVP Academic, 2018), 104.

which God knits together and calls us to use not for our own sake but for the sake of one another. In Jesus' kingdom, we celebrate and value interdependence with one another and with God as we mirror our triune God in his relational wholeness. God's kingdom is an upside-down kingdom in which there is a revaluation of lives and bodies as we find ourselves and all our weaknesses and shortcomings turned into strength because of what *God* does in and through our lives. Disability helps refocus everyone's perspective because disability requires intimate life on life, deliberate actions and commitments, and varied ways of seeing, hearing, speaking, experiencing, and engaging with the world.

The essence of Christian life should be about life on life, speaking and living the gospel message through meaningful relationships and through our lives of goodness (1 Pet 2:12). *We haven't always done this well, as we have promoted a passport out of this world while living lives not that much different from the world.* In a disabled gospel message we are brought to the heart of God's story and reminded of God's strength in our weakness, God's omnipotence in our limitation, God's life in our brokenness, God's perfection in our sinfulness, God's withness in our lament, and God's hope in our disablement. God came near, and he calls us to come near. There is no other way to enter into disability. There is no other way to love, speak, or live his gospel message.

DISCUSSION QUESTIONS

1. How does disability expand your understanding of the good news? What does the good news means for those with disabilities?
2. Have you ever thought about lament being part of the good news? How does this help or hurt your understanding of the gospel and how you relate it to others?
3. Have you ever thought of God as disabled before? Do you think this is a helpful image? Is this an accurate way to speak about God?
4. What might it look like for you to live out the disabled gospel in your church community? In your local community?

DISABILITY and the Practice(s) of Evangelism

6

Learning from Individual Stories

In his book *Disability: Living into the Diversity of Christ's Body*, Brian Brock says, "Grappling with the problems raised by the sheer diversity of the conditions lumped together under the single term 'disability' highlights the first and most significant theological point to grasp when beginning to think about disability: getting disability right means *paying close attention to particularity*." For Brock, this "really only means *listening* to people."[1] If we want to get evangelism among and with people with disabilities right, we have to start with the people and families who experience disabilities. In listening to their stories and getting first-person perspectives, we will be awakened to many of the things we and the church get wrong about disabilities and be pointed toward healthy, God-centered, and people-honoring dispositions and practices.

No matter who you are or what your experiences have been, you have more to learn. Even though my own life is steeped in the disability space, my experience has been limited to how one individual boy with Down syndrome interacts with the world. Every time I encounter a person or family with disabilities, it is an opportunity to learn from how they see and experience the world. We should be careful here to not assume that every person with a disability should take on the role of teacher for those who are not disabled or to turn people with disabilities into object lessons for our own purposes. However, as we genuinely interact with people from various disability spaces, we should yield to their perspectives and

[1]Brian Brock, *Disability: Living into the Diversity of Christ's Body* (Baker Academic, 2021), 20-21.

experiences and not assume we know what they need or that we know everything there is to know about disability.

I'm learning new ways to think and interact when I'm with someone who is blind, which is both similar to and different from how I'm learning to be with someone in a wheelchair, which is both similar to and different from how I'm learning to engage with someone autistic. As a scholar who writes about disability and the church, I am attuned to many of the experiences that people have and ways in which they wish to be treated. And I still have so far to go. If I ever lose this desire to learn, grow, and, most importantly, receive correction, I will close off my ability to engage people with disabilities well. It is less about getting it right all the time (as much as we desire that!) and more about having the right dispositions that set us up to speak and act in just and inclusive ways.

My goal for this book has always been to include voices of people who live in a variety of disability spaces. However, my original idea was to talk about various forms of evangelism and insert helpful quotes or tips here or there, with the occasional case study to better make a point. But as I sat down in my first interview, I realized that I was still approaching evangelism from an abled perspective. Here's what I mean.

Ableism, much like its close "ism" relatives (e.g., racism, sexism, ageism), assumes there is one way of thinking about and functioning in the world that is "normal." When a society functions according to a norm defined *by* those who are abled, the society is said to promote ableism. In such a world, systems, structures, practices, language, and attitudes all work to support the full inclusion of those without disabilities, leaving people with various forms of disability excluded from participation, partially or completely. When you think that your way is the normal way, you often aren't even aware of the biases you have in how you think and act. It requires intentionality to stop and consider whether this truly accounts for the variety of experiences out there.

With regard to this book, my aim has been to help us think about disability and evangelism; and yet when I first structured the book, I started with "normal" evangelism models and activities and assumed a tweak here or there would be sufficient. But this ultimately isn't sufficient. If the point of this book is to help us think about how disability intersects with evangelism, then we need to start not with the same evangelism practices we always talk about (as much as those are important and helpful categories) but with the themes and lessons that arise from the disability world itself.

My surprising discovery is not that people with disabilities do not engage in evangelism. They do, and they do so with great effectiveness. My surprising discovery is that when people with disabilities think about evangelism, outreach, and the church, their first impulse is less about individual activities and skills and more about dispositions and postures. We can do all the practices of evangelism, but if we fail to grasp these first-order ideas, we will still struggle to reach, much less incorporate, people with disabilities into the work and witness of the church. I will mention the kinds of evangelism activities you'd expect in an evangelism book, but in the remainder of this book, I will center disabled voices and use their thoughts and experiences to help shape the ways in which we talk about what is necessary as we engage in evangelism and outreach among, with, and by people with disabilities.

Let me introduce you to a few of my friends.[2]

CHRIS (HOLLAND, MICHIGAN)

I first met Chris at a Disability Symposium.[3] I was there to speak, and afterward we had a brief chat about some things I had raised in my talk and about the fact that he grew up not too far from where I now lived and worked. It was my first time having a sustained conversation with someone who uses augmentative and alternative communication (AAC). In Chris's case, he uses his big toe to navigate a computer device, selecting pictures and preset words and phrases to form his communication. The computer reads aloud the words or phrases as he goes, and when his full thought is formed, he hits a button, and the computer reads the thought aloud. In this way he can respond with a word, a sentence, or even full presentation.

---

[2]Each person introduced here was personally interviewed by the author. To enhance the readability of direct quotes from those interviewed, filler words and phrases such as *you know*, *um*, *like*, *and so*, etc., have been removed.

[3]Chris, interview by author, November 22, 2024.

It was a good conversation, but I know I made many of the same mistakes others do, such as trying to decipher what Chris was saying as he input words into the AAC and responding before hearing the full sentence together. My next conversation was better and honestly more enjoyable as I waited to hear Chris speak things to me. As I took the time to wait for full thoughts, I better appreciated what he was saying and how he was saying it, and it led me to have more natural and sustained responses to him. We enjoyed some good laughs, and I knew this wouldn't be the last time we would talk. Chris is insightful, direct, and not afraid to say the important things that need to be said. In fact, he believes his disability gives him the ability to say things others would not or could not say.

Chris came to disability through a traumatic birth. During labor, the umbilical cord descended into the birth canal before him, cutting off his oxygen supply. Failed attempts to release the cord led to a rushed cesarean section, in which he and the cord were finally freed from the birth canal. However, he was not breathing. It took forty minutes of CPR before he could breathe independently. The trauma of that birth, particularly the lack of oxygen, eventually led to a host of issues, which ended with a diagnosis of athetoid cerebral palsy, a kind of palsy that keeps his muscles in constant motion.[4]

Chris was fortunate to have an amazing family and some caring and thoughtful therapists early in his life who recognized he was smart. Over time, he received his first AAC, and this unlocked the world for him, allowing him to communicate with others and excel at school. Without minimizing the true challenges and pains he has experienced because of his disability, Chris lives with a strong sense that God has a purpose for his life, which gives his disability purpose as well.

Early on, Chris struggled with God and the church. The message he frequently heard was "God caused your disability" or "God willed your disability." How could a loving God cause such pain and limitation intentionally? Why should he serve a God like that? Over time, Chris concluded that God didn't cause his traumatic birth but saved his life in

[4]You can read Chris's entire story in Christopher J. Klein, *My Big Toe: A Story of Perseverance* (WestBow, 2024).

the midst of a traumatic birth. Chris believes that our pains and suffering aren't willed by God but rather are more a result of living in a fallen world. However, Chris is also convinced that God is not powerless in the face of suffering and uses everything in our lives for his purposes and glory. As we surrender our lives into Jesus, Jesus gives meaning and purpose to our lives.

Chris lives in the world of possibilities rather than limitations and pursued higher education, earning a bachelor's degree in kinesiology and a master's degree in theology. He is an author, a preacher, and teacher, and with his wife he also leads a small church online called Device Verses—an all-abilities church that includes seven to ten people who use communication devices. He thinks that when he gets to heaven, he'll be able to run and play football with his brothers; however, he does not personally ask God for healing, trusting that God is at work in the present and knows what to do with Chris's body now and in the future.

HANNAH (SUBURBAN ILLINOIS)

Hannah was an active thirteen-year-old, always on the go and always outside, until a spate of uncontrollable migraines stopped her in her tracks.[5] As the headaches intensified, she recalls that one particularly vicious migraine lasted for almost four months with no break. "Pretty quickly from there," she says, "I fell apart." She couldn't keep food down and began passing out. Immediate-care visits became routine, as did IV fluids and pain. Doctors were baffled by the symptoms and initially concluded that Hannah was making it all up. "It's school refusal," they said, which prompted her parents to keep her in public school for ninth grade. It was a struggle. She iced her head each morning to ease the pain and received help getting dressed. She picked which classes to attend on a given day based on need and spent the rest of the time sleeping in the nurse's office. Keeping attention in class was nearly impossible. "I just felt like everything stopped," she recalls. "Life stopped. It was lonely. It was really lonely." It wasn't until a weeklong hospital stay at age fifteen that Hannah was referred to a doctor who solves medical mysteries. He

[5]Hannah, interview by author, November 25, 2024. *Hannah* is a pseudonym.

was pretty sure she had POTS (postural orthostatic tachycardia syndrome), a condition that affects blood flow and heart rate. He referred her on to a cardiologist at a world-renowned children's hospital, and the cardiologist agreed. During her own tests, the cardiologist uncovered two other heart defects, both rare, and both ones she didn't think required surgery.

With POTS treatments, Hannah started to feel better but then unexpectedly plateaued. A new cardiologist reviewed her case and thought that perhaps one of the heart defects (an artery passing through a muscle) was exacerbating Hannah's issues and required surgery. But, as Hannah notes, the doctor wasn't positive and said it was really hard to know for sure. "That's really the summary of what my health has been," Hannah says. "None of my tests are normal, but they're not abnormal enough to point to something. Medications that you would take for one problem make a different diagnosis that I have worse. So it's murky and horrible, and you hope you make the right choice."

Hannah had grown up in the church and says she "took for granted how easy faith felt." When her body began to break, she got really angry with God. It didn't help that she received mixed messages from the Christians around her. In her very "Christian" town, people accused her of having done something to anger God or suggested that God purposedly caused her health crisis to teach her a lesson. In her small church where everyone knew her, they concentrated more on her physical appearance and health, even commenting on her fluctuating weight. "It was important to them that I was getting better," she says, and at times it even "felt like my church never actually acknowledged my disability." Putting these two sets of responses together left her feeling alone, unrepresented in the church, and confused as to where she actually "landed with God and in God's kingdom." In the end, she says, "it felt like everybody was talking to me about God, but I wasn't even hearing God. I felt really separate."

It was a slow journey back to God, one that Hannah says was mostly God's work. A few people stood by her and allowed her space to rage at God, be silent, ask questions, and reengage at her own pace. She felt like she began to hear God's voice again while working as an aide in the children's room at the church. Then she points to her heart surgery as the moment "that really kind of cemented it and was a really tangible point."

> I wasn't able to have any sort of pain medication following the heart surgery because I can't do narcotics. I don't react well to them. So I had to wait twenty-four hours to be able to get what amounts to like a jumped-up ibuprofen. My mom couldn't stay awake because she'd been awake for the whole surgery, which was over eight hours. She was exhausted. She couldn't stay awake. All I could think is, *Everybody has fallen asleep and I'm awake in agony.* And I really, I really felt connected to Jesus in his night in Gethsemane, when he knew it wasn't going to be easy. He knew there was going to be pain, and he still made that choice. Nobody stayed awake with Jesus. And so that kind of . . . I didn't feel alone. I really kind of sat with that, and since then, God's there and we're cool.

Perhaps the greatest challenge for Hannah is that her disability is hidden. She looks like any other young woman in her early twenties, which makes many people skeptical of her symptoms. "People just assume. They just make so many assumptions," she says. Family and friends still accuse her of being dramatic, of exaggerating heart problems, brain fog, fatigue, and the host of other things that go into her disability. Strangers judge her when she advocates for her needs, believing she's being a rude and entitled young adult. People who have similar diagnoses but less severe symptoms assume their experience should be hers. "People read things," Hannah says, "and then think they know more about my health than me."

Some people still pray for Hannah to be healed, but Hannah says with a laugh, "I remember praying, 'God, please don't heal me. God, please ignore everybody else.'" Having come to grips with the losses that her disability has brought, she says she is "actually okay with this body" and hopes that it's still this body in heaven. Though she doesn't believe God caused or even wanted her to go through this, she knows that "God doesn't see me as less. God does not see my body as being my limitation. And if God still expects me to do God's work and still expects me to enjoy God's creation and all of the good that God has, then I will." After all, she says, "A sinful, broken world impacts everybody. Everybody is going to have their own night by themselves, if you will. Mine just looks like this, and I don't know what other people's are going to look like."

ANDY (LOS ANGELES)

Andy, like me, grew up in a Pentecostal church and always felt like he knew Jesus and had a relationship with him.[6] He committed his life to Christ as a kid, was filled with the Holy Spirit at twelve, and, though he never walked away from his faith, recommitted his life to Christ as a teenager. At seventeen, he felt called into missions, a calling he believed was to an evangelistic life of reaching people who didn't know Jesus through ministry and church planting. Two years later, he was questioning that call as he began to lose his eyesight. He imagined that God would use him only if he was healthy and independent and wondered how God could use someone "broken." He began pleading with God for healing but over time recognized God had shifted his prayer from "Just heal me" to "Or use me until you heal me." Though it hasn't always been easy to reconcile his strong Pentecostal beliefs in healing with his continued blindness, Andy's mantra is "I'll just serve [God] in whatever capacity I have or lack. . . . I'll just make myself available."

Over time, Andy has begun to see his disability through the lens of Paul. It is a thorn in the flesh that gives even more platform for God to be at work. Noting that God's grace is sufficient, Andy says, "That's where I've really leaned into, where I felt, 'Okay, Lord, whatever I have or don't have, or whatever measures up or doesn't measure, or limitations in my life—that's all the more platform for your work to be seen or for your grace.'" In fact, he sometimes questions whether healing would be the best thing for him. Though he would embrace it if it came, he leans on Eva Kittay's idea that "in terms of vulnerability and dependencies, independence is a true impoverishment."[7] "To be healed to the point of 'I don't need anyone,'" he says, "seems like the wrong end towards the heart of God. What would that do between me and God too? Like, 'Okay, thank you, God. You gave me everything. I don't need anything.'"

God has answered Andy's prayer. Though he still receives prayer for healing from time to time, he is settled in his blindness and the ways in which God is using him both because of and despite his disability. After graduating from Bible college, Andy met his wife during his first youth

[6]Andy, interview by author, November 26, 2024.
[7]Andy's paraphrase of Kittay.

pastorate, and together they worked in Southeast Asia for several years. Now having earned a PhD, Andy teaches at his former Bible college and continues to serve in evangelism and witness through his life, church involvement, teaching, and writing.

ABBY (LOMBARD, ILLINOIS)

Abby doesn't know a time when disability wasn't a significant part of her life.[8] She has been a direct-support professional, earned a master's in disability studies, has three children with various disabilities, and has been autistic her whole life, though she did not receive a formal diagnosis until she was in her thirties and going through the diagnosis process for her oldest son, Andrew. She uses "identity-first language" when referring to herself, preferring "to just be called autistic because it's so ingrained in who I am that I feel like it's hard to separate out."

Being an undiagnosed autistic left Abby butting up against things in the church and the world that didn't make sense. "I went to a Christian college," she says, "and we had chapel three times a week. The sensory experience of chapel was very overwhelming to me. It was something I endured, and I thought, *Everybody's having trouble in this setting*, even though they weren't." Coming from a denomination that was steeped in missionary zeal, she struggled to find her place in the church. Her Bible school emphasized foreign missions and bold evangelism with the call to "Go! Go forth and speak the word of the Lord," but for Abby this made her feel extremely inadequate. It was only years later that she found her place in the church body as a children's director who organized workers and wrote curriculum others could teach. "I think at this point," she says, "I started to realize, '*Oh!* I *do* have a gift' . . . and started to relate the body of Christ image to *my* real life, work, and ministry."

Abby's oldest son, Andrew, is also autistic. Her youngest son, Silas, has ADHD. Her daughter, Sarah, who is in the middle, lost her eyesight in one eye to a rare condition that caused an extremely painful cyst to grow on her iris. Medicines given to treat the eye led to glaucoma and eventually blindness—and thankfully an end to the pain as well. Reflecting on her

---

[8]Abby, interview by author, December 6, 2024. Pseudonyms have been used for any named children.

and her family's journey, Abby firmly believes that God created each of them with their disabilities. For herself, Andrew, and Silas, she can't imagine any of them existing without autism or ADHD. It is too constitutive of their identities to be separated out. But even for her daughter Sarah, and others like her who have acquired disabilities, Abby says,

> It sounds cliché, and it's not something I would usually say to someone, but I do think God wasn't surprised by it. God wasn't like, "Oh, oops! There was a birth injury. I didn't plan on that." He did. He knew there would be an injury and worked through it. So I don't see a huge distinction between disabilities you have at birth and disabilities that are acquired. I think they're both part of God's design and plan. I can understand on an identity level how it can be more difficult to grapple with or more difficult to incorporate into your way of experiencing the world if it happens later. But I don't think that either one is the result of the fall.

In ruminating on John 9, she says that while we tend to relate sin to disability, God doesn't. For her own family, then, with some born with disabilities and others acquiring them later, she has never thought, "*This is because I sinned, or that [Sarah] sinned, or because of the fall.* I thought, *This is what's happening, and God will work through it.* I don't know if I'd say God caused it."

MEGAN (RURAL KANSAS)

Adoption was always part of Megan's plan.[9] Though the means and place took a while to figure out, she and her husband began fostering with the expectation that somewhere down the road they would adopt one or more of their placements. First came two brothers. A few years later came two sisters. "Before they came, [my husband] had been saying, 'If they call with two little girls, just say yes. You don't even have to ask me,'" Megan laughs. So when the call came to place two young girls, Megan said she immediately accepted the placement, the first time she had done so without consulting her husband. She was aware that the youngest, Joy, had some medical issues, but Joy was as yet undiagnosed, and no one really knew the extent of her medical challenges.

---

[9]Megan, interview by author, January 14, 2025. Pseudonyms have been used for any named children.

Just before the girls arrived, a worker called Megan to say Joy was getting out of the hospital after a choking incident and floated possibilities such as cerebral palsy and autism. Megan recalls feeling overwhelmed in that moment and thinking, *Oh no! What did I just say yes to?* Almost a year into the placement, they finally received the official diagnosis: Rett syndrome, a rare condition that primarily affects girls and causes rapid loss of language, mobility, coordination, and use of the hands. Joy and her older sister, Katrina, had been with Megan and her family long enough that when the time came that adoption was a possibility, the family was so in love that they said yes even without a full understanding of what that yes would mean. Though they hadn't initially thought they could handle disability, as Megan recalls, "We just kind of landed in it, and through a process of different things, that was what God brought to us, and we said yes."

Joy is approaching her tween years. She primarily uses a wheelchair and experiences repetitive hand motions that look like light, soft clapping. She has a G-tube and needs constant help with daily care. She understands things at an age-appropriate level and communicates through an AAC she activates with her eyes. Her responses, however, are delayed because she experiences apraxia, a motor-speech disorder that makes it difficult for her to form responses. Even though she knows the response, it can take a minute or more to answer a question because she struggles with executing the complex process required for intelligible speech. For many people, they don't have the patience or awareness to work at Joy's pace and wait for responses. "That feels like an eternity for one of us to stand there and be, like, 'What's she going to do?'" Megan says. In the church environment, people aren't trained to know how to respond, and Sunday school classrooms for young kids move quickly. This makes it hard for Joy to participate and interact in ways similar to her peers.

It's been a bit of a lonely road for Megan and her husband. The non-traditional path of adding kids two by two and never as infants meant that people in their church didn't always recognize they had children, and they lost opportunities to form close friendships with others who were adding infants to their families through birth. Disability has only compounded the loneliness because people are busy with their own lives and are not always aware or available to provide respite care. They received help early on while they were still fostering Joy and Katrina, but since adoption, Megan has only had brief help. As Joy has gotten older, her care needs have increased, leaving it impossible for her to be left with a teenage babysitter. Adults who might want to help are busy with their own families. There is never much of a break for Megan and her husband. It's tiring and isolating. Joy's care is full time, and the other children also need parenting and help as they work through their own struggles that are common with kids who have been in the foster system. Megan says, "We feel like we've been in a really weird season for a few years, several years now. There's no one that really fits, that can help us with our needs. . . . I hope that as Joy gets a little older that some of those will work itself out, and that maybe there will be the opportunities to have . . . a nurse-type person that could come and help some." For now, she says, "I just have to remind myself that doing the work of raising them and caring for them, it is—it's the ministry right now."

Megan hasn't thought too much about the cause of Joy's disability. "My general response," she reflects, "would probably be more, 'It's just the general fall, the sin in the world. Some people have this. Some people don't. We really do all have different things that we struggle with. It just comes in different forms.'" She looks forward to heaven, where Joy will be "healed, whole, and able to walk and talk and move freely." While she waits for that day and the opportunity for Joy to tell her everything they know they've missed in her communication, Megan already experiences many blessings from her daughter. Her daughter's joy, her love for people, her outlook on life, and her responses to people and situations have given Megan and others a glimpse of God's kingdom. Joy "just draws in your perspective on what matters in life and not being so easily tangled up in the things that we get stressed about and frustrated about." Megan says through tears, "It's a life-changing thing. She is such a light and such a joy . . . and she helps us see things the way God sees them."

RICK (FRONT PORCH CHURCH, NAPERVILLE, ILLINOIS)

Rick does not have a disability or a family member with a disability.[10] Through involvement with YoungLife, he accepted an invitation to participate in a YoungLife Capernaum event. YoungLife is an organization for high school students that seeks to "introduce adolescents to Jesus Christ and help them grow in their faith." The Capernaum branch of YoungLife carries out this mission by inviting "teens and young adults with and without disabilities to discover authentic friendship, growth, and purpose."[11] During his first camp, Rick arrived with the thought that he was there to minister *to* the boys in his cabin, but he left having received far more ministry *from* the boys instead: "I was going to tell them about how much Jesus loves them. They didn't tell me. They *showed* me how much Jesus loved me." The experience was life changing. He fell in love with the community and felt called to help them grow in Jesus.

In 2023, he opened Front Porch Church, an all-abilities church that describes its mission as "helping people of all abilities find their way back to God." The church mainly attracts people and families with disabilities, though several without disabilities join. As a micro–church plant from Community Christian Church (commonly referred to as the Yellow Box), the group follows sermon themes and worship sets used by all seven Community Christian Church locations. Every disability is welcome, and there is never a concern about how those disabilities manifest. "It looks different," Rick says. "There might be shoutouts and walking around and somebody going up and sitting on the stage," but in the end, he says, "there's no distractions, only interactions within our community."

Front Porch Church tries to be a church where everyone is welcome and given opportunities to participate. People of all ages and all abilities are present. When you attend, you will see nonverbal people giving the announcements and communicating in their own ways, and you'll see various people playing instruments or singing. One gentleman who loves music will occasionally walk up to the worship leader and shout her name with an enthusiastic, "Hi!" She will then lean back and, calling him by

---

[10]Rick, interview by author, November 25, 2024.

[11]"YoungLife Capernaum Home Page," YoungLife Capernaum, accessed December 7, 2024, https://capernaum.younglife.org/.

name, will respond just as enthusiastically, "Hi!" Another young man with Down syndrome who feels called to be a pastor is part of the preaching team and on the regular teaching rotations. For some families, Front Porch Church is their second church. For others, it is their only church family.

When I asked about the benefits and challenges of being separate from the main Community Christian Church body, Rick acknowledged that there are different opinions about disability ministry, and he receives emails that either support or criticize what he's doing. In the end, he says, "There's no perfect church. For our community, there's an opportunity to worship just how God designed them to worship . . . and in ways they never could in a traditional service." Reflecting on the Yellow Box, he says, "It can be too loud and flashy from a sensory perspective. There are a few in our all-ability community that would love to go to that that I know of. But for most of our community, it can be too loud and overstimulating, so a little quieter and standard room lighting works better for [Front Porch]." "Our church," he says, "is not a silver bullet for all. But I love the differences that people bring. It makes us a better church." Because the church's mission specifically mentions "people of all abilities," people are able to research that, and Rick says it's attracting families who are looking for a place of welcome. Families may feel lost or excluded in other church settings, but they come to Front Porch believing "our family's going to feel seen, feel loved, feel heard, feel valued."

DISABILITY AS PARTICULARITY

What these few interviews reveal is the true variety of experiences and differences of opinions that exist in the disability world. Some embrace disability as God-given. Some see disability coming about as a result of the fall. Others see it as simply a part of this world and something that has value and purpose because God is redeeming the disability for his own glory and the world's good. What this tells us about evangelism is that we cannot rush to a certain conclusion about what the person in front of us needs. Whether the person is far from Christ or on a journey of discovery, our beginning spot is always the same: *listening*.

For Chris, he never felt early on that people positively moved him toward Christ. He encountered resistance in the church. The message he heard over and over was that God planned his disability. This, along with a heavy emphasis that God needed to fix him before God could use him, pushed Chris away. "I came to faith in Jesus on my own," he says. When I queried further, "How did you persevere in seeking God? Everybody made so many barriers for you," Chris replied honestly, "I don't know, and I can't answer that other than God wanted me, and he kept pursuing me regardless." Had someone stopped to listen to Chris's questions and sticking points, perhaps they could have journeyed with him in a way that smoothed the path to Christ rather than blocking it.

Abby, however, receives the message that God planned her disability with open arms. She is comforted to know that God made her and her children as they are and sees disability as something that exists regardless of the fall and will extend into God's future kingdom. To approach her with a message that Jesus came to "fix" her so that she can be healed would be not just off-putting and confusing. For her it would be "an insidious message." She needs to know that Jesus created her and her children as unique beings and has a plan for their lives as they are, and not only if their disabilities were to somehow be eliminated such that they would become something she wouldn't recognize. "I don't know what's left. Would I recognize my Andrew with no autism? I don't think I would. It's *so* much a part of who he is. I *love* my Andrew. But it's part of him. I don't think he's going to stop having it when we go to heaven. You know, Christ's scars were still present in heaven. Why would I think that we're not still going to have [disabilities]?"

Hannah, like Chris, doesn't think God caused her disabilities. As God is merciful and loving, she doesn't think God purposely afflicted her, not even to teach a lesson. "We live in a broken world," she says, "and we are not made promises. We're not told that we're going to live protected bubble lives. I think eventually I came to the conclusion that what I've been through is not what God wanted. That God grieves when I grieve, and his heart breaks when my heart breaks, but that God doesn't see me as less." Unlike Chris, Hannah isn't so sure that heaven will give her a new body. Having learned to live with POTS, heart defects, ADHD, and other symptoms, she is at home in her body. Ruminating about messages she's heard that heaven will make her body perfect she asks, similarly to Abby,

"Are you just asking me to not be me, then? Am I just not going to be me in heaven? Because that's kind of what it feels like. It seems like people are saying you'll get this new body so that you can participate in society the way we do. But society is not going to exist like that in heaven. . . . It seems like everything that's different is wrong, and I just don't agree with that."

These are but a few examples of how disability affects people in different ways. The good news, as we have discovered, is that God's good-news story is big enough and powerful enough to handle all these variances and more. But if we aren't listening, we might be hindering rather than helping people on their journey. This leads to one last thought.

BRINGING DOWN THE BARRIERS

I will reveal more from my friends in the coming chapters, but as I reflect, even now, on the rich conversations I had with each of them, I am struck by the number of times they mention that the church and individual Christians either made the path to Jesus harder or didn't even think to point them to the path in the first place. This stands in juxtaposition to God's heart.

Toward the end of his book, Isaiah begins to announce God's promise to Israel that he is going to return the exiles and enact his great work of salvation by "his own arm" (Is 59:16 NIV). The prophet opens Isaiah 40 with God's call for his people to be comforted. "Speak tenderly to Jerusalem," God says. "Tell her that her sad days are gone and that her sins are pardoned" (Is 40:1-2). Then Isaiah announces with jubilation, "Listen! It's the voice of someone shouting, 'Clear the way through the wilderness for the Lord! Make a straight highway through the wasteland for our God! Fill the valleys, and level the mountains and hills. Straighten out the curves, and smooth out the rough places. Then the glory of the Lord will be revealed, and all people will see it together'" (Is 40:3-5). What do you notice about this passage? What posture in evangelism does this passage give us? What actions does it call us to?

God is coming with his message of salvation, deliverance, forgiveness, and restoration, and he calls us to prepare the way for him. How do we prepare it? By removing the obstacles and challenges that make getting to God harder. When you have a visual impairment, a straight, smooth highway is easier to navigate. When you have mobility challenges and other physical impairments, a road without big hills to surmount and valleys to conquer is easier to traverse. When you have cognitive and mental challenges, a road without twists and turns is easier to follow. Whatever the ability or disability, a straight, smooth road freed of rough spots is the easiest means for travel. This is the work God calls us to do as Christians who are walking the road with Jesus.[12] Why? So that as God is revealed "*all people will see it together*" (Is 40:5).

Many of our evangelistic practices are well intentioned, but they are often conducted from an ableist perspective. We see accommodations as something special, additional, burdensome, or costly. But God does not call us to the easiest and cheapest actions. He calls us to level hills, fill in valleys, clear away debris, relocate boulders, and reshape the roadways so that the path to God is straight and smooth *for everyone* so *everyone together* will see God's glory. As we consider the dispositions and postures we should have toward disability, I think you'll discover, like I have, that these will be some of our greatest means for doing the hard work of preparing God's highway through the wilderness so that when we engage in evangelism, it's on a smooth, straight path.

DISCUSSION QUESTIONS

1. Have you heard the stories of people with disabilities before? How do they resonate with the short introductions in this chapter? If you are disabled, share your experiences with your group.
2. Are you surprised at the diversity of beliefs people with disabilities have about disability? Which views do you most resonate with?
3. If you were to interview a disabled person, what questions would you want to ask?
4. Reflect on Isaiah 40:1-5 as it relates to evangelism and disability. What hard work do you and your church need to do so that people with disabilities are central to your church's life and witness?

[12]This imagery is drawn from how the First Nations Version speaks about following Jesus.

7

Evangelism Practice(s)

SINCE I WAS A CHILD, I have always dreamed of going to the Rose Parade in Pasadena, California. It is one of the most unusual parades in the world, featuring thematic floats that are covered entirely by organic material. When my brother-in-law moved to that area, it became our chance to go. The experience did not disappoint. Seventy-five degrees and perfectly sunny weather. Gorgeous and creative floats. Stellar bands. Horse troops. You couldn't ask for much more.

We casually walked to the parade around 7:15 a.m. and by 7:20 a.m. were setting up our camp chairs nearly in front-row spots at the edge of the road. The parade started at 9:00 a.m., but since we were located at the halfway mark of the parade, we would have some time to wait until it reached us. We sat down and began watching people. Some had camped out all night and were fixing breakfast on small grills or by pulling items from coolers. Street vendors walked up and down, selling everything from hot dogs and ice cream to Rose Parade merchandise, hats that looked like monsters, and other assorted kids' toys. A group of Hare Krishnas danced their way up and down the street, chanting and handing out tracts. And then came the street preachers. We probably saw twenty to thirty. They had big yellow, black, and red signs that read things like, "Accept Jesus as your Savior," or "Repent from you sins and you shall be saved." Some walked silently up and down the parade route holding their signs. Others walked in groups with a loud recording, playing a call for people to repent and turn to Jesus to be saved from their sins and the punishment of sin. Others carried a personal microphone and speaker and gave these messages themselves. A few handed out tracts as they went.

Rather than appreciating that people were trying to get the gospel message out, my first impulse was to roll my eyes in judgment as I asked, "Why do they do this when it never works?" And yet, my brother-in-law reminded me, "How do you know? Maybe that's the message that someone needs right now." I felt convicted. As I watched, with renewed sight, I saw people who loved Jesus and wanted others to know him. I saw people who were not pushy or rude. They never forced anyone to take a tract, and they responded with grace to any rejection. They simply used the time they had to give the thousands of people sitting in those blocks a brief moment of reflection on their own spiritual lives. Though it isn't my preferred method of evangelism, nor one that I am inclined to think is overly effective in many places, this is one way in which evangelism takes place.

This experience brought to light again the many ways in which we can negatively view evangelism, especially when we rely on tropes and stereotypes. Somewhere along the way we've corrupted the beautiful calling to showcase Christ and turned it into a forced sales pitch that makes Christians feel uncomfortable, fearful, and embarrassed, and makes non-Christians feel preyed upon. Judith Paulsen argues that our negative assumptions and opinions about evangelists, our evangelism methodology, and even our views of Jesus in an increasingly secular age have discouraged most Christians from wanting anything to do with evangelism. Worse yet, if we try to guilt people into evangelism (especially from the pulpit), we will only make the reticence worse.[1]

How should we think about evangelism and what our role in it is? We have already said important things about evangelism in the first section of this book; however, it is important here to make some explicit comments about what evangelism is, who is called to participate in evangelism, and what the end result we're looking for should be.

It may be surprising to many that the word *evangelism* isn't in the Bible. This isn't to say the concept is missing—evangelism is a key theme of Scripture—but the word itself isn't used. Rather, the Bible centers on the word *gospel* and how that gospel is shared. It is in examining a few of

[1]Judith Paulsen, *A New and Ancient Evangelism: Rediscovering the Ways God Calls and Sends* (Baker Academic, 2024), 1-10.

these nouns and verbs that we get a fuller picture of how the Bible sees evangelism.

The word *gospel* or term "good news" comes from the Greek word *euangelion*. It is used more than seventy times in the New Testament (at least fifty-four times by Paul) as a catchall term for the full story of Jesus. People who share this message are the gospelers, or evangelists (plural *euangelistou*), and the activity of sharing the gospel is *euangelizō*, announcing and proclaiming a good-news message. But this is not the only word associated with gospeling.

Kēryssō, used at least sixty-one times in the New Testament, means "to herald." This draws out the idea that we should faithfully share a king's message without adding in our own thoughts, interpretations, or commentary. There is a good-news story, and we should present it as a herald or mouthpiece for our King, the author, center, and end of this good-news story.

A third term is *martyreō*, "to witness." For Luke, this is testimony that comes from someone who knows Jesus personally and can testify to his life, his death, and especially his resurrection. John, however, is not so restrictive and uses *martyreō* to the exclusion of *euangelion* and *kēryssō*. Everything in John's Gospel is a witness to the person, nature, work, and result of encountering Jesus. The power of this kind of witness is that it "is non-coercive" because, as Richard Bauckham argues,

> It has no power but the convincingness of the truth to which it witnesses. Witnesses are not expected, like lawyers, to persuade by the rhetorical power of their speeches, but simply to testify to the truth for which they are qualified to give evidence. But to be adequate witness to the truth of God and the world, witness must be a lived witness involving the whole of life and even death.[2]

While this is not an exhaustive list of possible evangelism words, when we put these together, we could say that sharing the gospel (evangelizing) means *proclaiming, heralding, and living out a message that bears witness to good news about Jesus Christ*. Notice the emphasis here on the message

---

[2]Richard Bauckham, *Bible and Mission: Christian Witness in a Postmodern World* (Baker Academic, 2003), 99.

of Jesus. As Sam Chan affirms, "The essence of evangelism is in the message, the gospel of Jesus," not the methods, mediums, occasions, or audiences through and in which this messaging takes place, as much as those matter.[3] This is important to remember, especially when we consider disability.

First, our ability to evangelize comes from our understanding of and encounter with the gospel. A genuine encounter with Jesus transforms us and makes our lives an *evangel*—a witness—to his saving work. Every person who surrenders to the lordship of Christ is called to the work of evangelism both individually and corporately. While there are some people who are spiritually gifted to be catalysts of evangelism, no one can use "that's not my gift" as a free pass. If we have encountered Jesus, we have good news to share. This is not dependent on certain abilities or skills. Each of us brings witness to what we know and experience.

Second, because evangelism is focused on Jesus' story, when we do consider the methods and means of evangelism, we have the space to consider important questions about what evangelism requires and what a response to Jesus looks like. In part one, we examined the good-news story of Jesus with disability in mind and discovered some wonderful truths about how disability does not solely relate to the fall but rather is addressed in all parts of God's story in surprising and wonderful ways. We also considered four examples of how we can gospel with disability in mind. But here, in part two, we need to consider more deeply the methods and audiences through and in which our gospeling takes place and how we understand conversion, especially with regard to intellectual and developmental disabilities. Though evangelism and conversion aren't easily separated (indeed, Paulsen's *A New and Ancient Evangelism* considers how different conversion experiences reveal different evangelism strategies), for the sake of examination, we will separate them here.[4]

---

[3]Sam Chan, *Evangelism in a Skeptical World: How to Make the Unbelievable News About Jesus More Believable* (Zondervan Academic, 2018), 16.

[4]Paulsen, *New and Ancient Evangelism*.

WHAT CONSTITUTES EVANGELISM?

What does it mean to *proclaim, herald, and live out a message that bears witness to good news about Jesus Christ*? We often think of evangelism solely in terms of activities, models, and skills that lead to numerical results (i.e., new converts). But it is here that disabilities cause us to think in new ways. If we measure success by the quality of our evangelistic skills and activities and the results they produce, what role do people with disabilities have in evangelism? Are people with intellectual and developmental disabilities able to respond meaningfully to evangelism? If so, how? Can people with disabilities participate in evangelism, especially when their particular disability seems to detract from or limit them in employing evangelistic skills? If our goal in evangelism is numbers of converts, does this allow us to, for the sake of the greater good, set aside people we think may hinder others from making commitments to Christ and joining the church?

These are important and real questions well-meaning pastors and Christians ask. We cannot consider evangelism without considering these questions (or the other issues these questions raise). The remainder of this book will address these questions and concerns and argue that we need to take on dispositional evangelistic practices that embrace the fullness of all the people *God* calls into his kingdom, which in turn allows us to also demonstrate the fullness of God's kingdom in the world. To do this, we will finish this chapter by discussing evangelistic practice(s) and then turn, in the next chapter, to examine how disability interplays with evangelistic proclamation. This will lead us in chapter eight to address important questions about conversion. From here we will rethink the "burden" of disability in evangelism, which will lead us to our final chapters on specific evangelistic practices that will reshape our corporate and individual witness.

EVANGELISM AS PRACTICES AND PRACTICE

In his book *Evangelism After Christendom*, Bryan Stone asks, "Is evangelism a practice?"[5] At first blush this may seem like an odd question.

---

[5]Bryan Stone, *Evangelism After Christendom: The Theology and Practice of Christian Witness* (Brazos, 2007), 29-53.

Yes, we say, evangelism involves specific skills and activities such as articulating our faith to nonbelievers, inviting people to church, asking people whether they want to accept Christ as their Savior, and so on. While Stone would agree that evangelism necessitates these explicit activities that call others to know Christ and turn toward him, Stone says that evangelism also involves something deeper and more fundamental. Evangelism is a *core practice* of the church in which we implicitly witness of Christ's kingdom through the ways we live out salvation as a church body by responding to and living in God's continued work of mission in the world.[6] Evangelism, in this way, is not just acts we do; it is, more importantly, the way of life of the church as a new and distinct society created and perfected by the Holy Spirit for the sake of making God's kingdom known in the world.[7] This forces us to think more deeply about the telos of evangelism. While we cannot jettison either the implicit or explicit practice of evangelism—indeed, both are necessary for faithful witness—which side we emphasize will affect the questions we ask of evangelism and the ways we carry out evangelism.

In our postmodern, capitalistic society, we tend to view evangelism through the lens of productivity. From this perspective, evangelism becomes a "set of intentional activities that will achieve a particular end (conversion, initiation, baptism, membership, church growth, etc.), so that the logic of the practice of evangelism becomes wholly governed by that aim." We perform evangelism as a means to an end. It is the work of particular actors with particular skills to make converts. On the individual level, this requires certain means of reason, logic, articulation, persuasion, and charisma. On a corporate level, this requires attractive events, quality production, high energy, persuasive preaching, and radical hospitality. If what we do does not yield the kinds of results we hope for (conversion, church growth, etc.), we consider evangelism to have failed and often rethink our methodology, looking to other successful models or even hoping for a silver bullet. In this way, Stone says, "the means and the end of the practice are *external* to one another."[8]

---

[6]Stone, *Evangelism After Christendom*, 48-49.
[7]Stone, *Evangelism After Christendom*, 15.
[8]Stone, *Evangelism After Christendom*, 50, 18.

Many of the questions pastors ask unknowingly focus on this logic of production.[9] The earnest desire to reach people leads to capitalism-inspired phrases such as, "winning many for Christ," "reaching as many as possible," "finishing the task of evangelization," or "growing the church as quickly as possible." When this happens, we can easily slip into evaluative modes that leave people with disabilities excluded. If they do not contribute to explicit witness and proclamation, if they detract from corporate appeal, if they slow down or hinder progress, or if they do not have the cognitive or communicative abilities to receive and give clear gospel articulation, we can easily excuse, overlook, or exclude the disabled from evangelism. They do not seem central in the work and can be accommodated through other means or in other spaces.

What if we pull back and, instead of viewing evangelism at the granular level first, we consider evangelism from the "logic of bearing witness"?[10] This moves us toward a grounding of evangelism in the life and existence of the church, pulling activity away from what *we* plan, execute, and measure to what *God, through the Spirit*, enacts through our lives. "The most evangelistic thing the church can do today," Stone declares,

> is to be the church—to be formed imaginatively by the Holy Spirit through core practices such as worship, forgiveness, hospitality, and economic sharing into a distinct people in the world, a new social option, the body of Christ. It is the very shape and character of the church as the Spirit's "new creation" that is the witness to God's reign in the world and so both the source and aim of Christian evangelism.[11]

This changes the benchmark fundamentally. While we are still hopeful that faithful witness will lead to transformed lives, the measure of evangelism is not found in numbers but rather in how faithfully we are living into the witness of God's kingdom. In this way, witness can be rejected and the church still be faithful in evangelism because of its faithful (and even successful) performance. As Stone suggests, "There is only one criterion by which evangelism may be measured, and that is

---

[9]Stone, *Evangelism After Christendom*, 18.
[10]Stone, *Evangelism After Christendom*, 18.
[11]Stone, *Evangelism After Christendom*, 15.

whether or not it is a faithful, virtuous witness to God's peace."[12] In fact, as Stone argues, faithful witness to God's reign is both the source of our evangelism *and* the ultimate aim of our evangelism.

When we recognize evangelism as a wider practice of the church, one that is fundamental to a church's faithful existence in the world, this should change how we think about the role of people with disabilities in evangelism. If the church exists to be "distinct people in the world" and a "witness to God's reign in the world" such that the church showcases different values, virtues, habits, economies, and ways of being, it cannot do this without the witness and presence of the disabled. If we include only those with certain skills or we rank people by their perceived abilities and strengths, we cannot exhibit the kind of countercultural witness that showcases a different way of being and valuing. In this sense, we become just another social club that mirrors the world rather than prophetically speaking to it.

But if we are faithfully and virtuously living out the shalom of God's kingdom, the witness of the disabled among us becomes a central piece helping us live out the values, virtues, habits, and economy that mark God's upside-down world. When we live in this way, it turns us from asking "Can this person do [fill in the blank]?" to "How does this person help us bear witness better?" (or, said conversely, "What are we missing if this person's witness and work among us is absent?"). This also helps us rethink the ways we carry out individual actions of evangelism, opening us to new possibilities even while keeping us from making individual actions everything.

It is important to study the methods and models of evangelism because the church has been in the business of making Christ public through its work and words from the very beginning. As Priscilla Pope-Levison and Rick Richardson show, our evangelistic activities have included one-on-one conversations and large come-and-see events. Our practices of service help us show Jesus through tangible things such as neighborhood uplift, serving the homeless, or helping a shut-in neighbor. We have practices such as leading and participating in small group

[12]Stone, *Evangelism After Christendom*, 52; see 49.

studies that make space for people to seek and ask questions. We use power encounter and new church plants and various types of media to make the gospel known.[13] There is diversity in evangelism, diversity Richardson says we need to "integrate and celebrate."[14] Evangelism activities come in all shapes and sizes, just like people. This leaves space for everyone to participate in the activities of evangelism through the gifts and presence God has given them for the church (1 Cor 12).

But note, when we use *practices* solely in this way, we can often see them as actions we either do or don't do. However, by dropping the *s* off the word *practice*, we move beyond simply talking about *actions* to also include *dispositions*. It is not simply what we do; it is also about who we are. We are evangels because we are in Christ, who is making himself known in and through the Spirit's witness in the church. What this conversation about practices and practice leads us to discover is that evangelism is a wholistic way of life that requires living out God's new reality in community while explicitly calling people to join in this reality through the skills and activities we enact through our personal and corporate lives.

We can think of it a bit like spiritual formation practices. There are specific actions (disciplines) we participate in that are meant to form our spiritual growth, such as prayer, fasting, solitude, meditation, and study. As important as the disciplines are, our engagement with these activities is not about checking things off a list as much as it is practicing these formational tools as a way of intentionally loving God with our heart, mind, soul, and strength. There is work in the practice, along with self-denial. The goal is not achievement so we can boast in what we have done. The goal is formation of Spirit-formed dispositions that reshape how we go about living God-focused lives. Our engagement with spiritual practices should change our motivations, our dependencies, and our character. At times we will have great motivation to engage in a particular discipline. At other times, when our motivation wanes, our commitment

[13]Priscilla Pope-Levison, *Models of Evangelism* (Baker Academic, 2020); Rick Richardson, "Understanding Evangelism Through Time," Exponential, December 1, 2022, YouTube, 14:37, www.youtube.com/watch?v=ZzkLFu2URx8.

[14]Richardson, "Understanding Evangelism Through Time," 12:36.

to spiritual formation will bolster the intentionality of practices. The key to spiritual formation, however, is that the more we do it, the more it becomes our habit (or, as James K. A. Smith would call it, our love).[15]

The same goes for evangelistic practices. Yes, there are specific things considered evangelistic actions. But as important as these actions are, our participation is not about checking things off a list as much as it is practicing our roles in God's mission as a way of intentionally loving our neighbors. There is work in the practice, along with self-denial. The goal is not achievement so we can boast in what we have done. The goal is formation of Spirit-formed dispositions that reshape how we go about living evangelistic lives. Our engagement with evangelistic practices should change our motivations, our dependencies, and our character. At times we will have great motivation to engage in evangelism activities. At other times, when our motivation wanes, our commitment to the practice of evangelism will bolster the intentionality of our actions. The key to evangelism as a practice, however, is that the more we enact it, the more it becomes our habit, our love.

This is an important contribution from the disability world and one we cannot overlook. The people I interviewed, who live with disability in a variety of ways, talked so much less about the top actions churches can take to reach out to and with people with disabilities. Rather, when I asked them to speak to the church, they collectively voiced practices of *disposition*, even while giving some specific tips on how to put these into concrete actions within evangelistic activities. This resonates with Stone's argument that evangelism is much less about "translating our beliefs about the world into categories that others will find acceptable" and more "a matter of being present in the world in a distinctive way such that the alluring and 'useless' beauty of holiness can be touched, tasted, and tried."[16] Notice these words: *touched*, *tasted*, and *tried*. These are words of embodiment, physicality, and varied senses. Touching, tasting, and trying do not require particular abilities; if anything, they are the heightened senses of those we often label as disabled. If evangelism, as the psalmist says, is a call to "taste and see that the Lord is good" (Ps 34:8),

[15]James K. A. Smith, *You Are What You Love: The Spiritual Power of Habit* (Brazos, 2016).
[16]Stone, *Evangelism After Christendom*, 21.

we have quite a fresh and wonderful way of encountering God and God's good news that makes place and space for all people of all abilities in the practice and practices of evangelism.

DISCUSSION QUESTIONS

1. How does the definition of evangelism given here resonate or differ from how you've thought about evangelism in the past?
2. What are your initial thoughts about where people with disabilities fit into evangelism (as either recipients or participants)?
3. How does the distinction between practice and practices enrich your understanding of evangelism?
4. What challenges does this chapter raise for you? For your church?

8

Evangelism and Words

EVANGELISM, WE ARE DISCOVERING, IS MANY THINGS. It is the way of life of the community of Christ's body and a set of acts we intentionally perform that together make known God's reign as found in the life, death, resurrection, and ascension of Jesus Christ. This, I hope, is broadening and deepening our understanding of what it means to be evangels in the world. Through faithful living as Christians, we evangelize the world "by sheer presence," as Stone says. We also engage in very specific and explicit acts meant to reach the world, confront sin, communicate good news, invite people into God's reign, join in fellowship, and live as a distinct people guided by new values, loves, and habits. In fact, though much of his work emphasizes the lived witness of the church, Stone argues strongly that "to conclude that one can bear witness to God's reign without ever explicitly offering others an invitation to be a part of that reign is not merely half right; it is wholly wrong."[1]

This can inspire fear and concern for Christians who do not see evangelistic proclamation as their strong suit. It can also lead us to question the role people with cognitive and communicative disabilities have in this explicit offering. How do we explicitly proclaim and invite people to Jesus?

VERBAL PROCLAMATION?

Does evangelism require telling the full gospel story from Genesis to Revelation every time? Does it require offering every person we meet or

[1]Bryan Stone, *Evangelism After Christendom: The Theology and Practice of Christian Witness* (Brazos, 2007), 48-49.

talk to an opportunity to say yes to Jesus? Does it require people actually saying yes to Jesus for it to "count"? The answer to each of these questions is no. There is a flexibility in what we do, because each time we engage in evangelism, we're not entering into a formula; we're entering into a "conversation God was already having in the person's life," and we're just moving that "conversation toward Christ."[2] The most effective evangelism occurs when we discern where God is already at work and join in on what he is doing so people are one step closer to Jesus. This could mean introducing people to the person of Jesus. It could mean listening carefully to their story and asking probing questions about where they notice God at work. It could mean sharing our own story of transformation when God intervened in our life. It could mean demonstrating welcome, love, inclusion, and belonging in a way that explicitly makes God and God's love known. It could mean asking someone whether they're ready to commit.

But let me take this a step deeper and ask one more question: Does our explicit offer for people to know, embrace, join, and serve Jesus require words? This is not a trivial or inconsequential question. It is a question many Christians have and one many hope is answered with a no. Consider this oft-quoted saying: "Preach the gospel. Use words if necessary." Popular lore attributes this to Saint Francis of Assisi; however, Assisi not only never said this but also probably wouldn't have thought to say it. His own life was one of robust verbal proclamation accompanied by love. If Assisi never said this, why do we repeat it so often, and why is it so appealing?

One reason we like it is that it makes clear we cannot credibly bear *verbal* witness about Jesus if we are not living a life that gives credible *demonstrated* witness about Jesus. "Walk your talk and talk your walk" might be another way to express this. Why should anyone listen to us if we aren't living out the very things we're calling others to? Scripture has something to say about this. "Live such good lives among the pagans that, though they accuse you of doing wrong, they may see your good deeds and glorify God on the day he visits us" (1 Pet 2:12 NIV).

---

[2]W. Jay Moon and W. Bud Simon, *Effective Intercultural Evangelism: Good News in a Diverse World* (InterVarsity Press, 2021), 3.

Another reason we like this is that it seems to let us off the hook. We live in a day and age in which having an absolute truth and telling others we believe Jesus is "*the* way, *the* truth, and *the* life" (Jn 14:6) isn't popular. People are fine with you calling yourself a Christian and even okay with having spiritual conversations, but a postmodern mindset rejects the notion that one metanarrative should be imposed on everyone as the only metanarrative.[3] The claim of exclusivity through Christ is a key sticking point for twenty-first-century people. If it's true that we can preach the gospel without words, we are thrilled because it means we don't have to figure out how to share a verbal argument about an exclusive Christ. We can just hope "our unbelieving friends will 'catch' the gospel once our lifestyle is infected with it."[4]

While this feels good, there is a problem with this reasoning. First, it can keep us from having to make a clear statement that we belong to Jesus. We ride the "be nice" train in hopes we don't have to intentionally say we are Jesus people. Our desire to avoid awkward conversations and to distance ourselves from criticisms of intolerance and bigotry keeps us from bringing Jesus into conversations if we don't have to. Instead, we plan to say we're Jesus people *after* our friends catch the gospel from our good deeds and join the church, where we feel at ease talking openly about him. But this is not the call of Jesus, who told his followers, "In your going make disciples of all nations by teaching and baptizing" (Mt 28:19, my paraphrase); who reminded followers that he would be ashamed of those who were ashamed of him (Mk 8:38; Lk 9:26); who, through Paul, instructed believers to "do your best to present yourself to God as one approved, a worker who does not need to be ashamed and who correctly handles the word of truth" (2 Tim 2:15 NIV); and who, through Peter, said, "If you suffer as a Christian, do not be ashamed, but praise God that you bear that name" (1 Pet 4:16 NIV). Witnessing with our lives does not excuse us from witnessing with our words.

A second problem with this reasoning is that there are a lot of nice people in the world. How will others learn the true Jesus story, wrestle

---

[3]See Rick Richardson, *You Found Me: New Research on How Unchurched Nones, Millennials, and Irreligious Are Surprisingly Open to Christian Faith* (IVP Academic, 2019).

[4]Mark Galli, "Speak the Gospel: Use Deeds When Necessary," *Christianity Today*, May 21, 2009, www.christianitytoday.com/2009/05/speak-gospel/.

with the implications of what following Jesus means, and then come to an active and ever-growing faith if we don't tell the Jesus story? Might our living witness still require a verbal message that makes clear the good news story of Jesus? Paul seems to think so. Despite his living a deeply incarnated life among nonbelievers for the sake of bringing them to Christ (1 Cor 9:27), he does not say gospeling is in deeds alone. Rather, as he notes in Romans 10:13-17, people cannot come to faith in Jesus without hearing about Jesus through the work of one who preaches because faith comes by hearing. The apostle Peter agrees with Paul. He urges believers to be "eager to do good" *and* "prepared to give an answer to everyone who asks you to give the reason for the hope that you have" (1 Pet 3:13-15 NIV). Believers are an intentional part of God's plan to make Jesus known.

But here is where things get complicated. Often, when theologians, missiologists, and pastors argue for the necessity of verbal proclamation for being an evangelist and for receiving evangelism, they do so as if everyone in the world can give and receive verbal proclamation. Not having people with intellectual and developmental or other communication disabilities in mind, it is easy to make statements such as, "The gospel is inherently verbal, and preaching it is inherently verbal behavior. If the gospel is to be communicated at all, it must be put into words."[5] What does this say to and about people who may not be able to articulate the gospel well or listen to a verbal proclamation and make easy sense of what they hear? Does this exclude them from the need to hear about Jesus? Does this make faith impossible? If they do have faith, are they excluded from evangelism simply because they struggle to communicate verbally?

These are not unreasonable conclusions when we say the gospel is inherently verbal and must be put into words. For those with intellectual and developmental disabilities, they face judgments and assumptions on all sides. First, there are the questions of understanding: "How well will they really be able to grasp theological concepts? Will they get anything out of church? How can they make a confession of Christ?" Next, there are the questions of ability: "How can they tell others about Jesus if they

[5]Duane Litfin, "Works and Words, Why You Can't Preach the Gospel with Deeds: And Why It's Important to Say So," *Christianity Today* 56, no. 5 (2012), www.christianitytoday.com/2012/05/litfin-gospel-deeds/.

don't have a clear understanding of Jesus? How can they engage in evangelism if they can't speak clearly, quickly, or in full sentences?" Finally, there are questions of need: "Do people who cannot speak or understand in ways we expect really need Jesus? Aren't they accepted by God in the same way God accepts children who haven't yet reached the age of accountability? Do they really need to be involved in witness since others can do it faster, better?" Without revisiting the Bible to see what God says about his mission in the world and our place in it, we can easily dismiss the faith and the work of people with disabilities and the ways their witness in the world testifies of God.

EVANGELISM AS THE WORK OF A TRIUNE GOD

One reason Christians often dismiss the witness of people with intellectual and developmental disabilities is that they think of evangelism as a solely personal thing. When I was growing up, every evangelism class I had (whether in the church or in Bible college) was called *personal* evangelism. Sure, we had big come-and-see mass evangelism events, but the real emphasis was on our personal witness to others. I can't tell you how many times I heard, "You are the only Jesus some may ever see. If you don't tell everyone you meet about Jesus, they may never hear." While this rightly captures the idea that we are to continually let our light shine (Mt 5:16), the problem with leaving this perspective unexamined is that it can make us think evangelism is *our* work and requires certain skills. We should never discount the fact that we may play a vital role in someone's faith journey, but we should never see evangelism or the results of it as being up to us, and we should never assume there is only one way for evangelism to occur.

Perhaps the first and most important building block for understanding evangelism rightly, then, is the recognition that mission is always and ever God's. Paulsen argues that a careful examination of the conversion narratives in Scripture reveals "an ancient, respectful, and relational model of evangelism, one that understands evangelism to be initiated by God, empowered by the Holy Spirit, and Christocentric in focus."[6] It is through the empowerment of the Holy Spirit that we participate in

[6]Judith Paulsen, *A New and Ancient Evangelism: Rediscovering the Ways God Calls and Sends* (Baker Academic, 2024), 11.

beautiful and at times unexpected ways in what God himself is doing to draw people to himself. D. J. Konz even suggests that no human beings have the capacity to participate in God's mission in and of themselves. It takes Spirit indwelling to overcome our "inherent and absolute human incapacity" to participate and cooperate in God's divine actions.[7] This frees us from the assumption that evangelism is up to us or requires certain abilities for it to be done correctly. God is the one in the business of making himself known; we get the privilege of joining in what he is doing. But this does not give us another excuse to avoid engaging in evangelism. If we are indwelled by the Spirit, we can be assured that the calling to participate in God's witnessing work in the world is for us. The Spirit is always linked to mission, and if we have received God's Spirit, we are made participants in what God is doing (Acts 1:8; Jn 20:21).

Recognizing that evangelism is God's frees us from seeing evangelism as something we must initiate, produce, and bring to fruition. We join with God in whatever ways he wants. And this recognition that evangelism is the work of God also points away from the individualistic tendencies we bring to our understanding of evangelism. The triune God engages in witness within the communal relationship of Father, Son, and Spirit. Each member of the Godhead listens to, engages, and responds to the work of the others. The role of the Father is not the same as that of the Son or Spirit. The role of the Son is not the same as that of the Father or Spirit. The role of the Spirit is not the same as that of the Father or Son. Rather, it is in the harmony, interdependence, and community of Father, Son, and Spirit that mission takes place and God's work of reconciling the world to himself occurs (2 Cor 5:19).

EVANGELISM AS A WORK OF THE CHURCH COMMUNITY

If God's mission is one of interdependent community, we should not be surprised that our participation in God's mission through evangelism is also grounded in interdependent community. This can be harder for some of us to understand than others. Many of the evangelism models I grew up

[7]D. J. Konz, "The Even Greater Commission: Relating the Great Commission to the *Missio Dei*, and Human Agency to Divine Activity, in Mission," *Missiology: An International Review* 46, no. 4 (2016): 335.

with were responses to the hyperindividualism of modernity. The focus was on reason, logic, and argumentation that would lead to personal salvation. Only through this doorway of right belief would people receive the invitation to belong to the church community and begin the discipleship process that would help them toward right behavior, something George C. Hunter III has labeled the Roman model of evangelism.[8] Evangelism emphasized decisions: How many accepted Christ? In order to produce decisions, the work of evangelism focused on the ability to clearly articulate the gospel with such persuasive power that people were compelled to convert. While church membership and discipleship were encouraged, most were satisfied when people crossed the salvation barrier. Membership in the church was more optional, and at times the church was seen as a service provider for individuals seeking information, goods, and services.[9] Community had little to do with evangelism.

And yet, community has everything to do with evangelism! God's mission has always been about the creation of a people who enact his life and shalom in the world in a way that draws others into the witness and reign of God. From its inception, the church has consistently grown and expanded through community. Jesus' own model of sharing meals with sinner and saint, according to Robert Webber, "both embodied the kingdom and prophetically anticipated the kingdom. . . . Conversion was no prerequisite to fellowship at a common meal with Jesus. Instead, conversion became a consequence of eating with Jesus."[10] The early church grew through shared meals and shared life (e.g., Acts 2:42-47). Paul too understood the unity of diversity in the church as the means by which God makes himself known in the world.

After a robust discussion on how the church was part of God's original plan even before God created the world (Eph 1) and included a diversity of people God knit together into a unity without erasing diversity (Eph 2),

---

[8]George C. Hunter III, *The Celtic Way of Evangelism: How Christianity Can Reach the West Again* (Abingdon, 2000).

[9]David E. Fitch, *The Great Giveaway: Reclaiming the Mission of the Church from Big Business, Parachurch Organizations, Psychotherapy, Consumer Capitalism, and Other Modern Maladies* (Baker Books, 2005), 18.

[10]Robert E. Webber, *Ancient-Future Evangelism: Making Your Church a Faith-Forming Community* (Baker Books, 2003), 58.

Paul reveals God's singular plan for the church: to be the place where God displays his power, diversity, and wisdom for the watching world (Eph 3). "God's purpose," Paul says, in bringing Jews and Gentiles together into one body and one people, "was to use the church to display his wisdom in all its rich variety to all the unseen rulers and authorities in the heavenly places. This was his eternal plan, which he carried out through Christ Jesus our Lord" (Eph 3:10-11).

When people come together in the church and care for one another, encourage one another, sharpen and shape one another, and demonstrate God's kingdom values and practices in how they worship, serve, love, and speak to one another, they become a visible, tangible witness of God in the world. Witness flows from the open access to fellowship, which invites people from all backgrounds, ethnicities, and abilities to participate in community together. Witness flows from the enacted story of God through Scripture, prayers, songs, and teaching of a unified yet diverse group of people engaged in worship.[11]

This kind of robust, living witness is not something confined to the early church. In a postmodern world in which people are consumed by "individualism, isolationism, and consumerism," Christian community "becomes the post modern portal to truth" and "the vortex of evangelism."[12] Pierre Babin argues that in our present world, both the aim *and* the medium of evangelism are Christian community.[13] Stone similarly argues, "The embodiment *is* the heralding; the medium *is* the message; incarnation *is* invitation."[14] This means that instead of Christians merely imparting "universal truths to individual minds outside the church," rather "they live truth in God's power sufficiently to compel the lost to come and see his lordship in full display in a worship service."[15] This, Hunter says, is the Celtic way of evangelism. Belonging leads to belief and to behavior.[16]

---

[11]Webber, *Ancient-Future Evangelism*, 61-65.

[12]Webber, *Ancient-Future Evangelism*, 61; David Fitch, "Saving Souls Beyond Modernity: How Evangelism Can Save the Church and Make It Relevant Again," *Journal of the Academy for Evangelism in Theological Education* 17 (2002): 63.

[13]Pierre Babin with Mercedes Iannone, *The New Era in Religious Communication* (Fortress, 1992), 196.

[14]Stone, *Evangelism After Christendom*, 48.

[15]Fitch, "Saving Souls," 28.

[16]Hunter, *Celtic Way*.

While this does not take the verbal proclamation out of evangelism or dismiss the validity of personal evangelism, it does acknowledge the power of God's truth lived out in a community surrendered to the lordship of Christ and empowered by the Holy Spirit. Webber believes that when the unconverted experience the enactment of God's story in the context of relationships and worship of the Christian community, they are more likely to experience conversion gradually through the assimilation of truth and a dawning recognition of their faith in Christ. Webber is so convinced of the power of the community as the means for witness that he argues,

> Christian witness is not dependent on arguments or evidence. (Although reason may be used without being reliant upon it, reason is not what gives credibility to Scripture.) The Holy Spirit testifies to truth; God has not established reason or argument as the means of conversion. From the very beginning of the church it has always been the testimony of the Spirit that validates the Word and leads a person to Christ. . . . Somewhere along this trajectory, through an association with people who embody truth and a worship that proclaims and enacts truth, a genuine experience of faith in Christ will be acknowledged. A conversion takes place by the power of the Spirit.[17]

Note that reason and individual abilities of argumentation are not requirements for witness. While some may have the ability and opportunity to give a verbal proclamation that leads someone toward Christ and the church, a person who gives clear witness of Christ by their life, who invites others into Christian community, and who participates in the communal witness of the church does not have to "speak reasoned words" for evangelization to occur. Benjamin Conner calls this *iconic witness* and notes that such witness "does not speak" but "is never mute." "Even when the witness seems less active and intentional and more evocative," he says, "the iconic witness calls people to encounter Jesus," giving us a window into kingdom life and ethics.[18] "Those labeled the

---

[17]Webber, *Ancient-Future Evangelism*, 65.

[18]Benjamin T. Conner, *Disabling Mission, Enabling Witness: Exploring Missiology Through the Lens of Disability* (IVP Academic, 2018), 134; Benjamin T. Conner, *Practicing Witness: A Missional Vision of Christian Practices* (Eerdmans, 2011), 112.

disabled do have a capacity," Conner argues. Even though "they point differently, taste differently, sound and image differently . . . the Spirit whose witness they bear and the kingdom and Lord to whom they bear witness are the same."[19] In this way, they provide an intentional and explicit communication and invitation that succeeds where words fail. In fact, Conner suggests that one gift people with intellectual and developmental disabilities contribute to our articulation of the gospel is exposing how limited words are for conveying truth. Truth, he says is not "a product of the mind" but "an eschatological reality."[20]

We often place too much confidence in our words to articulate the mysteries of the kingdom when it is a reality that is meant to be experienced as much as known. We often also place too much confidence in our various activities of witness when our ability to mediate Christ to the world comes only by the enlivening power and work of the Spirit in and through us.[21] By our participation in the open welcome of others through hospitality and in the enactment of God's truth within a worshiping community, the Spirit enables people of all abilities to share in a clear proclamation that makes Jesus Christ known. This gives place to many different voices, bodies, and people without privileging one person, gift, ability, or role above another. Witness and proclamation are a work of the whole church empowered and brought to fruition by the triune God.

EVANGELISM REQUIRES EVERYONE DOING THEIR PART

One other thing to note about evangelism and community is that, much like raising a child, it takes a village. In their book *I Once Was Lost: What Postmodern Skeptics Taught Us About Their Path to Jesus*, Don Everts and Doug Schaupp reveal that the postmodern pathway to Jesus is a journey of crossing five significant thresholds that stand between skeptics and Jesus.[22] There is not a one-and-done evangelistic hit that gets people to the cross. Rather, it is a long journey with a community of people who each play their role in various threshold spaces.

---

[19]Conner, *Practicing Witness*, 113.

[20]Conner, *Disabling Mission*, 130.

[21]Conner, *Disabling Mission*, 126-27.

[22]Don Everts and Doug Schaupp, *I Once Was Lost: What Postmodern Skeptics Taught Us About Their Path to Jesus* (IVP Books, 2008).

The first threshold moves people from *distrust to trust* as they learn to trust a Christian.[23] When Christians lead with a sales tactic or try to scare people into faith, it turns people off. But when genuine love and friendship is the focus, people can move from thinking Christians and their Christ are suspect to experiencing an unconditional love and care that helps them trust people who follow Jesus. It should be a no-strings-attached relationship: We don't befriend people because they are evangelistic projects and quit trying if they reject Jesus. We genuinely befriend regardless of whether they take the next step even as we always pray and hope that by the consistency of our love, our care, and our life of Christian witness people will move through to the next threshold, where they become curious about Jesus because they see Jesus in the lives of people they now trust.

It is not automatic that people who trust Christians will be curious about Jesus, but being around Christians they trust gives them a place to experience new ways of seeing the world, to explore more options for living in the world, and to actively investigate and dialogue about their curiosities. Curiosity is something we can provoke, and Everts and Schaupp suggest that effective ways for doing this include asking questions, connecting people with modern-day parables that provide windows into Jesus' kingdom, and living curious lives.[24] The goal always is to get people wanting to know more and *moving from complacency about Jesus to active curiosity.*

While people might move rather seamlessly through these first two thresholds, crossing the third is one of the hardest: *from being closed to being open to change in one's life*. The reason this threshold is so daunting is that people often do not want to face their own lives or do the hard work of considering that where they are, what they believe, or how they live needs small and big changes. For any of us, accepting a new way of seeing the world, or finding ourselves contemplating a new commitment that requires giving something up or taking a risk and stepping into the unknown, requires that we count the cost. Not everyone can accept the terms, and when they don't, our goal as their friend is to keep on loving

[23]Everts and Schaupp, *I Once Was Lost*, 23.

[24]Everts and Schaupp, *I Once Was Lost*, 51-61.

and remaining steady in our commitment to them. We can support our friends, however, by praying earnestly, continuing to foster trust and curiosity, supporting them as they work through this threshold, and at times providing the right kinds of challenge that can nudge them toward a response. It is openness to change that helps people make a significant step toward faith.[25]

The wrestling and growth involved in threshold three sets people up well for the final two thresholds, moving *from meandering to seeking* to the point of *crossing the threshold of the kingdom itself*. People may trust a Christian, be curious about Jesus, and be open to change, and still not actively and purposely seek Jesus. It is in the experience of the friendship and community of Christians that people realize it is time to be serious about Jesus and make a final decision: *Do I believe and follow or not*? "True seekers," Everts and Schaupp say, "are on a quest" that is urgent. To this end, they are doing two things. First, they are focused on Jesus (not just God) and contemplating the demands that following him would have on their lives. Second, they are spending time with Christians to learn, grow, and continue their quest with and among believers.

Walking with seekers requires Christians to have open lives, to be patient companions who don't just spoon-feed answers but rather give confident support as others search the Scriptures for themselves, and to provide safe spaces for genuine exploration. We don't want to push too quickly, but as our friends seek Jesus, we should also be ready to invite them into the kingdom. People can't seek forever, and many need that extra nudge to make a commitment. This doesn't mean we are pushy or rude, but it does mean we help people come to points of decision and examine that choice when they say no or "not yet." For many, seeking can become that last safe space, but it is in facing the realities of what they have been seeking that they must make that last and final leap to trust in Jesus.[26]

Entering the kingdom is not the end goal. Living into the kingdom as a thriving, growing, and active believer should be the lifelong pursuit.[27]

---

[25]Everts and Schaupp, *I Once Was Lost*, 66-83.
[26]Everts and Schaupp, *I Once Was Lost*, 84-118.
[27]Everts and Schaupp, *I Once Was Lost*, 119-30.

Walking in community with one another is vital for individual and communal flourishing. When people walk the path to Jesus, they are not saying yes to a survey; they are saying yes to a new life committed to the lordship of Jesus, submitted to the work of the Spirit, and dedicated to the growth and flourishing of the Christian community. This is a communal life.

Notice that in each of the thresholds, different people are involved in a person's faith journey. It doesn't take a certain quality or ability to help people learn to trust Christians and become curious about Jesus, to walk alongside with active support and encouragement as people open themselves to change, actively seek Jesus, and accept the invitation to enter the kingdom. Women and men of every walk, age, culture, ethnicity, and ability can be a key player in helping people to and through each threshold. One person never bears the full weight of this process. It is in the community of believers that thresholds are experienced, and as people move closer and closer to entering the kingdom, community witness is essential.

Erik Carter, a professor and researcher from Baylor University, testifies that his own faith journey began when he was befriended by Wayne, Margaret, and John Ray. As he shared in a Wheaton College chapel,

> After the summer of my freshman year . . . God stumbled me into some new relationships with young men and women my age with intellectual disability—relationships I probably would not have pursued on my own. You see, at the time, faith and disability were probably the furthest things from my life and the furthest thing from my mind. But I quickly became captivated by the friendships that I formed with Wayne and with Margaret and John Ray. And as someone who had come to think that my worth was really measured most in my accomplishments and in my abilities, each of those friendships reminded me that neither is what makes me loveable or made me valuable. And I remember thinking, *How could someone befriend me and love me and not know all the incredible things I could do or think or say or had accomplished?* But of course, that's not how love works, is it? I experienced for the first time belonging. And it upended so much of what my young mind thought was important. But more than that, I was compelled by the testimonies that each shared about their deep love for

> Jesus. Though John Ray could not speak and Wayne struggled with words, their faith was deep and certain. They worshiped with a glad abandon. They trusted without seeming reservation. They knew for certain that they belonged to God. And how I longed to have that same kind of assurance. It was enviable faith. And so I followed their lead and I finally gave my life to Christ.[28]

Notice what happens in this story. Carter went from not knowing he even needed Jesus to making a full faith commitment by learning to trust three Christians who just happened to have intellectual disabilities. Though they could not speak or speak well, they caused him to be curious about Jesus through their life of faith. Their unconditional love and acceptance helped him experience a true belonging he had never known. This made him think about his life to the point that he began to realize and then question the fact that he found his worth, status, and meaning in his own accomplishments. He became open to considering another way. Their steadfast friendship helped him seek in earnest, and through their "enviable faith" they extended an invitation for him to enter the kingdom. Notice the ways in which these three friends not only walked with Carter through the thresholds but also helped him experience the Celtic model of evangelism: belonging, believing, behaving. Without the witness of these faithful Christians, Carter might not be a Christian today. And even if he had still found a path to Jesus, he would probably not have devoted his life to researching and promoting the flourishing, inclusion, and full participation of people with developmental disabilities in the life and witness of the church.

What Carter notes about his own story is that it shouldn't be surprising at all because "it's an ordinary story of how God's grace flows through his people to transform lives. All of God's people. No asterisks. No exceptions." However, he sadly notes, "It's a rare story still because our lives so rarely interact in our schools, in our workplaces, in our neighborhoods, and even in our churches."[29]

---

[28]Erik Carter, "Belonging: Psalm 67," Wheaton College Chapel, Wheaton, IL, March 22, 2023, YouTube, 19:37, https://youtu.be/-5gRfia1kW8.

[29]Carter, "Belonging: Psalm 67."

EVANGELISM REQUIRES AN OPEN SEAT AT THE TABLE

This leads us, then, to two important truths for evangelism. First, if so much of evangelism is done through relationships and within a communal space where people experience welcome and belonging around a table and encounter God's truth through the enactment of worship, how can the church expect to reach the disabled if their members never see or encounter people with disabilities in the community (or realize their need to)? How will disabled people know they are welcome if the church never invites them to come? How will churches fulfill their communal role in providing spaces of welcome, inclusion, belonging, or seeking if their communal gatherings and worship spaces are physically and socially inaccessible? How will the disabled experience communal belonging when the church hasn't anticipated their arrival? How will people with disabilities experience hospitality when the church segregates them from others or makes them feel like a burden or someone less-than? How will the church give credible witness that God's story is for everyone if worship excludes disabled voices and bodies, forefronts healing, and has little patience for interruption, noise, a change of pace, or new ways of doing things? When the church does not set the table with the disabled in mind, it shuts people off from community and prevents them from experiencing one of the most effective pathways to God. Community and belonging are vital in a kingdom journey, but so many people with disabilities are intentionally and unintentionally left out.

Second, when the church does have people with disabilities in the building but excludes them from serving, leading, and at times even being seen, the church also cuts the disabled out of the evangelistic work of the church and the calling of the Spirit. Those in Christ are to be evangels, but when people in the church believe that this requires a polished pedigree, a high intelligence, an ideal body, or a clear mind, they end up assuming the role of the Spirit in deciding who is and isn't part of the church and in judging the worth and value of people's gifts.

Receiving the spiritual gifts of others requires us to reject worldly assessments of status, power, skill, and talent, and instead be actively looking for and receptive of the spiritual gifts that are given by the Spirit and reveal the Spirit to others.[30] The Spirit is no respecter of persons. The Spirit actively places people in the church (Eph 2:19-22) to participate in the witness and work of the church (Eph 4:11-16). Such work and witness are distorted when only the most capable or esteemed are given places to lead and serve.

When the church does not release the disabled to serve in varied levels of leadership and service, those who come into the community and see God's story enacted through worship receive a distorted gospel message and do not experience God's upside-down kingdom in its fullness. This disables their own understanding of the full implications of the gospel and truncates their discipleship because they do not experience the reality that God's kingdom is for *everyone* and made known through *everyone* who belongs to Christ, disabled or not. When people in the church effectively hide the disabled members from others (e.g., forcing them to sit in the back and leave before everyone else so they can't talk to anyone, letting them worship only in separate spaces, telling people and their families that they are too demanding or too disruptive and asking them to leave), they do not give a proper countercultural witness of the true nature of God's kingdom, the wide expanse of God's family, or the value that God places in all people of all abilities.[31]

Jesus has something to say about this in Luke 14. We too often set the table for the wrong guests and then fight to get the best seats in the house. Instead, we should be compelling the poor, the crippled, the lame, and the blind to come, allowing them to access the seats that will help them best engage with the host. We should never make the feast about us, our position, or our "rights." Jesus' brother James notes that when we show favoritism and honor people by worldly standards, we not only demonstrate that we are "guided by evil motives" (Jas 2:4), but we also commit sin and become guilty of breaking God's law (Jas 2:9).

People with disabilities are invited to God's table. The only way they don't have the possibility to accept that invitation is if we block that

[30]Brian Brock, "Theologizing Inclusion: 1 Corinthians 12 and the Politics of the Body of Christ," *Journal of Religion, Disability & Health* 15, no. 4 (2011): 354, https://doi.org/10.1080/15228967.2011.620389.

[31]These are not hypothetical situations. I can give the names of the disabled who experienced these appalling responses and the churches where these occurrences happened.

invitation through our lack of participation in one another's lives and seek to preserve sabbath decorum in order to serve ourselves (Lk 14:1-14).

Carter asks, "How might we become communities where the friendship and the faith and the gifts of people with and without disabilities are readily exchanged and received?"[32] One way is to understand the true gospel message that is good news for everyone of every ability, and then participate together in the kingdom work that sets an open chair for everyone to sit at the table in true belonging. We do this as we together believe and together behave in ways that declare God's kingdom comes through the work, gifting, mutuality, reciprocity, and release of all God's (dis)abled people. Only when everyone is at the table will we be able to credibly *proclaim, herald, and live out a message that bears witness to (truly!) good news about Jesus Christ.*

DISCUSSION QUESTIONS

1. Do you agree with the idea "Preach the gospel. Use words if necessary"? Why or why not?
2. How does evangelism as a work of the triune God enrich your understanding of how you participate in evangelism?
3. Have you ever thought about evangelism as a communal work? Does this resonate with your own church experience?
4. In what ways does your church set an open seat at the table? What changes do you think should be implemented?

---

[32]Carter, "Belonging: Psalm 67."

9

Conversion

By now, you may be wondering how to put everything we've discussed into more concrete practice. "What's next? How can we start envisioning our churches as communities in which people of all abilities find their place in Christ?" Before we get there, there is another stop we need to make. A central part of evangelism and mission is working toward seeing women and men make faith commitments to Jesus Christ. For evangelicals, this is a hallmark of their belief and practice. People need to experience a personal conversion in which their life transforms from sinner to saint as their allegiance moves from Satan and self to surrendered follower of Jesus Christ. Though God is the only one who can call a person to himself and extend saving grace, people must respond to that offer in repentance and faith and through a life marked by a continual pursuit of God.[1]

For evangelicals, this idea of conversion is often recounted as a singular moment in which a person goes from not saved to saved. The standard evangelical conversion narrative—a must for every good evangelist—becomes the personal testimony of this moment in one's life. Key components of evangelical conversion narratives include admission of personal guilt and failure, God's irresistible pursuit, a moment of surrender, and evidence of new creation through a transformed heart and changed attitudes/actions.[2] The problem is that not everyone experiences conversion in this way.

---

[1]Miyon Chung, "Conversion and Sanctification," in *The Cambridge Companion to Evangelical Theology*, ed. Timothy Larsen and Daniel J. Treier (Cambridge University Press, 2007), 109.

[2]Timothy Larsen, "Defining and Locating Evangelicalism," in Larsen and Treier, *Cambridge Companion to Evangelical Theology*, 11; Gordon T. Smith, *Beginning Well: Christian Conversion and Authentic Transformation* (InterVarsity Press, 2001).

The summer between my freshman and sophomore years of college, I lived in Thailand, working with a missions organization near the University of Chiang Mai. As the newcomer, I was asked to share my testimony before a group of Buddhist college students who were visiting the Centre, where we taught conversational English as a bridge to sharing Christ. While preparing for my night in the spotlight, I became acutely aware that my conversion story didn't sound as exciting or dramatic as the others I had heard. I grew up in church. I had always loved Jesus. I couldn't remember a time I didn't believe. There was no dramatic Damascus Road experience (Acts 9). There was no sudden shift in my life. I just knew that I believed and asked, at age eight, to be baptized. As I worked to make my salvation story exciting, I remember trying to make it sound like I was this little hellion at the age of four when I had a clear sense of my rebellion and my need for God's forgiveness. In this moment, I placed my faith in Jesus and went from being a rebel four-year-old to a new creation. But honestly, I wasn't sure what to make of my conversion story.

For people like me, we sometimes question our own conversion narrative: What really makes me a Christian? If we can't remember the exact day or time or even year we crossed the boundary from out to in, are we really saved? Do we have a testimony? For some of my friends, this fear of not having a date written in their Bible led to multiple altar-call responses. They were at the altar every time the pastor made the salvation appeal just to ensure they had an exact date for when they got their ticket to heaven punched.

There is no doubt that conversion should be a desired outcome of effective evangelism. But for all of us, both those who grew up in the church believing and those who made a faith commitment later in life, it is important to examine what exactly we mean by conversion. We are Christians and we want others to become Christians, but what does that really mean? What must someone do to become a Christian? Are there certain steps or actions a person must perform? How much knowledge or understanding is required to be considered a Christian? Is conversion a one-and-done action that adds one's name to God's book, or is there something more to it? How we understand and answer these questions has significant implications for how we talk to people about Jesus and call them toward a response. It has a particular impact on how we understand the conversion of people with more profound intellectual and developmental disabilities.

THE CATEGORY "CHRISTIAN"

One of the best starting places for answering our questions is by considering possible ways to understand the category "Christian" itself. Here missiologist Paul Hiebert is particularly helpful. Hiebert was born in India to missionary parents, and after earning a PhD in anthropology, he returned to India as a missionary. Though he eventually took on seminary teaching roles after his wife's illness made it impossible for them to return to India long term, he never forgot the lessons he learned as he sought to grasp evangelism and mission in light of cultural understandings. Putting his own mathematics background to work, Hiebert applied set theory to missions to explain four views of the category "Christian" and the subsequent ways each view affects how we understand conversion, church, and Christian mission.[3]

Hiebert suggests that we assign something to a category according to two variables. The first variable considers the qualities that make something belong to one category over another. If we do this based on what something is by nature, we are looking at its *intrinsic* qualities. If we do this based on what something is in relationship to something else, we are looking at its *extrinsic* or relational qualities. Hiebert notes, for example, that an apple is labeled *apple* because it meets particular intrinsic qualities that either make it an apple or not. However, we understand son and daughter only with relationship to a father and/or mother.

The second variable considers how well defined the boundaries of a particular category are. *Bounded sets* have a clear boundary line that separates the things that belong from those that don't. Membership requires meeting a particular set of characteristics, which are rather static and homogeneous. Because the boundary matters for belonging, a

[3]Paul G. Hiebert, *Anthropological Reflections on Missiological Issues* (Baker Books, 1994), 107-36.

lot of time is focused on maintaining the boundary. You are either in or out. For example, you are either a member of the gym or not. Whether you attend and work out is less important. Having paid your dues and signed your contract is what guarantees belonging. *Fuzzy sets* are so named because the boundary line between in and out is fuzzy or graded, and "is based on attributes that vary along a continuum."[4] For example, it is not always clear when day ends and night begins. There is a gradual change during which both are present for a time until night has fully come and day has fully gone.

When we put these together, we have four ways in which to understand Christian: bounded set, centered set, intrinsic fuzzy set, and extrinsic fuzzy set.

While all four are possibilities, intrinsic fuzzy sets and extrinsic fuzzy sets receive less attention (as they will here). The reason we don't focus on fuzzy sets much is that being a Christian does have fairly clear boundaries. As much as they may try, people cannot be part Christian or Christian *and* something else. To be a Christian already suggests an exclusive allegiance to the Lord Jesus Christ. This doesn't correspond with the intrinsic fuzzy-set idea of people holding to some Christian beliefs and practices, belonging by degree, or belonging to two or more religions at the same time. This also doesn't correspond with the extrinsic fuzzy-set idea that people can be a Christian as a matter of degree because they follow Christ in some areas and not others and can view him as a guru or other spiritual philosopher.

Our main focus is on the differences between bounded sets and centered sets, as these are the two central ways in which evangelicals have understood Christian identity.

When we view "Christian" as a bounded set, we focus on specific characteristics that make a Christian a Christian and spend energy maintaining the clear boundary line between those who are Christians and those who are not. Since we cannot know for certain what is going on in the heart between the person and Christ, we focus on external intrinsic

---

[4]Michael L. Yoder, Michael H. Lee, Jonathan Ro, and Robert J. Priest, "Understanding Christian Identity in Terms of Bounded and Centered Set Theory in the Writings of Paul G. Hiebert," *Trinity Journal* 30, no. 2 (2009): 179.

qualities, such as orthodoxy (right beliefs) and orthopraxy (right actions) to make our determination.[5] Did this person pray a prayer that asked Jesus into their heart? Does this person call Jesus "Lord"? Can this person articulate certain beliefs? Does this person do certain things (e.g., prayer, Bible reading) even as they give up other things (e.g., lying, cussing)? Since in bounded-set thinking Christians do *a*, *b*, and *c* and do not do *x*, *y*, and *z*, you are either a Christian or you aren't. How long you've been a Christian doesn't matter since there is no gradation of belonging. Because of this, a particular emphasis is placed on the need for a conversion in which people pointedly move from non-Christian to Christian.

When "Christian" is seen as a centered set, everything in the set is dependent on a relationship to a specific center or reference point, in this case Jesus Christ. Christians, then, are those who are related to Jesus and directionally moving toward him. Said another way, Christians are those whose lives are centered on Jesus and actively following him as Lord.[6] Because belonging is dependent on a personal relationship with Jesus, while there is some knowledge about Jesus required (i.e., we are following the historical Jesus as revealed in the Bible), having copious amounts of biblical and historical knowledge or being able to articulate complex doctrine is not necessary. Rather, "Salvation is open to everyone, no matter who they are, what they know, or what baggage they bring with them, if they become followers of Jesus."[7]

This shifts the focus from maintaining a boundary to helping everyone grow in their pursuit of Christ. Conversion comes through one's turn toward Christ through faith and repentance (a process that can be gradual or dramatic) *and* through one's ongoing pursuit of Jesus at every moment and in every decision. This leaves space for Christians to have varying levels of maturity in matters of faith and practice, even as they all are moving ever closer to God's ideal.[8] This also leaves open the possibility of people positionally moving more distant to Jesus or abandoning their pursuit altogether. The crucial question, then, is,

---

[5]Yoder et al., "Understanding Christian Identity," 181.
[6]Hiebert, *Anthropological Reflections*, 125.
[7]Hiebert, *Anthropological Reflections*, 126.
[8]Yoder et al., "Understanding Christian Identity," 181-82.

"Is this person following Christ to the extent that they know him, and does this person desire to know Christ more fully?"[9]

DISABILITY AND THE CENTERED SET

Many of us (including me) were raised with a strong sense of "Christian" as a bounded set. We were very concerned about whether someone was in or out, and so our evangelism focused on getting people to the place of knowing, saying, and doing certain things we deemed as being requirements for becoming part of the in-group. Generally, this meant people had to understand that Jesus died on the cross to take away their sins and accept this as true. They acknowledged their understanding by audibly thanking Jesus for dying on the cross for them, praying to accept Jesus into their heart, and asking him to forgive them of their sins. They demonstrated their newfound belief by giving up what we considered to be non-Christian practices and taking on what we considered to be Christian ones. We were very concerned about responses and eager to ensure that someone checked the right boxes so we could be assured of their salvation. Often we were so eager for others to become Christians that we focused more on correct responses and less on what came afterward. Becoming a Christian was instantaneous, and if people acted the part, we were assured the salvation took.

Bounded-set thinking doesn't explain my path to faith. I grew up in faith, and while I acknowledge Jesus as Lord and know beyond a doubt I am saved, I don't have a date I can say I went from out to in. Rather, my testimony is one of how I have pursued Christ and how God was at work when I was positionally becoming more distant or struggling to be turned toward him in all areas of my heart, mind, and strength. Centered-set thinking makes sense of my conversion story.

Bounded-set thinking also doesn't work for my son or those who are more profoundly affected by cognitive disabilities. My son is still struggling to grasp basic math concepts my (at the time) two-year-old has mastered. Following two-step commands remains a constant on his IEP (Individualized Educational Plan), as does reading comprehension in

[9]Adapted from Hiebert, "Category Christian," 127.

order to answer basic questions of a text he has just reviewed. Will he ever get to the place of understanding something many Christians have not fully grasped: that, miraculously, God entered the world as a fully God, fully human man in order to die on the cross as a substitution for us and in so doing is able to forgive us of sin and impute his righteousness on us so we can be found blameless before God? Will having him simply "pray a prayer after me" be enough to turn his heart to Jesus? If his faith is dependent on orthodoxy and orthopraxy, as the famous quote goes, "Houston, we have a problem." It is doubtful that my son will ever articulate an orthodoxy that would satisfy boundary keepers or allow my son to then participate in the same articulation of faith so others can cross the same threshold into Christian faith. How might he come to faith?

For many Christians, the response is simply, "He doesn't need to. He will be considered the same way children before the age of accountability are considered: innocent." This is a real issue for people with more profound intellectual, cognitive, and mental disabilities. They are not counted in terms of needing Jesus because people assume they cannot express saving faith according to acceptable standards.

There are extreme disabilities for which faith and salvation are hard to parse out, and in these instances I absolutely trust in the grace of God. That said, my son needs Jesus. Pure and simple. So do the many people who are like him. How does faith come when someone cannot fully understand the ramifications of faith or perform the necessary tasks to be counted as in?

First, it is helpful to remember that "we are not saved by our knowledge and . . . our baptism is not dependent on our grasp of the mysteries of our faith."[10] Second, we are not saved by our works or abilities. Salvation is a matter of grace through faith and is a free gift of God (Eph 2:8-9). Centered-set thinking helps us on both points because it moves us from seeing salvation as a byproduct of individual attainment and knowledge (with everyone having to check the same boxes in the same way) to seeing salvation in a life that is centered on Jesus and moving toward him.

---

[10]A paraphrase of Alexander Schmemann in Scot McKnight, *It Takes a Church to Baptize: What the Bible Says About Infant Baptism* (Brazos, 2019), 45.

Centered-set thinking levels the playing field, if you will, because regardless of your IQ, your achievements, your physical appearance, your talents, your personality, or even how much you grasp about Christ, you don't have to check certain boxes; you simply have to embrace everything you know of Jesus and keep moving toward him.

But still, some say, doesn't this require some sort of verbal affirmation? Didn't Paul say you have to "declare with your mouth, 'Jesus is Lord'" to be saved (Rom 10:9 NIV)? Yes, Paul did say this, but if he meant this literally, then anyone nonverbal or those who do not understand what they are saying would be out. I don't think this is what Paul (or God) intended. The context of this passage alone reminds us that our works, our achievements, and our efforts cannot save us (Rom 10:1-3, 5). Rather, Paul says, salvation comes from trusting Christ, a message that is for everyone *and* "very close at hand" (Rom 10:4). In saying that people must confess with their mouths and believe in their hearts (Rom 10:9-10), he is quoting Deuteronomy 30:11-14, a passage in which Moses is calling Israel to "turn to the LORD your God with all your heart and soul" (Deut 30:10). Like Paul, Moses notes God's call for allegiance is "not too difficult for you, and it is not beyond your reach" because *God* has put it "on your lips and in your hearts so that you can obey it" (Deut 30:11, 14). What we see in these two passages is the reminder that God is the one who saves and who, through the Spirit, enables us to know and understand what he has put "within easy reach." Paul carries forward Moses' imagery by saying that this salvation is accessible for everyone because *God* has put it on our lips and in our hearts. Therefore, we bear witness to the work of Christ *in* us by the outward work of Christ *through* us to the extent that we are able by the power of the Spirit.

What about the means by which a person grows in their faith? Doesn't continued conversion (i.e., discipleship) require rational assent to truths about Jesus? Gordon Smith, in his book *Beginning Well*, affirms a centered-set view of conversion within the community of faith. When the Christian community bears witness to the center through word and deed, people are able to learn about faith and the person and work of Christ, "not through rational presentation so much as through conversation around life lived" within the "context of the worship of

Christ and a community that is seeking to live in the service of Christ."[11] This echoes Webber's belief that "God has not established reason or argument as the means of conversion."[12]

However, Smith (also using Hiebert) argues elsewhere that the minimal understanding required for initial conversion versus what is required for "mature Christian discipleship" is different.[13] Maturity in Christ requires a "radical Christianization of worldview"—a complete overhaul in thinking. Conversion should be all-encompassing and lead beyond a surface experience of Christ to one in which Christ becomes all and in all (Col 3:11). However, I believe that Smith, like so many of us, talks about this maturity of understanding in problematic ways. Consider his words here: "People will not experience ultimate transformation unless we take the human mind seriously, affirming from the beginning that understanding matters, that truth makes a difference, and that therefore true conversion includes, *and is inconceivable without*, a clear and decisive intellectual encounter with the gospel."[14]

Even with the most profound cognitive disabilities, we should take the mind seriously and affirm that understanding matters and truth is important. However, when we emphasize that this requires an "intellectual encounter with the gospel" or "rational" thoughts about faith, we must nuance our words and consider other ways that growth in belief, faith, and understanding can be expressed. Otherwise we can inadvertently cut people with cognitive and intellectual disability off from being considered able to make faith commitments or grow as mature believers with the ability to communicate their faith effectively to others. Yes, conversion is holistic, calling us to love God with all of our heart, soul, *mind*, and strength (Mk 12:30). However, conversion, the turn toward Christ, and the continued walk toward Christ is also situational and open to variance in what depth, maturity, and understanding look like.

Peter is clear that "[God's] divine power has given us everything we need for a godly life through our knowledge of him who called us by his

---

[11]Smith, *Beginning Well*, 39, 41.

[12]Robert E. Webber, *Ancient-Future Evangelism: Making Your Church a Faith-Forming Community* (Baker Books, 2003), 65.

[13]Smith, *Beginning Well*, 158.

[14]Smith, *Beginning Well*, 159, emphasis added.

own glory and goodness" (2 Pet 1:3 NIV). Perhaps that knowledge may be limited, but with God, such limits are never problematic. Rather, as Paul argues in 2 Corinthians, the God who said, "'Let light shine out of darkness,' made his light shine in our hearts *to give us the light of the knowledge of God's glory* displayed in the face of Christ" (2 Cor 4:6 NIV). Note that Paul says this wonderful knowledge is a treasure housed "in jars of clay to show that this all-surpassing power is from God and not from us" (2 Cor 4:7 NIV). Even the most feeble of clay jars can house this manifold treasure from God because it is not based on our ability but God's power.[15] God gives us knowledge of himself, and as we "with unveiled faces contemplate the Lord's glory," God transforms us "into his image *with ever-increasing glory, which comes from the Lord*, who is the Spirit" (2 Cor 3:18 NIV).

I think of this much like I think of my son's IEP. An IEP, or Individualized Educational Plan, supports my son's success in the classroom. As a collaboration between teachers, specialists, and us as his parents, this document evaluates his core strengths and areas for improvement and then establishes various learning, behavioral, and/or social goals for helping him succeed. It also lists the kinds of supports he will receive to help him in his achievement. While I know for some families the IEP process is painful, for us this has been a hugely helpful and encouraging experience.

One of the things I've learned with my son's IEP is that those in the classroom don't always lower the standards for him, but rather they make modifications to the ways in which he demonstrates achievement. For example, because of his low muscle tone, writing is an enormous challenge for my son. He cannot hold a pencil for long periods of time or write quickly enough to keep up with class dictations or other assignments that require writing letters or numbers. To help him keep up, he has separate time spent on his handwriting and instead, while in the classroom, has an aide to whom he dictates his answers. She will write them down verbatim (often using a highlighter, which he then traces). Another example of adaptation is that he is allowed more breaks during assignments to account for his short attention span and need for

[15]This thought was shared with me by Andy, one of the people interviewed for this book.

mental time-outs. While it doesn't keep him from completing district-required assessments, he is given the time and even classroom location needed to give it his best shot. In some circumstances, he will never achieve the exact thing his peers do, but he is given equivalents to show how he is growing in skills and moving in the right direction.

Centered-set thinking helps us see salvation in this same way. The standard of Jesus as Lord is never lowered, but there are a multitude of ways in which people can confess Christ, demonstrate their allegiance, and evidence maturity of faith. Like we found with evangelism, one significant way that people will receive Christ, declare Christ, move toward Christ, and show growth in Christ is through community. Why? Because it is in community that people experience the enactment of God's story, enter into his grace, and join the church in witness. We are never so wise or discerning as to know what the Spirit bears witness to in someone as they are exposed to God's story and experience God's saving community. As we noted in chapter three, faith comes as people are with Jesus and learn to trust him. For those who may lack the kinds of rational intellect that seems necessary for making a faith commitment or evidencing maturity of faith, they can experience Jesus in the community of believers and through them can learn to trust Jesus and move toward him. In the same way, as believers together experience the witness and withness of Christ within the church family, they have opportunity to use their gifts as they "grow in the grace and knowledge of our Lord and Savior Jesus Christ" (2 Pet 3:18 NIV). Community opens the door to faith, and community opens the door to discipleship. In this line of thinking, Smith even suggests that the church is to be "a midwife and nurturer" of conversion, with everything in the church serving "an evangelistic end, teaching people the language of faith and encouraging their faith, understanding, and commitment."[16]

THE MARK OF CHRIST

As we raise my son in a household of faith and as a member of Christ's church, we are trying to shape and mold him into possessing the dispositions and beliefs that characterize followers of Jesus. In our home and

---

[16]Smith, *Beginning Well*, 228.

our church, we are surrounding him with communal witness and demonstration of the life of Christ, giving him every opportunity to join in Christ-centered living with us as he learns to know and trust Christ through our lives and witness. As he does, he bears the mark of Christ on his life and walks ever closer to the center. I don't expect him to suddenly be able to articulate a deep doctrine; however, I do expect that he will be able to share, in his own ways, how Jesus has saved him and how the Spirit is forming him into a fruitful disciple. It might be verbal. But such confession might also come through actions and attitudes that display the mark of Christ.

This expectation that my son will show faith in ways unique to him has affected how I think about spiritual things because I am always on the lookout for how I can speak and show Christ in ways my son can better grasp. I am much less concerned about doctrine (even as much as I am steeped in it!) and more concerned with how, in this or that moment, my son is experiencing Jesus and either being moved toward or away from him. This is shaping me more and more into new dispositions according to which I am less reliant on my "correct knowledge" and more aware of whether I too am moving toward or away from Jesus. In this way my son's life is witnessing to me of the need for Christ to be center in my thoughts, words, and actions. As he draws nearer to Christ, he draws me nearer too.

Not long ago, I was telling my kids we had a visitor coming for dinner. Our guest was a recent graduate who returned to a powerful ministry in his home country of India. As I described this man's worldwide impact as a preacher, teacher, and musician, my son looked at me with a rather neutral and even puzzled expression. But when I said, "And this man goes around the world and tells people about Jesus," my son's face lit up and he exclaimed with great joy, "Jesus? I *know* him!" Can my son explain that Jesus died for his sins? Has he specifically prayed to "accept" Jesus? No. But does he know Jesus? You bet!

This confession (whether he could make it in audible words or not) is all it takes for someone to turn to the center and be on journey with Jesus. This personal knowledge happened not because we preached doctrine but because my son hears and sees Jesus within a community of love in which the Jesus story is our center and circumference. Is my son growing in the grace and knowledge of the Lord? Again, yes! He hasn't figured out how doctrine works, but he has stated his own beautiful truths such as, "Jesus is God" and "God-Jesus loves us." He also lives in worship music. As he takes in the many beautiful truths about Jesus through these songs (both ancient and contemporary hymns of the church), he can sing them to others as the Spirit makes these words alive in his own heart. The fact that he points me and others to Jesus, even in the simplicity of his faith, is evidence of a growing life in Christ. After all, isn't that a truth from Jesus as well? "I tell you the truth," Jesus says after pulling the little children toward himself, "anyone who doesn't receive the Kingdom of God like a child will never enter it" (Mk 10:15).

We sometimes forget that salvation is not dependent on reason or knowledge. It is in experiencing Jesus and learning to trust him that people are brought to the place of calling him Lord. They may never be able to give a verbal assent to their belief, but in their own way they too can make this declaration of faith and demonstrate the many ways in which "the Spirit of the Lord works within them, helping them to become more and more like Jesus and to reflect his glory even more" (2 Cor 3:18, my paraphrase).

DISCUSSION QUESTIONS

1. What is conversion? How do you know someone is a Christian?
2. Does your conversion experience resonate more with bounded-set or centered-set thinking?
3. Has your understanding of conversion changed over time? How? Why?
4. How do you think people with disabilities (particularly intellectual and developmental disabilities) can become Christians? How do they express faith?

10

Overcoming the "Burden" of Evangelism and Disability

AFTER ADOPTING OUR SON, I started reading all I could about Down syndrome. It was overwhelming to discover just how many areas of life this extra chromosome would affect (physically, cognitively, emotionally). Every book included pages of tips on things to try and ways to adapt to help our son flourish and our family to function. Visual aids, without doubt, were touted as the best and most important way to help our son learn routines, new skills, and emotional regulation.

With the zeal of new parents taking on a challenge, I was convinced I would be the best Down syndrome mom out there and we would breeze through life, meeting every challenge armed with strategies, skills, and charts. I was going to work ahead, I thought, and be ready even before we started hitting rougher patches. But then: *life*! Within a month of adopting him, I accepted a new teaching and administrative role that required a several-hundred-mile relocation. Before the dust could settle, my son's medical care increased, and our first year in our new home included over fifty therapy sessions and doctor's appointment and three surgeries. A couple of months later, Covid hit. All my best-laid plans to be proactive and active in making life as easy as possible for my son hit the reality of life that was filled with more than I could imagine. I knew visual aids were important, but because I saw it as an add-on to my parenting rather than the parenting itself, it felt like a burden and ended up losing out to all the other things I was doing to survive. With my capacity stretched to the max, I viewed this as just one more thing on the to-do list. Sometimes it gets done, but more often when my zeal wanes or I get tired, it's easy to keep pushing this down the list until I drop it from the list altogether.

We often have the same kinds of feelings about evangelism. It goes without saying that we live in a frenzied, fast-paced world in which the demands on us seem to exponentially increase over time. For many, the issue is not convincing them that evangelism is important work. The issue is convincing them they have the *capacity* to make this a *regular* part of their lives (corporately and individually). Evangelism too often is viewed as a burden. We may start with a burst of zeal, but when we see evangelism as just one more thing to do, something we need to check off our ever-growing to-do list, when we get tired and our zeal wanes, so will our participation.

If this is so much of a struggle for churches, how can I possibly ask churches to do the additional work of including people with disabilities in the evangelistic practice(s) of the church? We're struggling to just barely do church. We know all the things we *should* do and often feel overwhelmed and incapable of doing all those things. Adding evangelism to the list is another layer of complication. But if you ask us to also add a disability mindset, that's a whole new level of ask. How can we overcome the "burden" of evangelism and the additional "burden" of including disability within that evangelistic calling? How can we weigh the cost of evangelism among, with, and by people with disabilities?

FROM EVANGELISTIC BURDEN TO EVANGELISTIC DNA

In his book *You Found Me*, Rick Richardson explains why so many of our attempts at doing evangelism seem to fail or taper off after an initial burst of excitement. Richardson says we often look for a silver bullet to solve our stagnant evangelism and experience evangelism explosion. However, we then look for the latest model or trend that is working in a particular space and do not consider whether it fits our "church, culture, and philosophy." Though speaking specifically about church leaders, what Richardson says next applies to church leaders, church members, and churches as a whole. When going about mission and evangelism, "we don't have the bandwidth to add anything new, certainly not something that takes considerable energy, time, and people to accomplish." Even when we have motivation, we often fail to have margin. This can lead, then, to missional drift, in which our original passion for evangelism is gradually replaced by other things.[1]

For many pastors and churches, the pull of busyness is real. Personal priorities, church demands, events and meetings, and pastoral care needs fill up calendars. Congregants are pulled in many directions depending on the demands of their personal lives (work, family, home, community) and their level of involvement in church activities. Many pastors walk a precarious line trying to maximize participation without burning out volunteers. How can you increase the evangelistic impulse of pastors and churches in such an environment? We can say, "We need to do this" all we want, but if the margin's not there, as Richardson notes, such appeals "will go nowhere."[2]

What Richardson's research uncovered is that there is not a quick fix or magic pill that will move a church to become what he calls *a conversion community*, in which church growth happens largely through the creation of new Christians. Becoming a conversion community requires intentional steps over time to help churches change to the point that evangelistic impulses are the norm for congregational life and not an add-on. This requires *missional leaders* who model personal outreach and infuse evangelistic concern in the ministries under their purview. This also requires a *missional congregation* whose DNA is to engage those outside the church, bring them in, and extend "spectacular hospitality" when they visit. No matter when or where or what, when you visit the church, you feel engaged, invited, and hosted.[3]

When missional leaders and missional congregations work together, they become spaces where the church regularly grows (at least 5 percent per year); unchurched people come, commit to Christ, and stay (making up at least 10 percent of that year's church attendance); and every ministry and priority of the church includes outreach and witness. As more and more come to Christ, this will increase the *missional imagination* of the

---

[1]Rick Richardson, *You Found Me: New Research on How Unchurched Nones, Millennials, and Irreligious Are Surprisingly Open to Christian Faith* (IVP Academic, 2019), 104-5.

[2]Richardson, *You Found Me*, 105.

[3]Richardson, *You Found Me*, 107-8.

community, shaping the narrative of the community into one enchanted by Jesus' mission, expectant that the harvest is ripe and receptive, and filled with evangelistic faith and optimism.[4]

What is more, Richardson found ten *predictive* factors that lead to conversion growth. Placing these into the conversion church equation, Richardson says missional leaders lead the church into action by (1) a personal example of witness, (2) blocking out time in their schedule for outreach, (3) regularly inviting people to commit to Christ, and (4) investing in their own evangelism skills and inspiration. For their part, missional congregations will be marked by (1) growth through conversion and transfer, (2) sharing faith while engaging in the community through compassion and ministry, (3) a lead communicator who translates the regular weekly message for the irreligious and unchurched visitors, (4) investing money into evangelism and mission locally and globally, (5) a leader who regularly teaches a next-steps class to help visitors quickly move forward in commitment and involvement, and (6) an environment in which the unchurched stick around because the church really knows "how to invite, include and connect unchurched people to the congregation."[5]

Fundamental to Richardson's research is intentionality and accountability. Every step of the way requires people to intentionally block off time for outreach, to intentionally move out of their cliques and welcome the stranger, to infuse evangelistic outreach in each ministry of the church. The changes don't have to start out dramatic, but with each small, intentional step forward, you are forging a new lifestyle and establishing new habits. At the same time, without accountability, it can be easy to ease off the gas pedal when passion wanes, when motivation wavers because results aren't instantaneous, or when people naturally lose focus. Building in accountability with leaders and church members ensures we do not become passive.

Last year I decided that it was time to adopt a healthier lifestyle. My temptation was to look at the latest food and fitness trends to achieve my goals as quickly as possible. However, these didn't work. Many of these made me feel guilty and less-than. As an add-on program that didn't take

---

[4]Richardson, *You Found Me*, 108-9, 113.

[5]Richardson, *You Found Me*, 111-12.

into account my life stage (older working mom of two young kids) or what my body or mind actually needed, these ultimately were not sustainable or realistic. So I regrouped and tried again, but did so by incrementally changing my lifestyle, habits, and thought patterns in ways that matched my life and had goals that were much more realistic. This had good effect, but things became much more natural, sustainable, and enjoyable when my husband decided to join me in this healthy lifestyle pursuit. My personal intentionality only went so far when I could easily be tempted to fall back to old patterns. But when my husband joined me, we were able to motivate each other, do even more life together, and celebrate milestones when one or both of us achieved them. Amazingly, somewhere along the way what started out as a "We're getting older and need to be healthier" regimen moved from program to practice. Eating healthy and moving *is* everyday living for us now, not an add-on to everything else we're doing.

The same is true about evangelism. Being evangelistic is not a fad or a trend or simply one of the programs of the church. It really is a way of life that works best when you intentionally make space for it, when you intentionally let go of some habits and work to build others, when you make evangelism a part of your thoughts, and when you become accountable to others. In fact, as I have argued over and over, evangelism should be a core practice of the church—the faithful and virtuous living out of God's reign of shalom—so that everything the church does becomes infused with and a part of witness.[6] Not surprisingly, the more you do it, the more naturally it will come. This doesn't take all the work out of it—all of life is work in some ways—but it does mean that evangelism can move from add-on burden to nature. We do this not because we need to check it off the list. We do this because this *is* church living. We are evangels who practice evangelism through our practice(s).

DISMANTLING THE ADD-ON OF DISABILITY

But what about disability inclusion? Even when a church embraces its fundamental calling to faithfully and virtuously witness to God's peace, people often still have a lingering concern about the burden of adding

---

[6]Bryan Stone, *Evangelism After Christendom: The Theology and Practice of Christian Witness* (Brazos, 2007), 52.

disability to their life and acts of witness. If leaders are overloaded and already struggling to nurture evangelistic impulses into the life of the congregation, how can anyone receive an additional ask to also accommodate and adjust for people with a variety of disabilities without throwing in the towel? But even if a church does catch the vision Richardson lays out, and years of hard work have formed a church into a conversion community, some will still wonder whether disability inclusion would undermine what has taken years to develop. If disability inclusion is not part of the church's DNA, the thought of centering people with disabilities in the practices of the church, from evangelism and outreach to discipleship, will always be seen as something more, different, special, or burdensome. The response is often, "We don't have the bandwidth to add anything new, certainly not something that takes considerable energy, time, and people to accomplish." Something has to give, and it almost always is disability. While I would argue that not all accommodations require as much energy, time, or people power as you might think, this does summarize the dilemma I hear most often from churches leaders and members.

I think that, with one small tweak, Richardson's research will be an extremely helpful way to embrace disability within the evangelism practices of the church so that it becomes our way of living rather than an add-on. We get that tweak from Rick at Front Port Church.

Rick notes that as a microchurch plant of Community Christian Church-Naperville, Front Porch resonates with Community's mission of being "deeply committed to helping people find their way back to God." "When we say, 'Helping people find their way back to God,' that includes everybody," he says, "But when we add 'of all abilities,' it just gets a little bit more specific," so that when people research, they are able to find Front Porch Church "and say, 'Okay, this is a place that's going to be welcoming. Our family's going to feel seen, feel loved, feel heard, feel valued, and we're in.'"[7] It's a simple change that makes all the difference. Yes, *people* technically includes everyone, but it doesn't automatically lead to practices that include everyone. Do you feel the shift when "of all abilities" is added to the mission? It does something.

[7]Rick, interview with author, November 25, 2024.

What if we make this same shift when thinking about the conversion community equation? What if missional leaders *of all abilities* led the church into action by (1) a personal example of witness, (2) blocking out time in their schedule for outreach to people *of all abilities*, (3) regularly inviting people *of all abilities* to commit to Christ, and (4) investing in their own evangelism skills and inspiration, *intentionally including topics of disability* within this personal investment? What if missional congregations were marked by (1) growth through conversion and transfer, (2) sharing faith while engaging *people of all abilities* in the community through compassion and ministry, (3) a lead communicator who translates the regular weekly message for the irreligious and unchurched visitors *of all abilities*, (4) investing money into evangelism and mission locally and globally, (5) a leader who regularly teaches a next-steps class to help visitors *of all abilities* quickly move forward in commitment and involvement, and (6) an environment in which unchurched people *of all abilities* stick around because the church really knows how to invite, include, and connect unchurched people *of all abilities* to the congregation?

But aren't we still asking for more work when we add in "of all abilities"? What if we simply do not have the time, money, or people power to accommodate the range of disabilities we could encounter? What if we don't have the training? It is one thing to say "Just add *people of all abilities* to the conversion community equation" and quite another to do it. Let me see whether I can answer this in two ways: by way of my story and by way of God's.

EXPECTATION VERSUS BURDEN

When we felt our son was strong enough to join the nursey at the church we were attending, he was welcomed with open arms. Everyone thought he was cute and sweet, and they loved having him. When it was time for him to transition to his first classroom, however, we immediately encountered resistance. I still remember the smile freezing on the staff member's face when we asked to move our son up to the next room. The initial questions were: "Do you think he'll get much out of it? Can he follow directions?" (Can every two-year-old?) Picking him up that first day, we were told he did okay but that they still weren't sure he got much out of it even though he mostly kept up with the group plan. Then came the bombshell: "We're not sure the room is safe for him." Apparently, the TV wasn't bolted down, and until they completed that task, we were asked to keep him in the nursery. I was surprised. Shouldn't the TV be bolted down to keep all the two-year-olds safe? Every week we returned, hopeful we would be told the room was safe and he could return, but the excuses continued. Eventually we quit trying, and within a few months, we left this church.

What makes our story different from so many is that we didn't leave church altogether. We tried again. Unlike so many people with disabilities and their families, we struck gold. One of the first people to greet us at what is now our home church was the family ministries pastor. She spent time talking with us and asking about all the wonderful things she should know about our son. We were already impressed by the genuine interest she showed in him as a person, but what she said next made me cry. As she ended the conversation, she exclaimed *to our son*, "I can't wait to see what gifts God has for the church through you!" She didn't say it to us in the third person ("I wonder what God will do through him"). She said it directly addressing him in the second person ("I wonder what God will do through *you*!"). This exclamation changed the faith narrative for him. The church didn't approach him from a place of accommodation, burden, or cost. They started by seeing him as a valuable person through whom they *expected* God to work. This moved the conversation from "Can *he*?" to "How can *we* best help him grow so we can all receive what God has for us through him?"

In the days after we adopted our daughter, this same family pastor came to our house to welcome her on behalf of the church. She and her assistant spent time in our living room, doting on our daughter and watching as our son, who had just turned four, animatedly sang songs, danced, and talked to them about his books. Being on his home turf had opened him up, and they recognized new parts of his personality and how much he loved story and song. The family pastor got a strange look on her face, turned to her assistant, and said, "We have him in the wrong room!" Since our church was small, nursery ran from infants through age four, and then new classrooms started for those in kindergarten and up. The pastor turned to us and said, "I know he's just turned four and doesn't start kindergarten for over a year, but when we restart kids ministry this fall, let's move him up to the next class so he can engage with more story and song than we do in the nursery."

Did you catch what happened? Rather than holding him back (as our last church had done), this church promoted him *a year early* to the kindergarten-through-second-grade class because they recognized his love for and ability to engage with story and song. They didn't question whether he would get much out of it even though he was a young four year-old with a learning disability; rather, they trusted that as they played to his strengths, our son would get what God wanted him to get. They were right! In making this switch, my son, in just one year, learned the doxology, the Lord's Prayer, the Celtic benediction, the liturgy surrounding the Eucharist, how to pass the peace, how to greet people at the door, how to pray, and how to bless people in the name of the Father, the Son, and the Holy Spirit. When he prays, God hears; and people testify to how things change when my son talks to God.

Think about the seismic shift we experienced. One church saw disability as limitation, and they struggled to know how moving him into a class with his peers would help him grow. The other church saw an image-bearer who should be discipled into faith for the sake of having his gifts enacted for the benefit of the whole church and advanced him early to a new class, believing it would help him and others grow. One church saw disability as a burden to the teachers, peers, and setting that they either couldn't or wouldn't accommodate. The other church believed inclusion *is* the way of the church and proactively worked to set my son up for success in order to help him know and grow in Jesus.

Because they are looking for our son's growth, our church proactively seeks ways to help him. They made him a visual cue book so he can follow the classroom schedule. They invested in a chewy so we didn't have to worry when we forgot ours.[8] They enlisted a few people to serve as his personal buddy so he would remain safe and on task without being

[8]A chewy is a safe object that a child can chew on when they need increased sensory input or a way to self-regulate and calm intense emotions. They come in a variety of shapes and sizes.

a distraction to others. They also proactively look for ways to release his gifts. Knowing that he loves to help pick things up, they recently added him to one of the cleanup crews that tears down after service.[9] They've made this official by even sending him a text message, through us, so he will know when he's on the schedule.

Another thing our church does is regularly tell us ways God is using our son. Children's workers note things he says in the classroom. They tell us about growth in different areas. They mention times he helped a peer or prayed a prayer. They tell us how he is affecting his assigned buddies in a God-ward way, leading to their own growth in the Lord. They also share things he says and does with our lead pastor, who will sometimes include notes or videos in our churchwide newsletter so that others are aware of my son's gifts. Because all the leaders in our church are looking for our son's success, so are others in the church. People see our son as a vital member of the church and not just an add-on or a burden to be accommodated. They engage him in worship, draw him into the activities of the church, and do not give us side-eye or other off-putting gestures when my son is noisy or disruptive. Their welcome of him is the same welcome others experience, and it is drawing people of all abilities into the community as a regular part of our church's life.[10]

Perspective matters. Naming things matters. If we want to shift our evangelistic practices to include people with disabilities as recipients of and participants in our outreach, then we need to start with intentionally adding "of all abilities." This simple thing will awaken our imaginations to the questions and concerns that make implementing "of all abilities" possible. Yes, implementing evangelistic practices that account for things such as sensory needs, physical accessibility, Braille, sign language, visual aids, the need for buddies and helpers, and so on is vitally important. But if we start by thinking these things are burdens and extras we have to add on to our already overloaded life, we'll struggle to make this a lifestyle. If, however, we start with the belief that our mission is for, with, about, and

---

[9]Since our church rents space from another congregation, we have to set up and tear down our services each week.

[10]See Rochelle Scheuermann, "Learning and Living God's Story: The Power of Liturgy for, with, and Through People with Disabilities," *Missiology: An International Review* 52, no. 4 (2024): 415-26.

by people of all abilities, the accommodations will be seen as vital parts of the church's life and witness and a natural way to go about everything we do in the church.

My own church is small and lacks an abundance of human and monetary resources. We legitimately "don't have the bandwidth to add anything new, certainly not something that takes considerable energy, time, and people to accomplish." Our conviction that people of all abilities should be welcomed to the church and nurtured in faith leads us to many creative, inexpensive, and helpful accommodations that make all the difference for people and families with disabilities. This proactive spirit alone has made our church one of the safest and most welcoming places for my family to be. So much of our life is spent in advocacy that it is huge for us to find a church home where we are seen, valued, included, and genuinely embraced without our need to advocate for my son's right to participate, belong, and be nurtured. This leads us back to Richardson's discovery that the most effective conversional communities show "spectacular hospitality." Having experienced this kind of spectacular hospitality, especially with regard to our son, I am hard-pressed to find another evangelistic practice that is more powerful or all-encompassing.

GOD'S ACCOMMODATION

As inspiring as I hope my own church experience is for others, our commitment to inclusion of the disabled in our work and witness does not rest on human experience. If it does, we are always at risk of losing inspiration and drive. Our understanding of witness must always start with the triune God, who is on mission and whose accommodation to us is the pattern we are to emulate.[11] The Word made flesh is God's ultimate accommodation to our fractured, fraught, disordered, and disabled lives (Jn 1:1-14). Creator enters creation, taking on limits and vulnerability, moving toward us in ways *we* can understand, touch, taste, see, hear, and experience. Jesus did not consider moving toward us a burden, something to check off the list, something God added to the

[11] I am grateful to John Switon for emphasizing this point.

mission, or something that defined only parts of his life and only when he felt like it. Moving toward us *was* the mission. Being strong in our weakness was his delight. Making the invisible God known through physical embodiment was in a sense the message. The "I AM" (Ex 3:14), now the "I am with you" (see Mt 1:23), always the "I am with you . . . even to the end of the age" (Mt 28:20).

We tend to domesticate God in our own image and think we understand him on our terms. But we don't. God's "riches and wisdom and knowledge" are "impossible" to understand. "For who can know the LORD's thoughts?" Paul asks. "Who knows enough to give him advice? And who has given him so much that he needs to pay it back? For everything comes *from him* and exists *by his power* and is intended *for his glory*. All glory to him forever! Amen" (Rom 11:33-36 NLT 2015). If we are moved and captivated by God's story, it is because God first moved toward us because he loved us and knew we were incapable of reaching him on our own. Any knowledge of God we have, any experience of God we enjoy, is because God has accommodated our weaknesses and limitations so we can enter into him.

As we embody this witness through the Spirit, we too are called to a lifestyle that moves toward others and joins with others in responding to God's move toward us. Accommodation ends up going in all directions: God to us; each of us to one another. It is not merely *abled* to *disabled* but *everyone* to *everyone*, all because God made himself known to us and enabled us to move toward him.

Witness that excludes, overlooks, or makes burdensome the reaching of people with disabilities is a truncated witness that does not accurately account for the fullness and expanse of God's kingdom or his gospel. As we work to (re)ignite our passion for enacting evangelism as our way of living, both personally and corporately, let's also make sure that this includes people with disabilities front and center as part of the whole church taking the whole gospel to the whole world.[12] This will affect our practices, yes, but we will not be successful if we make this about only

[12]Rochelle Scheuermann, "Not Whole Without Us: Including People with Disabilities in Our Understanding of the Church, the Gospel, and the World," *Missiology: An International Review* 50, no. 3 (2022): 290-303.

accommodations to our practices. By reaching and incorporating people with disabilities in the life and work of the church, we will be awakened to *dispositions* that should be part of our life and witness as Christ followers but often aren't. We now turn to these dispositional practices that will make spectacular hospitality possible.

DISCUSSION QUESTIONS

1. Does evangelism feel like a burden? How well have you and your church addressed this common response to evangelism?
2. In what ways has or hasn't your church focused evangelism and outreach on people with disabilities? Are there certain disabilities they focus on? Are there disabilities that are missing?
3. How does adding "of all abilities" change perspectives on the ministries and focus of your church?
4. How does emulating God's accommodation of us affect or change your own response to disability and evangelism?

11

The Practice of Accommodation

THE AMERICANS WITH DISABILITIES ACT (ADA), signed into law in 1990, seeks to protect people with disabilities from discrimination by legally requiring reasonable accommodations that will allow the disabled to access and participate in public spaces similarly to those without disabilities. While this law applies to most entities in the United States, it is not well known within Christian circles that religious organizations (both places of worship and facilities controlled by religious organizations such as schools and daycare centers) are exempt. This exemption was not something pursued by lawmakers; rather, churches actively lobbied for this exemption when the law was under consideration in Congress in the late 1980s. In a letter to Senator Tom Harkin from Dr. Robert P. Dugan Jr., writing on behalf of the National Association of Evangelicals, Dugan closes with what he identifies as a *serious problem*: "The prospect of radical expansion of costs very often not warranted by the particular needs of anyone actually on the premises. In the case of voluntary religious activity, in which the participants have a constitutional right to engage, free of burdens (if such are not called for by health or safety considerations), the burdens are impermissible."[1] What is Dugan saying? Quite a lot!

First, Dugan is concerned that charitable organizations, especially smaller ones, will be so burdened by the costs of accommodations that this could force a reallocation of moneys from current ministries and perhaps overly stretch or even break small budgets that rely on voluntary

[1]Robert P. Dugan Jr. to Senator Tom Harkin, July 14, 1989, https://dolearchivecollections.ku.edu/collections/ada/files/s-leg_753_001_all.pdf, 114.

offerings. Second, he argues that the serious problem is not just about money. It is about spending money to make changes for people who are not "actually on the premises." Dugan assumes most churches do not have people with disabilities in need of these accommodations because he believes most churches do not have people with disabilities "actually on the premises." This, he believes, makes the expenditures unnecessary and overly burdensome. Third, Dugan suggests that religious activity is a voluntary one in which people can choose where they want to go and whether to engage, so when they do so, fourth, they should not become burdened by forced expenditures or accommodations that do not serve their own needs. Dugan articulates a singular understanding of accommodation that is common to most people: Accommodation is an adjustment we make to physical spaces and to the already established ways in which we do things. It is particularly burdensome when we do it for the sake of a few people, many of whom, as Dugan argues, aren't even present.

One of the most often asked questions I get is this: "We have *x* number of people in our sanctuary/church. Do we really need to adjust for just one person? What about everyone else?" Such questions come from very earnest pastors and church leaders who sincerely want to do the right thing but struggle to see how adjusting for one person is not simultaneously detrimental to the other people gathered to worship. How can pastors balance the diverse care needs of those in their flock? Here we need to be reminded that there will not always be easy, clearly defined solutions to the myriad of disability situations faced by churches. I do not want to minimize the work and questions that come when reaching and incorporating people with disabilities into the work and witness of the church. What works in one church may not work in another. What works for one person may not work for another. Knowing how to balance the needs and growth of all the people in one's care can be daunting and at times feel insurmountable. I commend and commiserate with all pastors and church leaders who start down this road and find themselves facing these obstacles. And I agree with Hannah, who says, "Cutting people out is not the choice."[2] What do we do?

[2]Hannah, interview by author, November 25, 2024.

In considering this dilemma, I wonder whether perhaps we are all starting from the wrong perspective. If we think of accommodation as merely adjusting physical spaces and the already-existing practices of the majority to include the few, if we wonder how much work or change or adjustment is enough to help the disabled assimilate while minimally affecting the abled majority, could we be approaching things the wrong way? God's kingdom has never been one of being first or power trumping service. God's kingdom is upside down and tends to center the marginalized, the least, and the oppressed. God's kingdom has also always been one of unity in diversity, with every person and part playing a valuable role for the sake of the whole body and the sake of whole witness. There should never be a stable majority for whom the rest must acquiesce. Who's to say which group gets to be the "majority" and which must be accommodated or not?

Viewing accommodation as adjustment of practice alone easily turns relationship with the disabled into one of transaction. How? First, it sets up relationship along an us-them binary in which the abled provide goods and services to the disabled other. Hannah observes, "When [churches] talk about how to reach out to people with disability, how to work with the disability community or whatever, it's othered. It's not 'your' community. It's 'this other' community."

Second, it subjects each adjustment to a cost-versus-benefit scale. How much distraction, cost, time, or adjustment can a church afford without asking too much of the majority? A church may be willing to provide a printed schedule each week but not tone down the worship volume or special effects. A church may be willing to install a wheelchair ramp but not rearrange the sanctuary to allow wheelchair users to choose seats close to the pulpit, to navigate the altar, or even to access the platform.[3] For many churches, if it fits within their budgets and mission, they will make adjustments that help disabled others assimilate as much as possible. Far fewer will be compelled to rethink practices, expectations, church culture, and even theology from a disability perspective. They are too locked into "This is who we are" without considering, "Is this who

[3]See Andrew T. Draper, Jody Michele, and Andrea Mae, *Disabling Leadership: A Practical Theology for the Broken Body of Christ* (IVP Academic, 2023), particularly xiii-xv.

we should be?" This keeps the balance of power with the abled and can lead to all sorts of actions that exclude rather than embrace.

When Abby was in college, she worked as a direct-support professional for a young woman who made a lot of vocalizations.

> She would kind of, "Ah! Ah!" And I took her to church. She wanted to go to church. And the way she would worship was to stand in the aisle and make these vocalizations. I was standing with her as her support worker. And the usher came up and asked us to leave, to go back out into the lobby because he thought she was distracting or disturbing the other people in the worship zone. We did. *And* we didn't come back.
>
> I have *never* felt so unwelcome in a church as at that moment. I don't know how much she was disturbing others or if it was making people uncomfortable. But I felt very much in that moment, like, "Maybe we *should* feel a little uncomfortable? Maybe it's okay to feel a little uncomfortable?" This is the way she's able to worship, and I don't think she needed to be segregated or separated from the rest of the body during that worship, even if it sounds different than what you're used to.[4]

Abby's story is one that is repeated thousands of times. My own mother, who suffers from intense migraines, once asked whether her church would turn down the volume and quit shining flashing lights on the congregation during worship because not only was the volume at a decibel that damaged hearing, but the volume and lights kept triggering migraines. The church responded by handing her earplugs and telling her to wait in the lobby until the worship was done if she couldn't take it. She notes that they didn't even say, "Worship in the lobby. They said, 'Wait.'" She soon found herself with a huddle of people who were similarly told to wait outside. My mom was devastated. "Am I not an important part of the body? Why is my worship not necessary? Why couldn't they see that by excluding people from the body of Christ, their worship wasn't whole?" When accommodation is transactional and based on making adjustments to already-existing practices, practices tend to prevail, leading to responses of exclusion. The resulting pain experienced by the disabled is not surprising. But, dear friends, these things ought not to be!

---

[4]Abby, interview by author, December 6, 2024.

What if accommodation is less about adjustments to our actions so we can assimilate the other and more about adjustments to *our own disposition* so we can receive one another? What if we begin *practicing* accommodation?

THE DOUBLE-EMPATHY PROBLEM

"Have you heard the phrase *double-empathy problem*?" Abby asked me. I hadn't. It's a theory from the autism space, she went on to tell me, that rethinks the communication impasse between autistic and allistic (non-autistic) people. Rather than following the typical framing of autism as people with a social deficit who cannot relate to others socially, the double-empathy problem suggests that autistic and allistic people communicate in ways that are merely different—not right or wrong, better or worse, just different. Perhaps, she says, "There needs to be a little bit more 'I accommodate for you and you accommodate for me.'" Giving an example from her own life, she notes that allistic people are typically offended by the direct communication of autistic people. However, the opposite also occurs. "It's a double problem," she says.

> I'm thinking you're not being very direct and that's rude because I don't understand what you're saying. And so we're kind of at this weird impasse where I'm communicating in a way that *really* makes sense to me, and you're communicating in a way that *really* makes sense to you, and we are missing each other in terrible ways. Maybe you could be a little bit more direct—that would help me. And I can ask for clarification, and that will help you. You know, there can be a little bit more of a two-way street in those social communications instead of just always assuming that there's this deficit. *You* are communicating wrong. *You* are relating to the world wrong. Let's put *you* in a social-skills class and fix it.

As I listened to Abby, I was struck by her conclusion.

> This is just a way of kind of recognizing it more as almost crosscultural. I think about the world in a different way than you, and you think about the world in a different way from me. *I can do something* to understand the way you relate to the world, and there's been a lot of that. There's been not much of "you have to understand how I relate to the world, too." It's this reorienting of the way we can relate to one another.

Hannah says something similar. "I think we see people who don't conform the way we think they should and automatically put them on a pedestal below us, in the sense of 'Oh, let me cater to you. Let me tell you about Jesus. Let me bring you to me,' instead of saying. 'I want to meet you where you're at and I want to learn from you because you have things to say.'" To practice accommodation will require that we reorient how we relate to one another. When we do, we will make overtures to one another from a posture of humility rather than superiority. We will check our own instincts that encounter different as *lesser*, *worse*, or *wrong*. We will see differences—in body, mind, communication, and action—as just that: differences, not necessarily problems to be fixed.

This posture, according to cultural anthropologists, is what we call *cultural relativism*.[5] "Whoa!" you say. "Now you've crossed a line. Aren't we against relativism as Christians?" If we're talking about *moral relativism*, yes. Moral relativism, Brian Howell and Jenell Paris say, assumes "something is only right and wrong according to context-specific criteria." Moral relativism says it's okay for people to behave and believe based on what each person and society deems acceptable. This is not what we mean by *cultural* relativism. Cultural relativism requires we set aside our instinct to immediately judge difference and instead adopt a posture of curiosity and investigation so we can understand others and how their given practices or beliefs developed and are understood from their context. We get into trouble when we forget to understand others on their own terms and instead "use the standards of [our] own culture to understand others, which invariably leads to misunderstanding rooted in ethnocentrism." Howell and Paris define *ethnocentrism* as "the use of one's own culture to measure another's, putting one's own culture (*ethno*) at the center (*centrism*) of interpretation, typically devaluing and invariably mischaracterizing the other culture."[6]

One of the quickest ways to recognize you're coming up against cultural difference is when your initial thought is, *You're weird! That's wrong! How bizarre!* When these thoughts and impulses come up, we

[5]Brian M. Howell and Jenell Paris, *Introducing Cultural Anthropology: A Christian Perspective*, 2nd ed. (Baker Academic, 2019), 33-35.

[6]Howell and Paris, *Introducing Cultural Anthropology*, 36.

need to recognize them for what they are: markers there is something we don't understand *yet*. Rather than simply acting on the judgment that this person or practice is weird, wrong, or bizarre, we can turn our exclamations into questions: What are you doing? What does this mean? How do you understand this? How do you experience this? Asking these kinds of questions will help us investigate what we are seeing and experiencing. Often, when we do this, we will find much more similarity than difference with others. In those places of difference, we might even be positively challenged by others and the principles, ethics, means, and modes behind what others do.

Cultural anthropology tells us that in our encounters with others, we are prone to elevate our own way of doing things, our own way of being embodied, our own way of speaking, and our own way of approaching others as the right way, leading us to easily devalue and mischaracterize others. What's more, we tend to want others to assimilate and conform to us rather than starting from a posture of humility and a desire to learn and value the other person's ways of being, speaking, and acting. Invariably, we hit up against the double-empathy problem, hoping others move toward us but not making a similar move toward them. Any attempt to practice accommodation must start with a humble view of self and a reorientation toward others.

Abby is right. This necessitates a crosscultural posture.

BECOMING RECEPTOR-ORIENTED

My son has entered the phase in which everything I do or say leads to a question. Just last week, as I was signing for a prescription at the pharmacy, he asked, "What are you doing?" When I told him I was signing the form because I had used insurance, he questioned, "What is insurance?" How *do* you explain health insurance to a first grader, much less to a first grader with a developmental delay? I finally mumbled something like, "It's this company we give lots of money to in hopes that they will help us pay less for doctors and medicine, but it's hard to know how much it really works, and I think it comes out in the wash." The pharmacy technician snorted, and I replied, "Some things just can't be explained!"

This encounter, like so many encounters with people, highlights the many challenges we have when helping someone understand a brand-new concept or trying to get a message across when speaker and listener have different cultures, languages, backgrounds, and experiences. Even when we come from the same culture and use the same language, our lives are fraught with miscommunication and misunderstanding because we tend to see the world through our own lens and from our own experiences and worldview, and we assume everyone else does too. If something doesn't get through, we often repeat ourselves over and over, getting louder with each round, as if repetition and volume were the key to communication. Let me let you in on a secret: They're not! How might we overcome these obstacles? By becoming receptor-oriented communicators.

If you think about what happens during a conversation between two people, at a given point you will have someone speaking and someone (hopefully!) listening (i.e., receiving the message). The speaker develops an idea she wishes to communicate and, using her knowledge and experiences, turns this idea into a set of words and nonverbal actions, which she then shares with the listener. If the listener is able to receive the words and nonverbal actions and interpret them in a way that corresponds with what was intended by the speaker, we say that communication has transpired.

When people share language, culture, worldview, experiences, and other areas of commonality, the likelihood of successful communication increases. But what happens when speaker and listener come from different spaces, backgrounds, experiences, cultures, worldviews, or languages? Where do we start adjusting to help the communication work? Too often we put the onus on the listener (the receptor). But that's not the correct starting point. The real work should happen on the side of the speaker.

Rather than forcing the listener (the receptor) to adjust, a good communicator will do the hard work of learning about the listener and considering the listener's knowledge, experience, worldview, and culture. The speaker will then consider how her ideas fit with the listener and start adjusting the communication so that as many barriers as possible are removed and the listener can more easily grasp the intended message. Being a receptor-oriented speaker is a posture that says, "I'm not watering down my message, but rather doing everything I can to make sure that what I intend you to hear is what you actually hear." It does require work on the side of the speaker, but the result is better for *everyone*.

Communication certainly matters for evangelism, and being a receptor-oriented communicator is a must for reaching people, especially those from different backgrounds from us. *And* this type of reorientation shouldn't start or stop with communication. Practicing accommodation requires that *our lives* are oriented toward others. Rather than starting from the belief that our way is best and should be universal, we should be other-oriented: asking questions about how others will experience a particular space, considering what our words or actions might actually communicate, and attempting to remove barriers that would hinder a person from receiving welcome and experiencing the love of God. "Are you even considering that there might be people in differentiated bodies, differently abled? We all have different places we come from," Andy says. "Are we even imagining what it would be like for them to be in our midst? What would we do differently?" Andy notes that when we don't start with the other in mind, we communicate the message, "You're not welcome."[7]

For Abby, two starkly contrasted experiences highlight the devastating effects of not being oriented toward the disabled and what happens when a small and simple attempt to be disability-oriented is experienced.

> I was at a small church for thirteen to fourteen years. My oldest took a long time to potty-train and the rule was you don't move into the preschool classroom until you are potty-trained. He just couldn't. He wasn't really potty-trained. He wasn't really speaking—kind of a couple words. And so, I was told he can't go into the preschool room by the preschool room teacher. So I kept him in the nursery, and then I was told he couldn't stay in the nursery because he was too old. He was too big. He might hurt the little kids. I had nowhere. I didn't know what to do. If I brought him into service, he was loud and disruptive, and I couldn't hear what was going on. If I brought him to the nursery, "He's too big." If I bring him to preschool room, "He's too small," or "He's not developed enough to be part

[7]Andy, interview by author, November 26, 2024.

> of that." Which . . . hmm. (eyeroll) That's all I'm saying. So I was really kind of stuck for a while.

The only resolution Abby found was to take over the preschool room herself. "*I* can accommodate these other preschoolers and my son, so I'll teach this class." But that too became a problem because no one would join the teacher rotation. "It became just me. Nobody else wanted to be in the preschool room with the different kid." Abby eventually took over the children's ministry and, with small adjustments to the curriculum, experienced an influx of families who had children with special needs. She was thrilled to be in this ministry but also found it isolating because she never was given a break to be spiritually fed.

Fast-forward several years as Abby and her family prepared for the long Easter vigil at their new (Anglican) church.

> I knew it was going to be a long service, and that has always been a problem for my family. So I packed fidgets. I packed noise-canceling headphones. I packed coloring books. I'm just anxiously ready to hunker down for this long service, worried about how my kids are going to behave during this long service because that's always been a challenge. And right at the door before we went in, someone had already arranged for noise-canceling headphones. I had my own so I didn't actually need that. But it felt like this . . . Oh. They're *ready* for me. They're *okay* with me. They—I'm *welcome* here. I'm not just *tolerated* here. Yeah, I'm being *invited* and *welcomed* as I *am*. My kids are being invited and welcomed as they *are* and not expected to sit rigid and not be bothered by the sounds. They're not expected to stay calm because they might freak out about the bells. They might. And it felt like a huge relief. A very small thing to set out these headphones, but nothing has felt more belonging, was more inviting me to belong, than that.

Aren't both of these stories about physical accommodations? Yes and no. It is true that the first church chose to not make physical adjustments to their children's program and the second church provided headphones. However, it was the advanced thought, the consideration of "How will this other person experience this space?" that made the difference. The first church lacked the imagination to think beyond their policies. The second church reviewed their service through an autistic perspective and proactively offered helps. This second church even toned down how loud the pastor shouts, "Alleluia, Christ is risen!" to ease the disruption that could be experienced by those with heightened sensory responses.

Receptor orientation is important because it is possible to make physical accommodations and still not practice accommodation. My own son took a long time to potty-train and the process was devastating. I remember crying in the daycare parking lot when an exasperated teacher made a judgmental comment about a new reward system we were trying. I remember my anger when the school nurse on the second day of kindergarten threw away my son's soiled clothes without telling us. At so many turns, we had to advocate for help and felt resistance and judgment and that we were asking too much, even when we were seeking accommodations that were required by law. Yes, we were technically accommodated. No, we were not loved or embraced.

Then came the unexpected email from our church's children's ministry. "We know that your son is potty-training (and doing really well for us!) and so we are wondering what you all are comfortable with when it comes to helping him with the bathroom." The email went on with some potential actions and included more questions to help gather information from us on how best they could support us in this. I cried and cried, but this time it was tears of relief and joy at being seen and welcomed. We didn't have to advocate and fight and face resistance. Instead, without knowing the solution or what accommodations to make, the church postured themselves toward us to say, "Let's learn from you so we can support you in helping your son succeed."

Being other-oriented moves us to action and leads to what we typically think of as *accommodations*. However, this posture changes us first, by decentering our ways and sharpening our focus on others so that the table we set is one of welcome (not resistance) and one of belonging (not othering). It leads us to hold practices more loosely and people more firmly so in everything we do we are forefronting people of all abilities and doing what works best for them as a matter of first importance. We can adjust our ways of doing things and still not be other-oriented in ways that help others feel welcomed. When we practice the disposition of being other-oriented, we will not merely say others are welcome; we will help them experience welcome. But note, just as with double empathy, being other-oriented is not a one-way street. It is not just a posture that moves you toward others. It is also a posture that requires you let others move toward you, having "an imagination of 'What ways could God do something *through* these people?"[8]

LEARNING TO RECEIVE

In *No Longer Strangers: Transforming Evangelism with Immigrant Communities*, Sandra Van Opstal notes what I have already talked about, that it is possible to practice hospitality without genuine welcome.[9] If we only ever make it about our extending welcome *to* others, "we will miss out on the gifts our global family have to offer." When hospitality is one-way, those offering hospitality retain the position of power. Consider this scenario:

> Imagine that your intent is to be a good neighbor to immigrants in your community: as a result, you perpetually invite them over. They come into your home, where you serve them food of your choice, play music (or not) of your choice, have them sit at a table or in chairs of your choice. In this setting, you have the power as the host. Maybe we've not thought about it that way before, but it is true. "Welcoming into" allows the one welcoming to preserve the power in the relationship while feeling as though he or she is doing something fantastic. . . . The problem is that if your relationships are one-directional, the people you are helping will not engage freely.[10]

True hospitality begins when the one who served as host allows the guest to become the host. Only when we become the guest and openly receive the hospitality and welcome of the other will we move from hospitality as transaction to hospitality as relationship.

The same is true for practicing accommodation. If we only ever move toward others but never receive from others, we truncate the relationship and retain the balance of power. In these moments, the very people we think we are accommodating and welcoming will feel left out, belittled,

---

[8]Andy, interview with author, November 26, 2024.

[9]Sandra Maria Van Opstal, "Beyond Welcoming," in *No Longer Strangers: Transforming Evangelism with Immigrant Communities*, ed. Eugene Cho and Samira Izadi Page (Eerdmans, 2021), 71.

[10]Van Opstal, "Beyond Welcoming," 72-73.

and discounted. Hannah recounts that her disability continues to make her feel "very displaced in the church."

> I'll kind of feel like I've reintegrated and I'm part of it. Then something happens, and all of a sudden, I feel like I'm either *the* voice for disability and I must know everything. And I'm like, "I don't, I only know me." Or people share a lot with me and then take it back. It's almost like they catch themselves word vomiting about a hard thing that's happening, and then they're like, "Oh! But you have it so much worse. I can't talk to you." Which I just want to say, "No. Just because I have things happening doesn't mean your things are not valid." But that's been tricky in trying to be there for people, but know that if I'm there, they might not actually be able to grieve.

It's these smaller interactions she thinks about the most. Hannah says again, "Just because I'm vocal and people know that I've gone through hard things doesn't mean that you can't come to me and that I think you're lesser, that I am sitting there while you're grieving thinking, 'Oh my gosh, this is so stupid. You don't even understand what grief is.' I want to be a part of the community, and that means supporting you as well." Hannah's experience can be multiplied thousands of times over. *I want to be part of the community, and that means supporting you as well.* When we do not receive the ministry of the other, we cut them out of the body and keep them from being part of the community. The result is that we lose out on the many blessings, gifts, talents, and comforts that come from the disabled. There is a mutuality and reciprocity that comes with practicing accommodation well. It must always be a two-way street.

As you allow others to move toward you, you will also find that practicing accommodation helps you see yourself more circumspectly, which in the end will help you see how much more alike you are to people with disabilities.

WE ALL NEED ACCOMMODATION

One of the paradoxes of practicing accommodation is that it isn't just about our practicing how to accommodate others. It is also about recognizing our own dependences and leaning into the accommodations we need. Decentering ourselves means recognizing we *all* have support needs that need to be met in order to thrive. The problem, however, is that because of the ways in which ideas such as independence, autonomy, and capitalism have entrenched themselves into our culture, we are not always able or willing to acknowledge support needs when we have them.

> Our country, our community, our culture is obsessed with independence. Just *obsessed* with independence. I think that obsession with independence has much more to do with capitalism than it does to do with Christ. But it seeps into our churches *a lot. A lot.* This idea that you need to be independent and autonomous and taking care of your own needs, it's, I think, seeped into the church in really gross ways, when we were *designed* to be interdependent. I think disability reminds us of that. We were *designed* to need one another. None of us was ever designed to live completely autonomous. That's absurd, actually.

In such a culture, Abby goes on to say, determining which needs are *special* and which are not can be quite arbitrary. "We differentiate between the people who need the extra and the people who don't need the extra," Abby says, "without acknowledging that *every single human* has a support need of some kind. And the way we differentiate between whether it's too much of a support need or just the right amount of support need is so absurd. It really has nothing to do with Christ, nothing to do with the way we were designed to live in community."

Some of our support needs are determined by culture or location or generation. My own need for strong corrective lenses in order to see things in focus is a special need that is supported by contacts and glasses. A century ago, my extreme nearsightedness would have been hugely disabling. However, because glasses are so commonplace now, we rarely consider vision correction as a support and certainly don't think of nearsightedness as a disability. If anything, it's simply an inconvenience.[11]

Some of our support needs, if we have money, can also be hidden. Abby observes,

> We're in a fairly affluent area where I think it becomes easy to hide our own support needs. "I need to be picked up from the airport, so I called an Uber. So I don't have that support need." But you *do* have a support need. It's just invisible because you can pay for it. You know, "I need to go

[11]Abby shared this idea of changing views on glasses with me.

> out, so I'll hire a babysitter." Well, you actually do have a support need for a caregiver for your child, but you're able to just buy it. You bought it. And so now it seems as if you have no need for interdependence because you . . . can hire people to do all of these things and make you seem as if you're very highly independent when really your dependence has just been commodified, right? It has just been something that you can use your wealth to hide. And that's not to say any of those things are bad. It's fine to hire a childcare provider. It's fine to hire someone to clean your house. But I think it gives this illusion that you are doing it all when really you're being supported in all kinds of ways. It just isn't free support, right? And so when the support has to come for free, it suddenly looks like a burden. It suddenly looks like something is wrong with you, when really I don't think it's wrong to need support. I think we all do.

Abby's words revealed this juxtaposition in my own life. When my husband and I recently went to a work event and needed childcare help, we asked a friend (and one of our son's former teachers, whom he *loves*) to come watch our kids. We were grateful but didn't see this as anything special. However, there are times when my husband is out of town and the morning routine is just too much for one person to handle. When I ask my parents for help (or especially when they volunteer help), I can't get over the feeling of being burdensome because I've got a need they have jumped in to meet. What's the difference? Nothing, really. Both are support needs. But society says that when you have the money to hire childcare, it is normal to go on a date. Society says that free help because you can't handle single parenting for a couple of mornings is burdensome because you should be autonomous and aren't.

The more I lean into my son's disability and the ways in which we need a village around us to raise him, the more I am attuned to the fact that it took a village to raise me too, and it *still* takes a village to keep me going. Somewhere along the way I bought into this fallacy that I need to be autonomous when all along I have needs that others meet, just as I help meet their needs. Practicing accommodation is helping me see myself much more honestly and humbly. The accommodations I make for others are no more or less than the accommodations I receive from others. They're just different. Sometimes what I need is easy to fill; other times it requires a lot from others. Sometimes what others need is easy to fill; other times it requires a lot. But when we come to realize we all need accommodations, it can reframe our attitudes and outlook to be hospitable toward the needs of others just as we hope they will be hospitable to ours.

PRACTICING ACCOMMODATION IN EVANGELISM

Practicing accommodation is a way of life that should realign how we view others, perceive their needs, and consider ourselves. Having double empathy, being other-oriented, and recognizing we all need accommodations will push us to a new way of being in the world. The more we practice accommodation, the more we will be on the lookout to proactively set up our church services, our teachings, our classrooms, our events, and our one-on-one encounters with disabilities in mind. We will be less worried about the cost or burden of making accommodations and more concerned with how we might intentionally make room for people of all abilities to know Christ, grow in Christ, and work for Christ.

Throughout his life and ministry, the apostle Paul practiced accommodation. Listen to his testimony.

> I have become a slave to all people to bring many to Christ. When I was with the Jews, I lived like a Jew to bring the Jews to Christ. When I was with those who follow the Jewish law, I too lived under that law. Even though I am not subject to the law, I did this so I could bring to Christ those who are under the law. When I was with the Gentiles who do not follow the Jewish law, I too live apart from that law so I can bring them to Christ. . . . When I am with those who are weak, I share their weakness, for I want to bring the weak to Christ. *Yes, I try to find common ground with everyone, doing everything I can to save some.* I do everything to spread the Good News and share in its blessings. (1 Cor 9:19-23)

Paul's continual refrain is that he moves toward others to the point of honoring as much of their life and perspective as he can, even giving up his own ways of being when possible, all for the sake of others knowing Christ. He did the hard work and was willing to give up preferences so that a welcome table could be set that would honor others and bring them to the knowledge of Christ. It was never superficial catering to others, all for a bait-and-switch. Genuine relationship for Paul meant giving others the best gift possible—an introduction to Jesus—but his continued relationship and practice of accommodation was never predicated on their response. Why? Because Paul's practice of accommodation was only ever possible because God first moved toward him.

The fact is, God moved toward all of us first. It was while we were the neediest of all, steeped in sin and brokenness, that he left his throne and entered our world (Rom 5:8), becoming a "disabled" God who took on limits and vulnerability and dependency in the body and flesh of Jesus. He did this for us, moving toward us in the most dramatic fashion of all, so that in giving up his life, he might buy us back. Perhaps this is some of what Paul recognized when he decided that everything that seems like gain and ability and strength is actually quite worthless. It was in giving it up, counting it as garbage, and relying solely on God's sacrifice that Paul knew Christ in the "power of his resurrection and participation in his sufferings" (Phil 3:10 NIV). As Paul learned to suffer with Christ and share in Christ's death, he also somehow could experience the resurrection from the dead (Phil 3:7-11). This alone made the practice of accommodation possible. Having buried himself in Christ, he was alive in Christ, which meant that he could follow Christ's example in burying himself for others so that they too could find their way to Christ and share in Christ's death and resurrection themselves.

In practicing accommodation, we find the heart of God. In laying down ourselves (including our rights and our ways) for the sake of others, we make it possible for them to come to God's table. In receiving one another's fellowship and gifts, as those Christ has "fitted together perfectly in his body," we "can each now do our own special work, helping each part of Christ's body to grow so that the whole body will be healthy and growing and full of love" (Eph 4:15-16, my paraphrase).

Perhaps, most importantly, we will all come to know God more deeply.

Though I have tried to reframe our typical notion that accommodations are about making adjustments that help the disabled get in the door to one of accommodations as an adjustment to our own ways of being in order to live lives of welcome, we can still be caught in a frame of mind that sees those with certain capabilities as conduits who take what they have received from God and give it to less capable others. We should be clear here: Everything we have received, any knowledge we have, we have because of "an accommodation on God's part."[12] If God makes himself known to us in ways we can receive, we can be assured that God is also making himself known to others in ways they can receive. Because evangelism is entering a conversation God is already having with someone, our posture must always be one of humility rather than dominance as we imagine and learn the ways in which God is already accommodating other people. In doing this, we don't just have the opportunity to join with God in what God is already doing and witnessing to the Spirit already at work in people's lives; we have an opportunity ourselves to be spiritually formed into new ways of knowing God, receiving the Spirit's work in our lives, which can become a witness for others. As my friend Ben Conner says, when we take the time to learn about how "God is already accommodating someone, for example, with I/DD [intellectual and developmental disability]," it will widen "our perception of God and the many communicative modalities God employs." By taking on the practice of accommodation, we not only make a space at the table for everyone to give and receive; we also come to understand God and his ways more fully.

DISCUSSION QUESTIONS

1. Did you know about churches having an exemption from the ADA? What are your thoughts on this?
2. What is the difference between making accommodations and practicing accommodation?
3. Using the double-empathy problem and the idea of receptor orientation, reflect on past encounters you've had with others. How do these concepts help you better understand interactions? Are there areas you need to work on to become more oriented toward others?

[12] I am grateful to Ben Conner for sharing with me this editorial feedback on God's accommodation and giving this point clarity. All quotations in this paragraph come from him.

4. In what ways will you start practicing accommodation? What things do you specifically want to start doing, keep doing, or stop doing?
5. How does the idea that we can learn from God accommodating us expand your thoughts on evangelism?

12

The Practice of Seeing People

During our premarital counseling, my husband and I were cautioned about ever using the phrases "You always" or "You never." *You always* and *you never* language, our counselors said, preempts true understanding because it gives us a lens that biases us toward some facts and away from others. It boxes others into stereotypes and tropes without taking the time to listen and learn. It allows us to hide behind a perceived injustice without taking ourselves into full account. It closes us off from new possibilities. It shuts down true communication. Ultimately, it cuts us off from each other. It is hard sometimes to fight that impulse to always/never my husband, but the counselors were right. When I give in, it hurts him *and* me, it takes a long time to repair the damage, and if I'm honest, it is rarely correct. When it comes to disability, we may not directly use *you always* and *you never* language, but we often follow the same patterns of assumption and grouping that shut us off from truly seeing, knowing, hearing, and receiving from the unique others right in front of us, which in turn also shuts others off from wanting to pursue relationship with us.

When I interviewed Chris, he began with this. "I guess you already know I think outside the box. However, it is the one thing I like people to know about me. I don't believe there is a box answer for anything. Not that we can't explore it. I guess I feel more that way when I discuss disabilities. Everybody seems to put people with disabilities in one box, and that is a disaster to fail." There was a pause, and then he added, "I had somebody call me Sammy yesterday and then said, 'Well, you all look alike.' I decided to roll away before I said something."[1]

I hardly knew what to say. Here is an individual person with unique features, unique personality, unique gifts and talents, unique ways of seeing and being in the world, and he was reduced to "you all look alike." What this really says is, "You, disabled person, are fundamentally different from me, are part of a monolithic disabled group, and are not important enough to be noticed as a unique person. What is more, I do not think you are worth my time to pay attention to you so that I can distinguish you from other people." I hope you find this viewpoint shocking, and yet even more shocking should be the fact that this is not a unique occurrence for people with disabilities. Such a grouping not only *others* people with disabilities; it also objectifies them in ways that make abled people feel licensed to say and do things to the disabled that they would never want said or done to themselves.

To reach, incorporate, and partner with disabled people in the work and witness of the church, we must practice the disposition of truly seeing them. For Chris, this is the only starting point. "See the person first," he says. "Unless you do that, you aren't going to do anything because you get overwhelmed when you see and welcome the person. Get to know them well and get to know their gifts. . . . Training is great, and I'm for that, but you have to see the person and gifts in order to move forward." Seeing people is a practice because it requires intentionality and effort to put our *always/never* language and impulses in check and to give deferential and genuinely interested audience to the other. Let's listen in as my disabled friends teach us about what the practice of seeing people is and isn't.

SEEING REQUIRES SEEING

Perhaps it seems like a non sequitur to say we need to see people in order to practice seeing people, but it must be said. Our tendency is to talk *around* people or *about* people but not *to* people. We direct our gaze to the interpreter or the caregiver. We address questions to others we think can speak for the disabled person. We talk in third person (he/she) rather

---

[1]Chris, interview by author, November 22, 2024.

than second person or first person (you/me). Perhaps even, in our discomfort in encountering disability, we purposely distract ourselves with phones, sign-in sheets, or other duties. When we do, we aren't actually seeing. We are ignoring, as if the person in front of us were invisible, incapable of, or not deserving of our full respect or attention.

When Chris was a kid, one of his worst experiences with the church was that people who knew he had a communication device and had even conversed with him would direct conversation and eye contact to his parents or family. "That was like a punch in the gut," he says, to the point that when he was home on summer breaks from college and had the autonomy to make the decision for himself, he refused to go to that church anymore.

Andy and his wife had worked as missionaries in another country, gaining fluency in the language and actively pastoring, teaching, and mentoring. When they applied for a missionary visa, Andy appeared before a group of people from the evangelical fellowship of churches in their area who helped to facilitate the missionary visa process with the government. When it was his turn to answer their interview questions, it felt more like an interrogation. They probed him on things such as, "How do you evangelize?" and "How do you preach?" Originally Andy thought they were asking him about his theology, philosophy, and methodology of evangelism, but then it hit him—they were asking him questions related to ability and possibilities. They weren't sure he was capable of doing the work simply because he was blind. *Oh*, he thought, *they* literally *want to know how I'm doing these things*, to which he responded, "Through relationships. I meet people at the universities. I meet people out and about."[2]

Later, as he recalled the experience, he realized the questions he was asked were in the third person. They were not "How do you?" They were "How does he?" His wife told him later, "Andy, they weren't even looking at you. They were looking at me." Not surprisingly, even though the couple met all of the criteria and should have been approved, their first application was denied.

---

[2]Andy, interview by author, November 26, 2024.

Andy tried again.

> I've got [this country's] language, I've got the credentials, seminary equivalency. I've got ministry training. And so I go back with a local pastor who will advocate for me. And the panel from the evangelical fellowship ask similar questions, "Well, how can you preach?" My pastor friend then interrupts and asks, "Wait, what do you mean 'How can you preach?' We just help walk Andy to the front. He preaches. We help him get back to his seat. He preaches." It's like, what do you mean?

The local pastor continued to advocate for Andy, and in a follow-up conversation with the denomination's national leader, he even noted that the local people were attracted to Andy, his wife, and their baby daughter. The local pastor had no problem imagining that Andy could effectively evangelize and minister. The visa was again denied.

Even within his own denominational circles Andy has remained unseen at times. At a prayer gathering, Andy's pastor tried to give his prayer slot to Andy. The organizer, a person Andy had met before, replied, "Can he pray?" His dumbfounded pastor listed off Andy's credentials and she simply responded, "Oh, okay." Andy concludes: "People think if you can't see—this is common—that you can't hear. So they speak louder or speak to my wife [as if I can't hear]. But I think they also think if you can't see, you can't know, because we have these metaphors of 'seeing is understanding,' like, 'Oh, I see.' And so there's this, 'Oh, they don't see. Maybe they don't even know anything.'"

Lumping disability together and assuming a person who is disabled in one area is disabled in all areas sadly is a common initial reaction when people encounter disability, but all this succeeds in doing is pushing people away and creating yet another barrier to relationship both ways. Seeing people means that we stop and intentionally direct our gaze, our body posture, our focus, and our questions to the person. Until you see this person, they will only ever be a *he/she*, a *them*, a person *about* whom you think or talk. Even when you're not sure whether the person can comprehend or respond, make the person the priority and subject of your attention. Speak in ways that honor their personhood and agency.

Megan notes that her daughter Joy can communicate very effectively with her eyes. You miss this if you aren't focused on her. During a church service at Front Porch Church, a teenager with Down syndrome gave a "Yay God" testimony.[3] Rick's eye contact was fully on the young man. Though Rick had difficulty understanding everything the teenager said, Rick kept his eyes on the young man as he asked, "And helper?" The boy's mom began to clarify what was said, but all the time she spoke, Rick never took his eyes off the teenager. It was as if he were still talking. When she was done, Rick responded not to the mom but to the son.

The practice of seeing people really does require seeing them. Note that this is not to say that the blind and those with other visual impairments cannot "see people." It is our posture of attention and focus that demonstrate whether we have validated the person in front of us as a human being worthy of our respect, time, and attention. People with disabilities have agency because they share in the *imago Dei*. Only by posturing ourselves toward them and intentionally directing our gaze on them will we receive the blessing of their lives and have an opportunity to build fruitful relationships.

SEEING REQUIRES SEEING PEOPLE, NOT BROKEN BODIES

The practice of seeing requires seeing. However, it can be easy to see the wrong thing, to focus on the wrong starting point, to focus on bodies (which we assume are broken). Seeing requires seeing people, first and always.

> Growing up so visible in the church and people knowing my grandparents and feeling really close to my grandparents, they felt really close to me. And all of a sudden, it was people saying, "We'll pray for you." Or "God told me you're going to be healed." There was no "How are you?" It was just, "You're broken. I'm going to pray for you. You're going to be healed. It's going to be great," on one hand. But then, on the other hand, I had people saying that I must have done something. I must have angered God.

[3]During each service, there is an opportunity for church members to share a good moment from their week that they want to thank God for. After each person shares their testimony, the entire congregation says, "1-2-3 yay God!" while punching their fist into the air.

> Or you know, this is a learning lesson and I'm going to be so much stronger in my faith.[4]

Words similar to Hannah's were repeated over and over by the people I interviewed. In chapters two and three of this book, we talked about common responses to disability, but it bears repeating here. Starting with unwanted prayer, unsolicited judgment, or pithy encouragement is the quickest way to tell a disabled person you do not see them. Each of these is a *you always* or *you never* statement that undermines the ability to see people because such statements push people to the background and instead foreground perceived differences, which are then judged as inherently bad, unwanted, and broken.

"What are you saying to me every time you tell me you want me to be healed?" Hannah asks. "You're saying that I'm broken, and that I'm not living a full life, and that you're sorry for me." We may counter, "This isn't what I'm trying to say at all," but in reality this is what so many people with disabilities receive. "It can come from a good place," Hannah says. "It can still cause a lot of harm."

> For me to hear that people are still praying that I outgrow it or that I get better feels like a slap in the face because this is my body. This is who I am. This is how I was made, and I've decided it's not going limit me. When people say that "I'm gonna pray for you to be healed. I'm gonna pray for you for this," they're not asking me what *I* want. They are *assuming* they know what I want, and it feels like they're coming from the stance of "Oh, poor you. Your broken body." It's just not helpful. It makes me feel small when there's other things I would rather people be praying for, but they don't ask.

For Abby, the message that cure is God's will is antithetical to the gospel. "I don't think Christ taught that we need to be cured of our disabilities," she says, while noting that neither she nor her kids needs healing. To be told "you don't have enough faith, or that needs to be fixed, that needs to be cured, that needs to be healed," Abby says, is "an insidious message" that pushes people away from Christ rather than toward him.[5] Andy

---

[4]Hannah, interview by author, November 25, 2024.

[5]Abby, interview by author, December 6, 2024.

reminds us that healing and cure are two different things and that healing often is less about our physical selves and much more about a restored relationship with God and others.

When we start with bodies over people, it can lead toward theological judgments about others that are rarely true. It can lead us to assumptions about what a person wants and needs. It can lead us to assumptions about God's will for that person. It can keep us from considering whether the perceived difference is indeed bad or broken. It can keep us from taking time to listen to others to find out what they think about their disability and what they feel they need most. When we take the posture that we are normal and that others are broken and need to be fixed in order to come to God and experience God fully, we can even become oblivious to our own brokenness and to the places God wants to be at work in us (Mt 7:3-5).

Chris often feels like people "are looking for a show" when they forcibly pray for his healing.[6] Andy, who has been left questioning his own relationship with God from these encounters, has wondered whether sometimes these encounters are less about him and more about the other person. After a stranger at a conference kept praying for him and admonishing Andy to believe more and ask God for more faith, Andy, in his humble and kind way, was finally able to say "something that was deep in my heart for years. 'I *have* faith, and maybe *you* need more faith.'" Though he tried to be soft and meek in how he said it, Andy notes that underneath, "there was a little bit of an edge in how I felt about it. I was wanting to say, 'Leave me alone. I *have* faith. I feel fine between me and God. I'm not, this is not me that's begging this to be changed. It's *you* wanting to see some kind of sign and wonder. It's to grow your faith or to remind you that God is still at work.'"

Foregrounding "broken" bodies is an othering posture that turns the disabled into objects of rather than subjects in God's story. True evangelism never objectifies. When we practice seeing people, we will move from seeing differences in physical bodies to recognizing similarity in people just like us. This opens us up to listening before speaking, learning before acting, loving before all else.

---

[6]Chris, interview by author, November 22, 2024.

SEEING PEOPLE REQUIRES SLOWING DOWN

My grandmother was always on the go. She never did anything slowly. On vacation in Hawaii, the only Hawaiian word she picked up was *wiki*, which means "quick!" In fact, she could never say it once. It was always, "Wiki! Wiki!" Along the way, I picked this up too. When my kids ask what I'm doing I note, "I'm going to [insert task] real quick." I often chide my kids, "Hurry! Quick! Faster!" It was in watching a *CoComelon* song with my daughter that I uncomfortably saw myself. In the video, a dad is quietly sitting at the kitchen island enjoying his morning coffee when his alarm goes off. 7:30 a.m. Time to get the kids ready for their day. He rushes off singing, "Go, go, go!" and frantically shepherds the kids through various tasks in their morning routine. Every chorus from Dad declares, "There's no time," which is why hurry is the order of the day. At the end of each chorus, the kids turn up in a state of disarray, and with their exclamation of "Dad, uh oh!" they sing back the truth in a counter-chorus that they really do have the time in their day to slow things down and do them well.[7]

I took an immediate dislike to this song. (Okay, I take a dislike to most *CoComelon* songs, but that's another matter!) Too much of life is spent in the fast lane. Our cultural mantra is, "Go, go, go, there's no time. Speed up! Hurry!" We are stressed by details, deadlines, and destinations, and in this harried state we cannot and do not focus on the things that truly matter: people, presence, and the present. Disability forces us to slow down. If you don't, you simply will not engage. Period.

In his book *Becoming Friends of Time*, John Swinton breaks down the function of time and the ways we have commodified it to the point of sinfulness. "The time of the clock," he says, "has taught us to pay attention to the realm of time in ways that are grasping, utilitarian, instrumental, focused, selfish, and ultimately idolatrous."[8] When we live in a state of speediness, believing time is under our control and able to be wielded for progress, gain, wealth, and power, we inevitably view anyone who interrupts our time or slows it down as less-than. We cannot understand

[7]*CoComelon*, "School Morning Routine," written by Jessica Jean Kelly and Joshua Zimmerman.
[8]John Swinton, *Becoming Friends of Time: Disability, Timefullness, and Gentle Discipleship* (Baylor University Press, 2016), 57.

how less or no productivity or profit can equal a quality of life that is worth preserving, worth living, or worth learning from. In a worldview of "industrial, commodified evolutionary time" that believes people "should not be a burden or a handicap on others (we must not retard the progress of others)," the people who do slow us down become disposable and expendable.

> How could you possibly enjoy your time on earth and be enjoyable to others if you cannot produce anything? How could you possibly be the person you used to be if you cannot do or think in the way you used to think? How could you possibly enjoy life when you move so slowly and cannot think quickly? The suggestion that we are a burden on others because we cannot contribute is simply another way of saying that the way in which persons with profound disabilities use their time is incompatible with current temporal assumptions and expectations.[9]

We saw this only too clearly during the days of the Covid-19 pandemic, when overwhelmed hospitals were in threat of running out of lifesaving ventilators and other equipment and medicines. Much like in wartime triage, they prioritized people according to who would be most likely to survive given the treatment. In setting up their ranking, people with intellectual and developmental disabilities, regardless of age, were always put on the rejection list. The reason? People with disabilities had no quality of life and contributed little to society. Why use up precious lifesaving resources that could be given to an otherwise healthy, productive adult?[10] For some, they denied care even when rationing was not even needed.[11]

We may distance ourselves from this extreme view that disabled life is expendable and even better off dead. However, we often move at a speed that places every other person and priority above a mind or body that slows us down or disrupts our goals. We move as if time were ours and

---

[9]Swinton, *Becoming Friends of Time*, 52.

[10]Samuel R. Bagenstos, "Who Gets the Ventilator? Disability Discrimination in COVID 19 Medical-Rationing Protocols," *The Yale Law Journal Forum*, May 27, 2020, www.yalelawjournal.org/forum/who-gets-the-ventilator.

[11]As one example, see Joseph Shapiro, "Oregon Hospitals Didn't Have Shortages. So Why Were Disabled People Denied Care?" NPR, December 21, 2020, www.npr.org/2020/12/21/946292119/oregon-hospitals-didnt-have-shortages-so-why-were-disabled-people-denied-care.

as if the outcomes of controlling it were what matters most. We want to move and we want to move now. This is as true in the church as it is in the world.

Though Joy can understand many things she hears at an age-appropriate level and can communicate through an AAC using her eyes, her apraxia causes a slowness to her response. "It can be difficult for her to respond in some ways because people have to wait, really give her a chance to answer," Megan says.

> *It takes time to tell somebody that*, "Well, you may need to give her *up to a minute* to respond." That *feels like an eternity*, you know, for one of us to stand there and be like "What's she going to do?" It's also *hard not to repeat a question over and over*, but you really are not supposed to. You're supposed to say it and assume that she's understood and *wait for her to respond.* But it's like her mind knows the response and wants to, but to carry it out, whether that's getting her arm to reach out or getting her to choose which thing she wants or whatever, *it just takes time and it varies.*
>
> And *it's giving her the opportunity* to do that. That's a challenge, you know. And of course, in the church environment, you don't have people that are highly trained in something. They've just wanted to help and so you're kind of giving them the basics. But in the young kids' classroom *things move quickly*. So that's a real challenge anywhere that we are, *to give her that time and space to be able to keep up*.[12]

Notice how many *time* thoughts are in Megan's account (see the italicized phrases). To interact with Joy, there is a need for time to train, time to wait, and time to respond. But note that it's a challenge because there is only time to give *basic* training to others, waiting one minute for a response makes everyone feel antsy, and things move quickly in the children's classroom. Everywhere Joy goes, she experiences people that struggle to "give her that time and space to be able to keep up." Megan, who knows the beauty of the perspective, pace, and pure love that "just exudes" from Joy, says,

> It can be hard because if people don't give her the time to show that. They never see that. But we see that because we're with her in the day-to-day

[12]Megan, interview by author, January 14, 2025.

> and we have to slow down and give her those opportunities. And it's just, I don't even know the word to describe it. It is a life-changing thing because you're watching her and it just brings a new perspective and kind of aligns that perspective more with the heart of God.

What is that new perspective Joy gives? "Really taking time for other humans and seeing their value, that we don't need to be caught up with all the things of the world so easily that we get distracted with."

In a similar way, Swinton argues that disability moves us toward the heart of God when it slows us down to the speed of God. He notes, "Time is not an impersonal, free-floating commodity intended for the satiation of human desire. It is an aspect of God's relationship with the world, a gift from a loving Creator. . . . As an aspect of God's love, *the purpose of time is to facilitate and sustain love*."[13] In fact, we find time redeemed in Jesus. Jesus steps into the world at "the fulness of time" (Gal 4:4 KJV), a moment Judith Shulevitz says "is the moment when God (through Christ and the Holy Spirit) invades the present and fills it with his presence."[14] Jesus' incarnation tells us that "time matters eternally because Jesus opens its fullness up to the world and draws creation into the heart of God. In Jesus we have the opportunity truly to become timefull people."[15]

Scott Bader-Saye notes how the ways we "experience, name, and interpret time contribute to the kinds of communities we imagine and inhabit."[16] Where the world's view of time pushes us to discount, dismiss, and even dispense of the disabled, in Christ, "Christians are called to learn to inhabit the world in quite particular ways and come to engage with time in ways that are distinctively different from those of people who have bought into different narratives that produce different kinds of time."[17] Namely, we are called to share in Jesus' redemptive work by shaping and forming our communities according to God's view of time. Only by recognizing time properly will we move

---

[13]Swinton, *Becoming Friends of Time*, 58, emphasis original.

[14]Judith Shulevitz, *The Sabbath World: Glimpses of a Different Order of Time* (Random House, 2011), 98.

[15]Swinton, *Becoming Friends of Time*, 63.

[16]Scott Bader-Saye, "Figuring Time: Providence and Politics," in *Liturgy, Time, and the Politics of Redemption*, ed. Randi Rashkover and C. C. Pecknold (Eerdmans, 2006), 98.

[17]Swinton, *Becoming Friends of Time*, 63.

> away from idolatry and violence toward faithful timefullness. Those who are made in God's image have time for one another. To give generously of one's time—to care, notice, value, and appreciate time—is to adopt the attitude of Jesus and to begin to tune one's body into the cadence of God's time and the redemption of all time. To live into God's image is, at least in part, to learn what it means to live within the Creator's time. When the world is looked at in this way, those things that we name "disability" begin to look very different.[18]

Offering us a new option, Swinton says that instead of thinking of time as money (power, productivity, fill in the blank), we should think of time as love. God's own unique relationship with time (with time occurring in God, not the other way around) means that God takes the time he needs to complete his work.[19] The apostle Peter reminds us that God "is not slow in keeping his promises, as some understand slowness. Instead he is patient with you" (1 Pet 3:9 NIV). Many of us have shared this lament at God's slowness, wondering why, in our world full of days, hours, minutes, and seconds, God has not already stepped in. But God's promises and work are steadfast even if we perceive his actions to take a long time. Only by learning to walk the same speed as God will we be able to live within the Creator's time. Listen, once again, to Swinton:

> The average speed that a human being walks at is three miles per hour. In his earthly experience, Jesus, who is God, who *is* love, walked at three miles per hour. There is nothing to suggest that he has speeded up following the ascension. We may choose to live our lives very quickly. "When time is money, speed equals more of it." We may choose to stigmatize, alienate, downgrade, and exclude people for taking up too much of our time—for being slow in pace, speech, wit, or intellect—but in the face of the three-mile-an-hour God, such ways of being in the world become revelatory of what it means to love and to be fully human. The reality is that, when time is love, speed equals *less* of it. The love of God is inexorably slow. Jesus walked slowly: Love takes time.[20]

---

[18]Swinton, *Becoming Friends of Time*, 65.
[19]Swinton, *Becoming Friends of Time*, 61.
[20]Swinton, *Becoming Friends of Time*, 68-69, emphasis original.

Too many church leaders, church members, and church functions are in the fast lane. Sundays and special events are broken down into minutes so that we can accomplish the many goals we've laid out for classes, worship services, and outreach. We feel pressed to get through the material and to keep things moving. There is little or no space built in for pause. We become impatient with those who disrupt, slow down, or impede our plans, and we become upset, even angry, when our plans get upended completely. Our enslavement to time shifts our gaze from people to production quality, leaving less space for people we perceive as slowing, disrupting, and derailing our agenda. We justify our speed and its many consequences by saying "we're just doing the Lord's work to reach as many as possible," but when our speed leaves out large swaths of people (many of whom are judged as the last and least), we do not do God's work.

"I think the world's watching how we treat others," Andy says, "and I think we communicate things to the world. And the way we design church for efficiency and so on. Who is welcome? If these people are not welcome, there's implicit communication that then maybe others who don't have it all together aren't welcome, or others who would take more time to care for." Love takes time, and "faithful discipleship is slow and attentive to the things that pass us by when we insist on traveling at high speed. There is a great power in slowness."[21] The practice of seeing people is also a practice of slowing down.

SEEING PEOPLE REQUIRES RESPECT FOR BODIES AND BOUNDARIES

When we take the time to slow down and see people, we will inevitably see bodies. I have already admonished you to see people first and always, but this does not negate the fact that when we slow down enough to travel with others, we will become attuned to bodies. In one sense, this is nothing new. We notice bodies all the time. We notice people's skin color, hair styles, weight, physical fitness, smiles, gait, and so on. Perhaps certain bodies stand out (as when a young man notices a girl he'd like to

[21]Swinton, *Becoming Friends of Time*, 69.

ask out on a date), but overall, even when we may make a few internal judgments, we are relatively unbothered by other bodies. People come in all colors, shapes, and sizes. However, people with disabilities find their bodies scrutinized all the time. What is their disability? How debilitating is it? Is it enough of a disability? Do they even have a disability or are they making it up? How does it compare to my experiences? How is it affecting their appearance? How is their appearance changing? Because people with disabilities are seen as fundamentally *other*, their bodies are deemed fair game for the abled to judge, speak about, and touch. These violations of bodies and boundaries are demeaning, unwanted, unjust, and just plain wrong.

My son has become very aware of his size. Both his inherited genetics from his birth parents and the added effect of Down syndrome mean that my son will always be much shorter than those of his age. He rarely appears on the average growth chart and is in only the twenty-fifth percentile for the Down syndrome chart. At age seven, he was just reaching 5T clothes and toddler size-ten shoes. My son is perfectly proportioned and growing in expected and even ways. His size is not problematic until it is compared to others with the assumption that their height/size is best. Without considering whether tiny really is problematic or just different, people everywhere feel free to comment on how "tiny, small, little, short" he is. Strangers and friends ask, "How old are you?" When my son responds they say with shock, "Oh! You're so tiny!" When he hears this, I notice now that his face falls and he gets sad. Others don't always perceive this, but I do. Every once in a while, I accidentally call him "little boy" in the same way I call my daughter "little girl," but he now pushes back. "I'm not little. I'm big." We may dismiss this as something that happens when we talk about kids, but this matters immensely to him and will be a pain point going forward as long as people continue to focus on size as a matter of importance. If people aren't careful, this and other judgments about his appearance and abilities will become barriers that keep him othered in our minds and ostracized in his.

In US culture, we rarely find weight gain and weight loss an open topic. Unless the person initiates or we are such intimate friends that we regularly have this conversation, we just do not talk about weight. It is a sensitive topic. And yet, for people with disabilities, their bodies are on display and people often make comments as if their bodies were open for discussion. "I encourage people to think about what they're saying before they say it," Hannah says.

> I've had lots of people come up to me and say, "You look great. You've gained weight. You look great. You've lost weight. You look great." And they're trying to be encouraging and I understand they're trying to say you look great. But to have somebody basically say what amounts to, "I'm constantly watching you and I've seen that you've gained weight, you've lost weight" . . . it just, that's not kind. That is damaging.

People with disabilities also find their own experiences questioned and judged. Hannah faces constant skepticism from family and friends who believe her health issues are just her being "dramatic." It has taken time for her immediate family to get to a place where they believe her without question when she says she can't do something (with the understanding that she won't say she can't do something when she can). Others, however, constantly question her conditions and are skeptical of the diagnoses and their severity.

One girl in her youth group early on dismissed Hannah's four-month migraine by saying, "I have migraines and I go to school. I don't know why she can't just go to school." Post-Covid has led to an increase in POTS diagnoses, and many tell Hannah, "I have POTS, and it's not that bad." The problem is that Hannah has more things going on than just POTS, but even if it were just POTS, as she rightly points out, the symptoms and severity differ from person to person. Hannah says with hurt and frustration, "I should not have to give you every single diagnosis for you to be, 'Oh, her POTS is her POTS, and mine is mine.'" This invasion of medical history, symptoms, and experience is a regular occurrence for the disabled. With access to things such as WebMD, everyone has become an expert in diagnosis and treatment. For people with disabilities, it is demeaning and dismissive of their experiences.

People with hidden disabilities also face judgment when asking for accommodations others deem unnecessary. The assumptions can be brutal. Hannah recalls,

> I was in the city for six weeks. I was doing rehab, and my mom and I were taking the bus back and forth from where we were staying in the hospital. And we got on the bus, and it was packed, and I am not able to stand for a long time. So I needed a seat, and there was one seat available. It was next to a mom who had a stroller, but you couldn't get to the seat. All of a sudden, I think she realized I needed it, and she just got up and let me sit. But there were two women who were saying horrible things under their breath about me, about how dare I make a mom get up. I just don't understand. I got horrible looks and I had to sit there and try not to cry. And all I could think is, *Fine. You know what? Let me stand, and I'll pass out, and then we'll have to call an EMT and you'll be late to wherever you're going. But then at least I didn't take the seat and you'll feel better. I'm sorry I don't look the way you want me to.* But it's . . . do you think I would make a mom get up out of her seat? Does this seem like I want to? Does this seem like I love this?

When we turn people with disabilities into objects of scrutiny, they can even face unwanted touches. Uninvited prayer leads many to place hands on the disabled without consent. When trying to solve access dilemmas, some may pick up a person in a wheelchair and physically move them to a new space or floor without having first consulted the person to find a collaborative solution or ask permission. None of us welcomes unwanted touch, but when we objectify disabled people, we can easily cross body boundaries we would never want violated for ourselves.

In the practice of seeing people, we must honor the bodies before us as sacred, made in God's image, and deserving of the utmost respect. We should not pry into people's medical histories to accommodate and welcome. We should not comment on how much weight a person has gained or lost. We should not express shocked opinions on someone's appearance or height. We should not initiate touch without permission. We should not pray for healing without invitation. By honoring bodies and boundaries, we honor people and the many diverse ways they are embodied.

SEEING PEOPLE REQUIRES LISTENING

In seeing people, there is one thing we should be quick to do: listen. In James 1:19 we are admonished to be "quick to listen, slow to speak, and slow to get angry." Too often we reverse this and are quick to anger, which leads to rash talk and closed ears. Or we strategize our reply while the other person is talking, which keeps us from hearing and often leads to incorrect responses. Or we start to listen but, without taking the time to understand what is said, get defensive and respond harshly. Being quick to listen, accompanied by slow speech and slow anger, will require humility to listen with wide-open, nonjudgmental ears, circumspectness to see ourselves and our churches in new (and often painful) ways, and a willingness to enter into the pain of others to the point of repentance and collaborative action. Genuine listening is one way we follow Paul's exhortation to mirror one another's emotions, weeping and bearing together in suffering (Rom 12:12, 14). Only through the kind of listening that beholds "the pain and the suffering disabled people and their families have felt and continue to feel in their daily lives" will we ever be able to have authentic ministry among the disabled.[22]

When I asked what she would want to say to pastors and churches about disability if given the chance, Hannah reflected for a moment and then said,

> For those who are entering *truly* because they want to, *truly* from a good place, they're entering an already-old conversation for that person that they're speaking to or that community that they're trying to connect to. It's new to you. You've just started. You're new to the conversation. But I'm already hearing everybody's who's told me I'm lesser, I'm sinful, I deserve this, I'm not a part. I'm already hearing all of that, and so they're working with us, but it's our voice. It might be painful for them. It's hard to hear that you or the church that you're a part of might have caused harm. I can think of several churches who are great places for some people and are deeply damaging in my story. There are churches I cannot step into any more. And so for churches that are stepping into this to know that it's painful and it's . . . I have fought tooth and nail to get where I am in my relationship with God, in my relationship with the church, and that there's a lot of voices at the table and not all of them have faces. There's a lot of ghosts whispering in my ear. [pause] And space and grace and kindness and understanding that it's not you. And that I might not know, we might

[22]Erin Raffety, *From Inclusion to Justice: Disability, Ministry, and Congregational Leadership* (Baylor University Press, 2022), 67.

> not know. You have to go in to actually listen and to talk to the person instead of from whatever [pause], wherever you think it's going, it's not going. It's just not. It's a conversation, and you can't have a goal.

Hannah has said a lot in this comment. It is important for us to hear and understand what she's communicated. First, for any person genuinely desiring to engage in relationship and ministry with people with disabilities, you can't come in thinking you know what people's experiences are and with an action plan you're ready to implement. That is not listening. That is simply trading "pain for problem-solving, so eager are we to resolve this pain, sweep it under the rug, and move forward."[23] Instead, Hannah, says you have to start from the place that you don't know.

Second, Hannah notes that this conversation and space that is new to you is an old, ongoing conversation. The disabled have their own stories of disablement, their own experiences of exclusion, rejection, pain, suffering, isolation, and injustice, and they share in the experiences of others in the disabled community. There are stories and experiences that need to be told and that you need to hear, which means, third, you have to be willing to hear and receive the hard things. This is where James 1:19 comes into play. You will want to defend, deny, deflect, defer, and disagree, but you can't. The only starting place is willing acknowledgment of the pains, hurts, and harm people have experienced, not just in the world but in the church. In this moment, you will be tempted to jump to solutions. Stop. Be quick to listen, slow to respond in ways *you* think are appropriate, and slow to defensive anger. Rather, as Hannah suggests, it is a time for space, grace, kindness, and understanding.

Hannah's words beautifully and powerfully reflect Erin Raffety's call for listening beyond inclusion and beyond rebuke. "In our breakneck, problem-solving culture," she says, "even churches have jumped too quickly to trying to fix disabled exclusion, isolation, and ministry without really listening." As we learned in the last chapter, this can lead to accommodations without having practiced accommodation. Genuine listening, Raffety argues, will "involve not just active reflection but also

---

[23]Raffety, *From Inclusion to Justice*, 67.

introspection, repentance, and confession if the church is to move [forward] in doing justice with disabled people."[24]

To reach people with disabilities, we must take on the practice of regular, genuine listening sessions with the disabled among us. This can be hard and painful, but only in receiving their lament, their rebuke, and their wisdom will we, in partnership with the disabled, become places of gospel hospitality for people of all abilities. Raffety says,

> Churches cannot afford to sell the gospel for inclusion but must do the risky work of turning toward God by not turning away from disabled people's hurt, pain, and even critique. It is also important to be clear that what warrants lamenting is the way in which the church has participated in the isolation and exclusion of disabled people, alongside other experiences for such people in the world. What is not being lamented is disability itself.[25]

PRACTICING "SEEING PEOPLE" IN EVANGELISM

In Mark 5:21-42, we have the story of two people simultaneously vying for Jesus' help. Jairus, a prestigious leader in the synagogue, asks Jesus to heal his twelve-year-old daughter, who is dying. Jesus starts to go with him. It's likely the pace is even slower than the normal three miles an hour because Mark tells us a large crowd is pressing all around him.

As he walks, an impoverished women pushes her way through the crowd toward Jesus. For the same twelve years Jarius's daughter has been alive, this woman has suffered from a debilitating bleeding disorder that has resulted in her poverty and isolation. Everywhere she goes she must announce her unclean state. Her desperation has led her to doctor after doctor, but instead of a cure, she has suffered in their care, spent all the money she had, and grown worse. As she approaches Jesus, she thinks, *If I can just touch the hem of his robe, I'll be healed.* She reaches out, and immediately her bleeding stops, and she knows her suffering is done.

But then, with great fear, she notices Jesus has stopped moving. He realizes healing power has gone out of him, and he turns in the crowd asking, "Who touched me?" Everyone is incredulous. He is in a press of

---

[24]Raffety, *From Inclusion to Justice*, 85, 81.

[25]Raffety, *From Inclusion to Justice*, 84.

people. Everyone is touching him. But Jesus is not satisfied, and Mark says Jesus keeps looking to see who has done it. The woman finally steps forward, trembling with fear, and tells him her story. Jesus responds, "Daughter, your faith has healed you. Go in peace and be freed from your suffering."

At the same moment Jesus is having this conversation, people from Jairus's home come with the news: "Forget it. Don't bother with Jesus. Your daughter is dead." But before Jairus can respond, Jesus says, "Don't be afraid, just believe." Taking Peter, James, and John with him, Jesus travels on to Jairus's home and enters the daughter's room. Jesus takes her hand and calls to her, "Little girl, get up." Immediately she stands up and starts walking around the room.

I love this story for so many reasons. I tell it here because it demonstrates so many of the things we have said about the practice of seeing people. We have two people in dire need. One is a powerful, able-bodied man who has a dying daughter. The other is a disabled woman without money. Jesus is in the middle of a crowd by the lake, no doubt healing and teaching. When Jesus hears Jairus's desperation, he immediately responds. But in his going, he is not distracted by his goal, by the power of the person he is helping, or even the press of this ministry need.

The moment he feels healing power leave his body, Jesus stops. He is looking, searching, eager to find the person. He never asks, "Why did you touch me?" He asks, "Who touched me?" He individualizes the encounter and searches until she is found. When she comes forward, Jesus doesn't back away or tell her to leave or tell her to clean up. He does not call her unholy. He also doesn't ask, "Why did you distract me? Don't you know I'm going to heal a little girl?" In that moment, he has eyes and attention and listening ears only for this woman. He listens to her story. The whole story, Mark says. And again, Jesus doesn't rebuke or discount it. He doesn't tell her, "You should haven't touched me because you were unclean and you've made everyone else unclean by being here." No, his first word is one of fellowship and community. He gives this nameless woman a new name, "Daughter." He says she belongs, and then he passes the peace to her, sending her off healed (not just cured). Only then does

Jesus resume his response to Jairus, which leads to the daughter being raised from the dead.

What happens in this scene is what should happen when we practice seeing people. Sadly, so much in our practice of mission and outreach has failed to do this. We see broken bodies that need to be fixed before they can belong. We see disability as a detriment to our mission, our plan, or our production quality, and we either move the disabled aside or ask them to leave. We fail to listen to the pains and hurts people with disabilities are experiencing and try to accommodate our way over them. We become so enslaved to *doing* that we cannot hear people with disabilities calling us toward *being*. Said another way, when encountering people with disabilities, we don't see people; we see distractions.

But the practice of seeing people in Jesus' own example with Daughter calls us to just the opposite. Here I love something Rick says over and over at Front Porch Church and whenever and wherever he talks about encounters with people of all abilities: "There are no distractions, only interactions."

There are no distractions, only interactions. This gets to the heart of seeing people. When we look at every person we meet as an interaction rather than a distraction, we are not bothered by the noises and disruptions. We are not closed to their experiences of joy, pain, celebration, and hurt. We are not concerned by our agenda, plans, and tasks. We are not afraid to listen and receive tough corrections. Rather, we are turned to see people and ready to encounter God in new ways as we stop, listen, respect, and respond together in Christ and for Christ. Only then can we ever reach out. In seeing and receiving the ministry and work of the disabled already among us, we will be ready and able to see and receive the disabled who are still on that journey to Christ.

DISCUSSION QUESTIONS

1. How hard is it to see people? Does disability make this easier or harder? How do you think you should respond to people with disabilities so that you see them, see their bodies, but don't problematize their bodies?

2. Are you caught by the spirit of hurry? In what ways do you need to slow down? With whom do you need to slow down? How might slowing down be practiced as a spiritual discipline?
3. Imagine you're listening to a disabled person, and they tell you that you have hurt or offended them through actions that promote ableism (even though you try to be intentional about inclusion). How can you practice listening so you can receive the hard information while being slow to respond (with a fix) and slow to get angry and defensive (Jas 1:19)? What listening and receptive skills do you want to work on?
4. How can you and your church practice the idea that there are no distractions, only interactions?
5. In what ways will you practice seeing people? What things do you specifically want to start doing, keep doing, or stop doing?

13

The Practice of Interdependence

Our first two practices, the practice of accommodation and the practice of seeing people, call us to look beyond ourselves to genuinely recognize and honor the people of all abilities we encounter. The last practice calls us to reorder our own lives. In a nutshell, the practice of interdependence says we are not whole without the disabled. I hesitate to write this in a way that sounds as if the work of interdependence were only the work of the abled to receive the disabled. This is not at all what I mean. Interdependence is a two-way street; everybody needs everybody else. I stick with this phrasing for the moment to highlight that too often the abled view disabilities as something to manage, accommodate, avoid, or reject. It is rare that abled people and churches recognize they are not whole without having the disabled in their lives and receiving the true mutuality and reciprocity of those relationships. But without the disabled as part of our church's work, withness, and witness, our churches are disabled and unable to witness to the fullness of God's kingdom and to receive in full those God wants in his kingdom.

Many of us struggle with interdependence because it calls us to embrace vulnerability and dependence, things our world says are antithetical to successful, meaningful lives. The best stories are those of self-made people who beat the odds, work hard, and end up as champions. The tragedies are those who can never muster the willpower or physical power to overcome, or those who lose their independence through accident, violence, or illness. The saddest stories are those who must depend on others, robbing those others of independence without ever gaining their own. But interdependence, as a major part of God's upside-down kingdom, flips the script on the world and says what the world promotes is myth.

Andrew Draper notes, "People are neither self-made nor simply recipients of the good graces of others. People exist in community; we are necessarily mutually interdependent. Nobody creates herself; we are who we are according to God's Word revealed in the particularity of our circumstances, families, cultures, places, and histories."[1] We become who we were meant to be by submitting to the mutuality of the *whole* body of Christ. If we have only able bodies around us, we are disabled from seeing the world fully and as God sees it. We are interdependent whether we realize it or not. It is in practicing interdependence that we begin seeing ourselves and others as God intended, and only through doing this can we enter into the gospel story, able to show, share, and live the full gospel in the church and in the world.

BELONGING TO ONE ANOTHER

In our best efforts, we may work for disability inclusion, but if this is our sole lens and goal, we will fail. Inclusion language maintains an us-them divide that retains power on the side of the abled. Inclusion makes space for the other to come into *our* space, receive accommodation, and participate from the position of a subordinate beneficiary. The Bible calls Christians to something different. We are to be members of one another.[2]

After his robust theological argument in Romans 1–11—that Jews and Gentiles alike are fallen into sin and that God's grace, not our works, is the sole means for saving and justifying us before God—Paul moves his letter to the implications this saving work has for how we live "in view of God's mercy" (Rom 12:1 NIV).

> Offer your bodies as a living sacrifice, holy and pleasing to God—this is your true and proper worship. Do not conform to the pattern of this world,

---

[1]Andrew T. Draper, Jody Michele, and Andrea Mae, *Disabling Leadership: A Practical Theology for the Broken Body of Christ* (IVP Academic, 2023), 65.

[2]Brian Brock, *Wondrously Wounded: Theology, Disability, and the Body of Christ* (Baylor University Press, 2020), 201; see also Erin Raffety, *From Inclusion to Justice: Disability, Ministry, and Congregational Leadership* (Baylor University Press, 2022).

but be transformed by the renewing of your mind. Then you will be able to test and approve what God's will is—his good, pleasing and perfect will.

For by the grace given me I say to every one of you: Do not think of yourself more highly than you ought, but rather think of yourself with sober judgment, in accordance with the faith God has distributed to each of you. For just as each of us has one body with many members, and these members do not all have the same function, so in Christ we, though many, form one body, and each member belongs to all the others. We have different gifts, according to the grace given to each of us. If your gift is prophesying, then prophesy in accordance with your faith; if it is serving, then serve; if it is teaching, then teach; if it is to encourage, then give encouragement; if it is giving, then give generously; if it is to lead, do it diligently; if it is to show mercy, do it cheerfully.

Love must be sincere. Hate what is evil; cling to what is good. Be devoted to one another in love. Honor one another above yourselves. Never be lacking in zeal, but keep your spiritual fervor, serving the Lord. Be joyful in hope, patient in affliction, faithful in prayer. Share with the Lord's people who are in need. Practice hospitality.

Bless those who persecute you; bless and do not curse. Rejoice with those who rejoice; mourn with those who mourn. Live in harmony with one another. Do not be proud, but be willing to associate with people of low position. Do not be conceited.

Do not repay anyone evil for evil. Be careful to do what is right in the eyes of everyone. If it is possible, as far as it depends on you, live at peace with everyone. Do not take revenge, my dear friends, but leave room for God's wrath, for it is written: "It is mine to avenge; I will repay," says the Lord. On the contrary:

"If your enemy is hungry, feed him;
  if he is thirsty, give him something to drink.
In doing this, you will heap burning coals on his head."

Do not be overcome by evil, but overcome evil with good. (Rom 12:1-21 NIV)

In every way, this is countercultural. It is important we sit with this chapter.

The first thing Paul notes is that everything about us is in view of God's mercy. It is not our work, our abilities, our appearance, our talents, anything about us. It is God's mercy toward us that makes our lives and work possible. Already this levels the playing field because whatever we thought we could offer God is not enough to save us (Rom 3:23). Rather, we "all are justified freely by *his* grace through the redemption that came by Christ Jesus" (Rom 3:24 NIV).

But next, note that Paul (Rom 12:1) pleads with us to present our *bodies* to God as a living sacrifice. We are to give of our whole selves to God and present our bodies in all their diverse abilities, shapes, colors, and sizes to God as an act of "true and proper worship" (Rom 12:2 NIV). Again, there is not a distinguishing of able bodies from disabled bodies. Rather, having been found equal at the foot of the cross, we now equally offer our bodies (and thus the ways in which others experience our embodiment) to God. It does not seem surprising, then, that on the heels of this Paul admonishes us to "not conform to the pattern of the world" in our thinking (Rom 12:2 NIV). Our bodies and our minds are not to be at the mercy of the world, living into the exaltation of self and the diminishment of those we deem lesser. Rather, our minds and bodies should be conformed to the new pattern of God's kingdom.

In this kingdom, Paul says, we should be honest about ourselves, not thinking better of ourselves than we are (Rom 12:3). We are only because Christ is. If this is true, then our place in the church, in Christ's body, is not because we have earned a spot or been promoted to ever higher positions through our gifts, abilities, or popularity. We are in Christ's body because he has placed us there, and in his grace and by his Spirit he gives us the gifts we need to participate in a healthy, functioning, body of Christ (Rom 12:4-8). But note, Paul does not use "serve" language with regard to our gifts. He does not say we have gifts in order to serve one another (as much as the use of our God-given gifts *should* serve one another). Rather, Paul says our gifts and functions are given to us because "each member *belongs* to all the others" (Rom 12:5 NIV).

Each member—in all their strengths and weaknesses, in their maturity and immaturity, in their wealth and poverty, in their abilities and disabilities—each member belongs *to all the others*. There is no way around this. If we are in Christ, we belong to all the others. We need each other. We are bound to each other. We are broken without each other. This is a hard message.

Belonging is simultaneously beautiful and challenging. The only way this belonging to one another works is for us to sincerely love by hating what is evil (e.g., dismissing, avoiding, rejecting, or looking down on disability and difference) and clinging to what is good (Rom 12:9). We do this by devoting ourselves and being loyal to others, honoring people of all abilities *above* ourselves (Rom 12:10). We do this by serving the Lord (and thus others) with zeal (Rom 12:11). We do this through dispositions that respond to one another's circumstances and suffering, with hope, patience, and faithful prayer (Rom 12:12; note that it says faithful prayer, not unwanted prayer for healing and deliverance). We do this by sharing with others in their need and practicing true, two-way-street hospitality (Rom 12:13). We will bless in the face of persecution and curses (Rom 12:14). We will enter into the experiences of others (Rom 12:15). We will live in harmony, surrendering our pride and conceit to become true associates of those the world calls least (Rom 12:16). We will live righteously and peaceably, repaying evil and vengeance with good (Rom 12:17).

If you haven't caught the vision yet, reread this section again and again until you do. God says we are missing something if we only ever have one type of person in our midst. We are failing to be the body of Christ if we have ranking in our midst. We are failing to be the body of Christ if the abled do not belong to the disabled and the disabled do not belong to the abled. We are failing to be the body of Christ if we do not receive the ministry of one another. We are failing to be the body of Christ if we look around us and see hostility, judgment, cliques, self-promotion, impatience, stinginess, inhospitality, cursing, disharmony, pride, and unchecked independence.

It can be easy to dismiss this difficult list and think, *Of course we are welcoming, hospitable, and loving.* But Brock surmises that one of the most likely reasons "why there are not more disabled people in our churches is that our unredeemed feelings and attitudes toward individuals with disabilities have somehow leaked out, through our looks and maybe even our actions, a message that people with disabilities are somehow not *really* welcome in our churches."[3] One of the prophetic gifts that

[3]Brian Brock, *Disability: Living into the Diversity of Christ's Body* (Baker Academic, 2021), 27.

people with disabilities bring to the church is the revelation of how well the church is actually living into its calling. Brock says,

> Stop asking about people with disabilities, especially those with learning difficulties, "What are they thinking? What are they intending?" Instead, start watching what *happens* to people around them.
>
> Don't ask, "Does Johnny with autism really understand what is going on in church?" Watch who responds when he seems to be agitated. Watch who squirms when he makes funny noises and complains to others. Who accompanies him to church? How does the pastor relate to Johnny? Such questions reveal the nervous connections that define the essence of the church—or what the church lacks.[4]

Think about how you respond differently when someone belongs to you. You are watching for their presence. You are ready to help when they need a hand. You are generous with your time and money. You can anticipate how they will experience some situations. You come ready with tissues and open arms when they are upset or hurt. You make sure they are safe and where they need to be. You protect them. You fight for them when they are mistreated. You make allowances for them that you might not for others. You look for them when you have needs and hurt. It's their presence that calms your anxious heart. You are ready to receive their love, their time, their gifts, and their wisdom. At times our actions in belonging may feel lopsided. As a mom, I give and do and am for my kids without equal reciprocity of actual time and action in return. But lopsided actions do not mean I somehow belong more to my kids than they do to me. I may give more in some areas, but their gifts back to me are monumental in their own ways. There is no gradation in our belonging.

Imagine this kind of mutual belonging at work in the church. It is not easy. Being family can bring friction, which is why Paul admonishes us toward love, deference, and humility. But when we capture the true nature of Christ's body, we cannot do anything else. This perspective challenges our conformity to the world and calls us to look for others to be present and to honor them when they come.

---

[4]Brock, *Disability*, 128.

Think about how the practice of interdependence would have changed the church's response to my mom. Rather than telling her to wait outside until worship was done, they would have asked, "Who is being excluded by the ways in which we are doing this practice? How can we ensure that people aren't forced to the lobby and left out of the body?" Think about how the practice of interdependence would have changed the church's response to Abby and her friend. Rather than seeing a young girl's vocalizations as a distraction to others, if she belonged to them, they would have welcomed her worship and sought ways to join in the diversity of praise being offered to God rather than sitting in judgment over their disrupted decorum. A church with this kind of focus would make sure that in all they did, including their outreach and evangelism, they would be asking, "Who does this include, and who does this exclude?"

Who in your church do you need to be intentional about claiming and belonging to? Only when we can say Chris, Abby, Joy, Hannah, Rick, and Andy *belong* to us and us to them will we have the space to reach out to the many people with disabilities who should also belong in God's house.

EMBRACING VULNERABILITY

One of the challenges of belonging "to all the others" is that we are forced to reckon with vulnerability. We are uncomfortable with others who openly display vulnerabilities and often hide our own because we are taught that vulnerability is bad. Vulnerabilities reveal weakness and imperfections—again, qualities that are antithetical to a culture that values productivity, achievement, and ideal bodies. This is one reason we so often resort to the medical model of disability and try to fix disability and pray for healing. However, "The evasion of vulnerability is fatal to the church," Brock says, because "it hurts disabled people directly. . . . It also falsifies the life-giving gospel of Jesus."[5]

In talking about things she's heard from the pulpit, Abby says the ways we preach healing narratives are problematic. Not only do they elevate bodily fixing (cure) over community restoration (healing), but they also

[5]Brock, *Disability*, 27.

lead us to preach that "we shouldn't have any limitations, and we should never admit a limitation and never be vulnerable." But Abby reminds us that vulnerability is God's way.

> God taking on those limits gives us this permission to be the vulnerable beings he created us to be, who are dependent on him, who can't live apart from God. We can't live apart from God. He didn't come as a strong man. He didn't come as what we would accept, think is successful. I mean, he flipped all of that on its head. We get so enmeshed in our culture that we forget about that part.[6]

When God came into our world, John tells us, "The Word became flesh" (Jn 1:14 NIV). The Word became human with a fully human body, taking on all the weaknesses and limitations that human flesh entails. Jesus could not do everything everywhere all the time. He needed rest. He needed solitude. He needed friends. Jesus got hungry and tired and bruised. Jesus suffered. We can be tempted to beautify Jesus' life and rush to resurrection, but when we do so, we fail to see the vulnerability of his humanness, the very means by which he identifies with us. God did not come as a strong man (as we understand it); he came as a suffering servant (Is 53).

It was Jesus' suffering that made the difference for Hannah finding her way back to God. Originally she was angry when people told her Jesus gets it, that he suffered and so he can identify with her pain. "Jesus cannot possibly suffer," she replied. "How can Jesus suffer if Jesus knows that he's going to be fine in the end, he's going to be resurrected? That's not suffering. He's not sitting with this unknown, 'What even is going on?'" But after her heart surgery, when she was in terrible pain, struggling to breathe, and unable to take any pain medications, she found herself utterly alone, her mom physically unable to stay awake with her through the night. In that moment, Hannah was brought to the Garden of Gethsemane. "And then I don't know what it was, it just felt like, 'Oh, you grieved. You just wanted your friends to stay awake and they couldn't do it.' And it just all of a sudden, it clicked, and Jesus was accessible to me. And by default, God felt accessible again." It was his limitation and

[6]Abby, interview by author, December 6, 2024.

suffering that "humanized Jesus" and became Hannah's way back to God. "Finally, I was able to say Jesus did suffer. Jesus does get it."[7]

God reigns supreme. In the midst of all our turmoil and brokenness, we know he wins (he has already won!). But we often forget that God's means for victory have been upside down from everything the world says is victorious: humility, service, pain, suffering, weakness, limitation. He did not come by force, violence, or prominence. It was as a baby in a manger to a poor couple who became refugees. He never held power in the synagogue or a seat among the ruling leaders in the temple. He walked the dusty road with people, serving, loving, feeding, and crying. When we deny these things and gloss them over as if to say vulnerability is not God's way, we discount the very means of God's victory. In so doing, we also discount our own stories, that vulnerability is also our way in God.

In writing to the Corinthians, Paul notes that the amazing gospel of God is a "great treasure" we house in "fragile clay jars" (2 Cor 4:7 NLT 2015). Andy notes that the metaphor of clay jars is clearly speaking of "our human, frail, fragile creatureliness, our limitations, our vulnerability . . . of weaknesses."[8] The ways in which our bodies are buffeted, knocked down, and pressed allow us to "share in the death of Jesus so that the life of Jesus may also be seen in our bodies" (2 Cor 4:10). It is in weakness that God shines. It is in sharing in Jesus' death that *Jesus'* life is seen through ours.

When we try to polish up our lives and hide weakness and vulnerability, we project the message that we have saved and sanctified ourselves. We have little space for weakness as something good. It is to be overcome so we can show ourselves strong, put together, in control, productive, and powerful. But hiding weakness and living in our own strength is the world's way. In God's way, we have his treasure in clay jars, perishable containers, weak bodies, which "makes it clear that our great power *is from God, not from ourselves*" (2 Cor 4:8 NLT 2015). Andy wonders whether

> maybe there's a commentary on that as Paul gets to chapter 12 when [he says], "When I'm weak, I'm strong," that power is perfected in weakness

---

[7]Hannah, interview by author, November 25, 2024.

[8]Andy, interview by author, November 26, 2024.

> and so on. This whole thing that *when I'm weak, the gospel is strong* is how I interpret what Paul is saying there. Paul is saying not "when I'm weak that I'm strong," that there's some kind of paradox there. But it's really a reversal that when I'm weak, God is strong. When I'm weak, the gospel is strong.

So often we think Paul's message and exhortation is that when we have weakness, God makes us strong. But in reality, Andy is right; it is when we are weak, it is through our weaknesses, that God is strong. Our dependence on God allows everything to be by, through, and with God (Rom 11:36) and not of ourselves (Eph 2:8). We become reflections in which the power is seen as from God and not us. When we try to live in our own strength and refuse to accept the weaknesses of our own flesh, we do not become a conduit for God's power. We become like Israel, who sought to power their way through the keeping of the law and in so doing became veiled from Christ (2 Cor 3:10-15). It is only by turning to Christ in our weakness that we find the veil removed (2 Cor 3:16-18) and God's power, God's gospel, made strong in and through us, not because we suddenly become strong but because God has a place in our weak and perishable bodies to be strong in and through us.

This renewed perspective will reshape our understanding of the gospel and one another. Andy continues his commentary:

> The gospel does not belong to us. We as the church are not the protectors of the gospel or the guardians of the gospel or the owners of the gospel. The gospel is at work in us and through us. If it can be at work in and through us, all of us as humans, relativized before God—that we are all weak, lowly, needy, vulnerable, before God—then how could I not also have the same grace for someone else who might be differently abled, in differentiated bodies? It can speak to how people would see God, because not only does the gospel not belong to us, but as the gospel shines through us, it would point to God because of how our life is postured or because the disposition of our life is that God will use us in all that we *do not* bring to the table. God is seen not because of what we have but because of what we don't have. And that allows for interdependency,

Instead of discounting others for not bringing more to the table, we should recognize that God is at work through what we all, in our various mixes of abilities and disabilities, do not bring to the table. Instead of working hard for perfection, projecting strength, and fixating on production quality, we should recognize that God is at work through what we all offer to him in our weakness. God is not seen because of what we have but because of what we don't have. And that, Andy says, allows for interdependency. It also makes love possible. As Draper, Michele, and Mae note,

> One of the things we learn by being with people with disabilities is that we all have limitations. People with disabilities regularly experience the awkwardness or difficulty of not being able to do everything independently. Including people with disabilities means that the limitations of nondisabled people will be shown as well. Love requires vulnerability.[9]

REALIZING GOD'S KINGDOM

It is in belonging to each other and leaning into our vulnerabilities that we will be able to live into the reality of God's kingdom. Even though God's kingdom is an already-not-yet kingdom, breaking into the present without being fully realized, everyone grafted into God's family is called to kingdom work through kingdom means. It is important to understand what this means. Too often we try to shape God's kingdom into our own image rather than recognizing that God's kingdom is ordered by different loves and different priorities. Abby argues that in God's present and future kingdom,

> Sin is atoned for. That doesn't mean, I don't think that means, that our bodies are going to be perfect. But what do we mean by perfect? Who decides what perfect looks like? I think that to see sin eradicated and to live—I sound like a broken record—but I think a disability can and does exist in the kingdom of God. And it also, I think, was part of God's intentional design. I don't think he accidentally made people disabled. I don't think he necessarily sees fixing those disabilities as honoring or glorifying.

The reason Abby is a firm believer in disability within God's kingdom, both now and in the future, is that God is looking for different qualities

[9]Draper, Michele, and Mae, *Disabling Leadership*, 141.

and practices to be on display. It is not perfection in body as much as it is mutuality and deference in our relationships with one another.

> He sees us treating one another with kindness and love and compassion and interdependence as fulfilling his kingdom goals. Not [snaps fingers], "Fixed you all and now you all can do your own thing." I don't think that's what the kingdom of God looks like. I think our picture of the kingdom of God is very influenced by what we would like to see based on our own image.
>
> It's the same thing where so many people expected Christ to come as a conqueror, and then he didn't. And it was like [gasps]. Now what? He's not the king, but he *is*? But he's a servant? That doesn't make sense. And I think the kingdom of God is the same way. It's not that suddenly everyone is this perfect being who doesn't need anybody else and who just serves God, whatever that means. Serving God involves a lot of that kind of messy stuff. We need to have a vision of the kingdom of God that is *God's* vision of the kingdom of God instead of our own.

It is easy to build God's kingdom our way, but such creations often are inconsistent with God's principles and irreconcilable with God's economy. Abby admits that if she were planning the kingdom of God,

> I never would have picked some of the things I've built my whole life on. I never would have picked to be a servant. That's terrible. I never would have picked to love my enemy. That's awful. If I got to pick, I would hate my enemy. I would have nothing to do with my enemy. But that's not what I was taught. That's not what Christ came to accomplish. And so many of those things, I do it because I was given this example from Christ. And he said, "Love your enemy." So, I have to try. And I think the kingdom of God will look like loving your enemy. And you're just gonna have them. There's still going to be people you don't like. There's still gonna be people who are offensive to you and who depend on you in ways that you don't want them to depend on you. And I think all of that is part of the design. That's part of how we were made. I don't see any of that disappearing in some otherworldly new body, whatever it is. And I don't know that the new bodies are going to look like we would think of as perfect.

Interdependence is the design and the means of God's kingdom, and we are called to participate in that kingdom in the now. Such a practice is a countercultural statement that upends the falsehood that power, production, profit, and perfection are the principles by which we demonstrate our own worth and meaning and have grounds to discount the worth and meaning of others.

Interdependence also upends the telling of God's kingdom story as one that centers perfection as God's crowning achievement. God's story has always been one of working in and through diversity and limitation. Without that, we can't realize God's kingdom. "If you only have able-bodied people and perfect health, perfect mental capabilities, whatever, you're missing *so many* people," Hannah says.

> You're missing whole slices of the world, whole experiences, whole places of ministry, and God and parts of God's story. Because you're only one voice. And if all like-minded people are running a church, then you're missing Jesus, who ministered and was friends with a *variety* of people because he saw them as equals. Jesus enjoyed their company. Jesus learned from them. And. I think it's just sad and boring to have people who all experience the same thing leading things because that's not a conversation. That's just a monologue. And church is supposed to be a place where we can wrestle and come to Jesus. And if there's nothing to wrestle with, then what are we doing? If there's nothing to talk about, then no one's conversing with God and Jesus. And no one is—we're not inviting God into the space.

God's kingdom is not in one person or through one type of person. "We are all reflections of God," Hannah concludes. "We all hold a piece of God, and you can't ask somebody to not be a part of that conversation just because you don't like [disability], or because you don't understand it, or because you think it's less, or a result of the sinful world or whatever you want to call it. We reflect God, and we get a place at the table too." None of us is a people by ourselves. It takes others to make a person into a people. There is nothing that disqualifies or diminishes the role of disabled people from making others into a people.

RESTORING COMMUNION

By leaning into the interdependence of God's kingdom through our belonging and vulnerability, we will be moved to reach others with intention and purpose. Practicing interdependence will help us to notice who is present and who is absent, whose voices are heard and whose are overlooked, who is participating and who is not, who is leading and who is not. And it will move us to respond with acts of justice (Mic 6:8), making sure we have set a table for people of all abilities and purposely waiting until they are there to feast.

In his own work on 1 Corinthians 11, Andy notes that beyond the violence in the Eucharist in terms of Jesus and the cross, "there's a violence that the church perpetuates when we're not welcoming all to the table." Paul tells the believers they're participating in the Lord's table in an incorrect fashion, but we often individualize his comments in a way that misses Paul's true intent. Andy explains,

> I think we miss it in Pietist ideas of "we need to examine our heart." Like, "Oh, think about where you sinned this week." And that's not what he's saying. In *examine*, he's talking in context of, "You come to the table as ones who are rich and eat everything and drink everything to the point of drunkenness before those who are working and poor and can't get there yet." And so he's saying, "Examine yourself, how you approach the table or approach the Lord's Supper." And people are dying. . . . The Lord is taking [this] so serious that people are being judged in that moment. But I want to say, when it comes to the Lord's Supper, the question Paul is basically asking or implicitly asking here is, "When you come to the Lord's supper, ask who's not here. And wait until they are there." He's saying, "Wait. Wait for the people to all be there." And that's an issue of rich and poor. But I think the same thing goes in anything. We could think about, "Well, why is a homeless person not here? They don't feel welcome to just wander in stinky and whatever. Why? Why is a single mom maybe not here? Because she's overwhelmed and has her hands full. Who else isn't there, then? Has different vulnerabilities or needs?"
>
> Disability helps us think, like if we think in terms of disability, who else might need help? That helps the church think, "How else can we be more attentive to others in our community that have needs or who aren't here? Maybe this person doesn't feel welcome?"

This leads us back to Jesus' rebuke of a prominent Pharisee in Luke 14. "You keep inviting the wrong people. Seek out the poor, the crippled, the lame, and the blind, people who may not be able to repay you in kind.

This is what God's kingdom looks like and the only way you experience God's kingdom blessings." Interdependence helps us recognize our own disabilities and teaches us to live out the truth that we are not whole without others.

THE PRACTICE OF INTERDEPENDENCE IN EVANGELISM

The practice of interdependence becomes a practice of justice because it adjusts our gaze toward others and ourselves as we contemplate belonging to all others, embracing vulnerability and weakness as the means of God's kingdom, and anticipating others to be present with us in order for wholeness to be experienced. In every way this affects our posture and message as we contemplate evangelism.

In Luke 10, we find a very familiar parable, the story of the good Samaritan. A man is taking a trip, and as he passes through a particularly dangerous stretch of road, he is ambushed by a gang, who robs him, beats him, and leaves him for dead. As he is on a well-traveled path, other people soon happen upon this poor, beat-up soul; however, the Jewish priest and the temple assistant see the man but walk by—on the other side, no less—and leave the man in his misery. But then the hero of the story, the Samaritan, the one person Jews would see with contempt, stops when he sees the man. He stops because, unlike the priest and the temple assistant, who are unmoved by the man's suffering, the Samaritan is filled with great concern for the man who is beat up and is moved to action. He begins by tending to the man's wounds. He then places the man on the Samaritan's very own donkey and takes him to an inn, where he pays for the man to continue to receive care until he is well.

We know this story but often fail to contemplate the implications of it in light of the surrounding context. Jesus tells this story in response to a question.

The encounter starts when Jesus is confronted by an expert in religious law who wants to know how to inherit eternal life. "What should I do?" he asks. Jesus turns the tables and has the man answer his own question. "What does the law of Moses say?" The man replies, "'You must love the Lord your God with all your heart, all your soul, all your strength, and all your mind.' And, 'Love your neighbor as yourself.'" Jesus commends the response and admonishes the man, "Do this and you will live" (Lk 10:25-29). But then the story takes a turn.

The man does not seem to have a problem contemplating that he must love God completely. But he is bothered by the next part. Something pricks his conscience because Luke says he wants to "justify his actions" (Lk 10:29). He wants to know that how he's been narrowly reading this command is okay. Here's what he asks: "Who is my neighbor?" (Lk 10:29).

It is a bit puzzling that he would need to ask this. As an expert in religious law, he would know that the law is pretty clear on what *neighbor* means. In Leviticus 19, for example, the law instructs us to care for the poor, the foreigner, the deaf and the blind, our literal neighbors, our relatives, the elderly and aged, and anyone, for that matter. Leviticus 19:18 specifically says to never seek revenge or bear a grudge against anyone but love your neighbor as yourself. It seems pretty clear here that *neighbor* means everyone.

So why does this man not accept his own words at face value? Why does he know enough to say he should love his neighbor but then need to justify his own actions by asking what *neighbor* really means?

I would posit that if he has to justify his actions, he already knows that there are people he has considered in and others he has concluded are out. He sees their faces. He knows what judgments he made about them. He knows why he thought each person deserved to be ignored, overlooked, distained, or excluded. What he wants to hear Jesus say is that there are parameters about whom to include and whom it's okay to exclude. He wants Jesus to explicitly name what characteristics disqualify someone from being called a neighbor. Ultimately, as Walter Liefeld poignantly states it, the man wants to "limit the extent of the law's demands and consequently limit his own responsibility."[10]

The expert in the law knows what the law says, but he wants to limit the law's demands so he can limit his own responsibility toward his neighbors. He is hoping for a loophole. Who is my neighbor?

It is good for us to pause here and sit with the question. It is rare that we ask this question as one of true inquiry with a view to widening our

---

[10]Walter Liefeld, "Luke," in *The Expositor's Bible Commentary with the New International Version*, vol. 8, *Matthew, Mark, Luke*, gen. ed. Frank E. Gaebelein (Zondervan, 1984), 942.

circles. More often we share in the same spirit as the religious expert, "wanting to justify" ourselves and limit our own responsibility toward others. We may not have asked this in such bold terms, but we do ask it when we exclude the disabled because "they're not the group we're targeting." We do ask it when we look at our budget and say, "Disabilities do not fit into the priorities of this church." We do ask it when we ask a person or family to leave because "we're not called to disability ministry" or "you're disrupting us, so you need to go somewhere else." We do ask it when we give a side-eye, take a different route, avoid eye contact, and exclude others from entry, participation, or leadership because of how they look, speak, think, or move. Making our excuses religious sounding doesn't excuse us because every time we make excuses, Jesus tells us this parable. Note that the first two characters who happen upon the scene are Jewish religious leaders who both ignore the man's plight and find religious justification for doing so. And Jesus flatly says no.

Lord, who is my neighbor? Consider a Samaritan man who exemplified the heart of God's law by showing care for a man society tells him he should ignore. Jesus has made his point that loving our neighbor means crossing ethnic, social, economic, and physical boundaries and seeing our lives so bound up in someone else's good and worth that we receive as our own kin those the world says should be left on the wayside. We offer them the fruits of kinship: love, time, generosity, and embrace.

We often stop here, but we're not done. This encounter is a tale not of one question but two. "*Who is* my neighbor?" is an outwardly facing question that is important but incomplete. If we only ever stop with "Who is my neighbor?" we will never move past concerns of boundaries and differences.

Jesus ends the parable by asking the religious expert a different question. "*Who was* the neighbor?" Forget trying to figure out who is in and out and how you are or are not obligated to them. The real question is, "What about my own heart? Am I the neighbor? Is my life one of enacted mercy?" By asking who *was* the neighbor, Jesus moves the focus from "What are the limits of love?" to "Am I loving enough?" "Who was the neighbor?" was answered by a kind of mercy that says, "This man belongs to me and I to him."

This is what the practice of interdependence does in our evangelism. It removes an othering that limits our love, limits our embrace, and justifies exclusion, and instead calls for the deep heart work that moves us to be the neighbor. We cannot be a neighbor if we're isolated from others. Neighbors become such only through living in communities with other people. You don't always get to choose your neighbors, but that doesn't negate your responsibilities or postures. As we get to the heart of God, understanding that everyone is our neighbor and we need to be the neighbor, we get to the heart of interdependence. We need each other. We belong to each other. We cannot be satisfied with a house of God that is missing large swaths of people. Practicing interdependence will change our own hearts to beat like God's and believe that we are not whole without the "one anothers" of all abilities.

DISCUSSION QUESTIONS

1. How interdependent are you with others, especially within the church? Where do you resist interdependence? What makes interdependence so challenging?
2. Consider Romans 12 and the "we are failing" list. How would you evaluate you and your church in light of these items? What would it mean for your church to catch the vision of Romans 12?
3. How can you embrace your own vulnerabilities? How might this change the ways you interact with people with disabilities?
4. How does disability reshape your understanding of God kingdom?
5. Who is missing at your church's table? What would it look like to wait for others to be present?
6. How can you be the neighbor (Lk 10)?
7. In what ways will you start practicing interdependence? What things do you specifically want to start doing, keep doing, or stop doing?

Conclusion

"The whole picture of the kingdom gets lost," says Chris when I ask him what is missing when we exclude the disabled from the work and witness of the church.

As the most salient living picture of God's kingdom, the church should be enacting God's good-news story in the world by serving as a sign, witness, and foretaste of all that is and is yet to come. Paul argues for this kind of radical witness in Ephesians, a book Timothy Gombis argues is both a narrative account of God's cosmic victory *and* "a script for churches—gospel players—to perform the drama of the gospel that magnifies the triumph of God in Christ."[1] We often believe victory comes through a show of power, dominance, force, strength, intelligence, and wealth, and our evangelistic practices tend to follow this path toward "triumph, growth, and expansion" as we look to win the lost, build the church, grow our budgets, and transform cultures by taking (back) power.[2] But Paul argues that Jesus, as cosmic Lord and Victor, has won by losing, and as those who "imitate God" (Eph 5:1 NLT 2015), we too should "live a life filled with love for others" through sacrifice and giving up of self (Eph 5:2), living "cruciform and subversive" lives.[3]

Our best witness, then, does not come from the latest methods, the slickest productions, the most cultural relevance, or a message that exudes respectability.[4] Our best witness is the radical and countercultural

---

[1]Timothy G. Gombis, *The Drama of Ephesians: Participating in the Triumph of God* (InterVarsity Press, 2010), 181.

[2]Bryan Stone, *Evangelism After Christendom: The Theology and Practice of Christian Witness* (Brazos, 2007), 315.

[3]Gombis, *Drama of Ephesians*, 182.

[4]Stone, *Evangelism After Christendom*, 11.

life of God's kingdom on display in and through the church. We prove to the world that Jesus has won, not by force but, through the power of the Spirit, enacting the values, virtues, habits, and economies that mark God's gospel and God's kingdom as something different, upside down, and beautiful.

The only way in which we can faithfully and fully do this is if people with disabilities are included completely in the gospel we enact. This is not the way we have done church or considered evangelistic strategy. Disability, we have too often contended, is tragedy, judgment, and brokenness that detracts from the power of the gospel, upsets our comforts, and hinders our progress and appeal. We may make accommodations for disability, but we rarely submit to disability as a valued part of knowing Christ, living in his fullness, and bearing witness. But Lesslie Newbigin argues, "It is *only* when the witness of the handicapped is an *integral* part of the witness of the whole Church, that this witness *is true to the Gospel* of the Crucified who is risen, the risen Lord who is Crucified."[5] Why?

Bryan Stone argues, "Whatever else evangelism may be, it is the practice of giving the world something to see—and to touch, and to try." The question is whether we're giving the world something distinct.[6] Is our offer something that counters the "latent idolatries the powers are peddling," or is our offer one that mimics and sustains the state and is "disciplined by the logic of the market"?[7] We give in to the powers when we idolize perfect bodies and minds and problematize imperfect ones, and when we value speed, efficiency, economy, time, and production over people who may delay, slow, or disrupt. When we live this way in the church, we become just another community that honors self, power, and prowess over others, especially those the world calls weak. Andy correctly says,

---

[5]Lesslie Newbigin, "Not Whole Without the Handicapped," in *Partners in Life: The Handicapped and the Church*, ed. Geiko Müller-Fahrenholz (WCC Publications, 1979), 24, emphasis added. Note: Newbigin's use of *handicapped*, acceptable language at the time of his writing, is no longer the preferred way for referencing disability. It is likely that my own terminology will undergo similar scrutiny as language changes and further refinements are made by future generations.

[6]Stone, *Evangelism After Christendom*, 315.

[7]Gombis, *Drama of Ephesians*, 183; Stone, *Evangelism After Christendom*, 48.

> The church isn't fully being the body of Christ if we're only accentuating certain members of the body. . . . The world's watching how we treat others, and I think we communicate things to the world, the way we design church for efficiency and so on. Who is welcome? If these people are not welcome, there's implicit communication that then maybe others who don't have it all together aren't welcome.[8]

So much of what we have valued, craved, and centered in the church has sadly distorted the gospel we seek to profess. We have made the gospel one of comfort, efficiency, and self-service because we have made our churches places of comfort, efficiency, and self-service. Nothing showcases this more clearly than disabled people's absence from, marginalization in, and exclusion from the church and all of its practices of withness and witness. When we exclude the disabled from evangelism, we may think we're making the gospel palpable and convenient for the world, but the witness we end up offering is corrupted, truncated, and not God's good news.

But God's story is good news! It is just not good news in the way of the world. In fact, as Paul argues, the gospel is foolishness to those who are perishing because it upends the world's values and ways (1 Cor 1:18). Paul argues that when God calls us into Christ, few of us possess the wisdom, influence, wealth, or power the world esteems (1 Cor 1:26). *God chooses us in what we lack rather than what we possess.* He does this for two reasons. The first reason is to keep us from boasting in anything but the Lord (1 Cor 1:29). The second is to upend the human standards of wisdom, influence, wealth, and power the world traffics (1 Cor 1:27-28).

There is nothing we possess—not intelligence, not physical power, not social position—that gives us merit before God. In fact, in comparison to God, the smartest, strongest, and most popular among us are foolish, weak, and despised. We are all on the same level before God. By taking away any grounds for us to boast in our own worth or ability, God brings about a kingdom with eternal foundations "whose architect and builder is God" (Heb 11:10 NIV). Because of this, Paul says the good-news story we preach "is not ourselves, but Jesus Christ as Lord" (2 Cor 4:5 NIV), a

[8]Andy, interview by author, November 26, 2024.

treasure housed in jars of clay, which "makes it clear that our great power is from God, not from ourselves" (2 Cor 4:7 NLT 2015).

Notice that God specifically puts his knowledge in fleshly, limited jars of clay for the express means of displaying his glorious and incomprehensible power. Too often we preach ourselves by honoring certain bodies. We preach ourselves by valuing certain minds. We preach ourselves by crafting churches of convenience. We preach ourselves by not being bothered by the absence of people who do not look, sound, move, or present like us. We preach ourselves by eschewing weakness, vulnerability, and limitation for pretenses of power, togetherness, and strength.

But when we remember that God chose all of us in what we do not have, we can embrace the truth that weakness, limitation, and inability are actually a key part of gospeling. In our weakness, God is strong. In our human limitations, God's power is revealed. We preach Jesus Christ as Lord when we learn from God's accommodation of us all and live in the way of cross.

We have not often embraced disability in the church because we think that having a church shaped significantly by disability will push us to the margins, make us unpopular, and, if we're honest, cause us to be unattractive. For a post-Christendom church that was once center to cultural, political, and economic power, this is not a comfortable or familiar place. We resist this space. We plan, spend, organize, and act to avoid the periphery if at all possible. But as Stone contends, "evangelistic refusal of vulnerability, particularly, and marginality is finally a refusal of the way of the cross, a way that forgoes the privileges and security allied with winning and opts instead for costly obedience, incarnation, and gospel nonconformity." This is a bit of a gut punch, but if we're willing to receive this conviction and listen to the way forward, we have the opportunity to practice evangelism in a way that "inescapably counters and disarms the world's powerful practices by unmasking the narratives that sustain them and by offering a story and a people that are peaceful and beautiful."[9]

[9]Stone, *Evangelism After Christendom*, 11-12, 20.

That way forward, as I have contended here, is by the welcome and open embrace of all people of all abilities into the good news of God's kingdom.

Disability gifts the church the means for living and speaking a gospel story of God's shalom that runs counter to much of what our world promotes. Disability gifts the church an opportunity to learn about humanness, vulnerability, and what it means to depend on God.[10] Disability gifts the church new ways of thinking, seeing, hearing, being, tasting, and touching the gospel. Disability is powerful in the church because if we get this right, it seems like we can get a lot of other things right too. When we make space for people the world discounts and center the disabled, "we'll just naturally, intuitively come to these other questions like, 'If we have to adjust to make things work for somebody here, maybe we can adjust in another way for multi-ethnic, intercultural, or the poor, those that need extra help, or whatever,'" Andy says. "Disability is redemptively fundamental," Reynolds argues, because "by welcoming people with disabilities in our church communities, our churches become communions bearing witness to God's creative-redemptive power, a strange power that works not through strength but weakness and vulnerability to give life. And when our church communities traffic in such power, they cannot help but spill outward to transform the world in a God-ward direction."[11]

Ultimately, disability is redemptively fundamental because it (re)shapes our churches and communities into a greater Christlikeness. Newbigin argues, "As mission goes its way to the ends of the earth, new treasures are brought into the life of the Church, and Christianity itself grows and changes until it becomes more credible as a foretaste of the unity of all humankind."[12] Disability is indeed a treasure to church if we are willing to receive it. By embracing people with disabilities in the life and witness of the church, we can more clearly and more faithfully live into our evangelistic calling of proclaiming, heralding, and living out a

---

[10]Andy, interview with author, November 26, 2024.

[11]Thomas E. Reynolds, *Vulnerable Communion: A Theology of Disability and Hospitality* (Brazos, 2008), 249.

[12]Lesslie Newbigin, *The Gospel in a Pluralist Society* (Eerdmans, 1989), 124.

message that bears witness to good news about Jesus Christ that is extremely good news for *all* people of *all* abilities.

DISCUSSION QUESTIONS

1. How does disability show up in God's story?
2. How does disability enhance our understanding of God's kingdom?
3. What has changed for you after reading this book?
4. What are your next steps personally? As a church?
5. Who will you share this message with?

Appendix

A FEW WORDS ABOUT GETTING STARTED

WHILE THROUGHOUT THIS BOOK I have outlined many different practices we can take on, many people still find themselves a bit stuck on how to actually do this good work as we move to include people with disabilities in the life and witness of the church. How do we get started on accommodations? Where can we go for ideas and resources? How do we train our people to practically and physically love and partner with people with various mental, physical, social, and emotional capacities?

There are a lot of good resources out there, and I have been hesitant to create a list of practical to-dos that simply parrots what others have crafted. I have decided that instead of creating pages and pages of resources, I am going to list some more general principles that may even seem common sense and then leave you with a few resources to get you started. I hope these will spark some tangible ways for moving forward as you embrace this beautiful place of incorporating disability in all you say, do, and think.

- *Pray.* Ask God for guidance and for the ability to humbly listen, wisely discern, practically act, and be personally shaped and reformed. You want to enter and remain with the right posture as you engage and embrace a new way of life.
- *Engage people and families in your community who have a variety of disabilities.* Have listening sessions to understand the people and the experiences of disability already present in your congregation or other social spaces. Most people with disabilities and their

families welcome opportunities to share their experiences and their expertise. This doesn't mean you should force people into the role of teacher, but it does mean inviting others to share the good, the bad, and the ugly of their experiences and expectations. But don't just make this a one-and-done event. Revisit these conversations regularly to make sure you are working together.

- *Enter into disabled spaces to learn, share life, and experience others' accommodation of you.*
- *Pull people with disabilities into leadership teams.* If you have the opportunity to work in leadership at your church, make sure people with a variety of abilities are active in leadership roles. This is not a token appointment but a genuine invitation for people to use their gifts of leadership and perspective to help the church live into her witness.
- *Revisit church mission, vision, and other guiding documents to better align with your vision for disability inclusion.* How can you make disability more explicit? What steps do you need to take to make sure everyone knows and is committed to disability in the church?
- *Bring in disability experts to do an audit of your community.* Have an audit that helps you understand your space from the perspective of disability. This isn't just about parking spaces, wider doors, and ramps; it is also about messaging, sensory experiences, and attitudes.
- *Consider incorporating universal design into your teaching, preaching, worship, and activities.* Everyone you encounter has a specific learning modality. Some prefer hearing words; some prefer reading them. Some prefer watching; some prefer doing. The more ways you can develop what you do to meet a variety of learning modes, the better the experience is for everyone, regardless of what disabilities they may or may not bring with them.
- *Learn from other churches and people.* There are a lot of people doing a lot of great things. You don't have to reinvent the wheel. My friend Rick copied some of the structure, methods, and activities he uses in Front Porch Church from other ministries that have seen

people with disabilities thrive. Have conversations, take field trips, and share resources with one another.

- *Invest in training for yourself and others.* Look for classes, symposiums, and seminars on disability, especially disability and the church. There are many organizations in the community and the church that are eager to partner with you.
- *Study, study, study.* Make sure you regularly read books, listen to podcasts, and watch videos that help you understand disability and make it a natural part of your thoughts, experiences, and actions. Not sure where to start? Find a source (such as this book!) and plunder the bibliography. What books, articles, and other resources are referenced? Find those and engage with them. And then start again! Look at that resource's references and follow the trails. (To make it easy, I will suggest a few people and books below to get you going.)
- *Keep adding "of all abilities" to everything you do.* How does this change your approach? Who will this exclude or include? What will you want to prioritize? As you plan events, ask questions about who they will include and exclude. Though you will never be able to plan for every disability or need, consider what sensory, auditory, visual, cognitive, and mobility needs might be present and how you can set a table that is welcoming and ready to respond. What needs, beyond Sundays, can your church meet (e.g., respite care, transportation, advocacy)? As you welcome people into your home, consider how intentionally adding "of all abilities" might reshape your invitations to be more welcoming and inclusive.
- *Expect that God has gifts for the church in each person you meet.* How can you help this person know Jesus and grow in Jesus? How can you play to this person's strengths in order to release and receive those gifts? Watch for gifts from this person and learn to receive and celebrate them.
- *Highlight disabilities in all the ministries of your church.* Make disability a regular part of the experience, conversation, discipleship, witness, and celebration in all you do as your church's way of life.

- *Receive the ministry of those with disability.*
- *Remember that for all you can do, including disability is not an add-on.* Lean into the practices that help you develop the kinds of values, patterns of thinking, habits, loves, virtues, and economies God wants.
- *Intentionally enter into friendships with disabled people and learn to do life together.* Celebrate having people with a variety of abilities in your life. Learn to value and appreciate their presence and participation. Miss them when they are absent. Receive their hospitality and friendship. Give them hospitality and friendship. Do life together!

HELPFUL RESOURCES

Baylor Center for Developmental Disabilities. https://bcdd.soe.baylor.edu/. In particular, review the ministry guides found in Faith and Disability Resources.

Brock, Brian. *Disability: Living into the Diversity of Christ's Body.* Baker Academic, 2021.

Carter, Erik W. *Including People with Disability in Faith Communities: A Guide for Service Providers, Families, and Congregations.* Paul H. Brooks, 2007.

Center for Disability and Ministry at Western Theological Seminary. www.westernsem.edu/beyond-the-classroom/center-for-disability-and-ministry/.

Conner, Benjamin T. *Amplifying Our Witness: Giving Voice to Adolescents with Developmental Disabilities.* Eerdmans, 2012.

Draper, Andrew T., Jody Michele, and Andrea Mae. *Disabling Leadership: A Practical Theology for the Broken Body of Christ.* IVP Academic, 2023.

Joni & Friends. https://joniandfriends.org/.

Wheaton Center for Faith and Disability. www.wheaton.edu/wheaton-center-for-faith-and-disability/.

With Ministries. https://withministries.org.

Yong, Amos. *The Bible, Disability, and the Church: A New Vision of the People of God.* Eerdmans, 2011.

General Index

Scripture Index

Center for Disability & Ministry

The Center for Disability and Ministry at Western Theological Seminary exists to support ministry leaders of all abilities in nurturing and receiving the gifts and contributions of persons with disabilities through formational opportunities including theological education, consultation, forums, and publications. For more information visit www.westernsem.edu/center-for-disability-and-ministry/.

www.ingramcontent.com/pod-product-compliance
Lightning Source LLC
LaVergne TN
LVHW091127080826
845145LV00008B/2076

9781514009789